Library of
Davidson College

THE MACHIAVELLIANS

THE MACHIAVELLIANS

DEFENDERS OF FREEDOM

JAMES BURNHAM

Essay Index Reprint Series

 BOOKS FOR LIBRARIES PRESS
FREEPORT, NEW YORK

Copyright © 1943, by James Burnham

Reprinted 1970 by arrangement with The John Day Co., Inc.

INTERNATIONAL STANDARD BOOK NUMBER:
0-8369-1785-5

LIBRARY OF CONGRESS CATALOG CARD NUMBER:
70-117762

PRINTED IN THE UNITED STATES OF AMERICA

THIRD FISHERMAN. Master, I marvel how the fishes live in the sea.

FIRST FISHERMAN. Why, as men do a-land; the great ones eat up the little ones.

Pericles, Prince of Tyre

CONTENTS

Part I.—Dante: Politics As Wish

1. The Formal Meaning of De Monarchia — 3
2. The Real Meaning of De Monarchia — 11
3. The Typical Method of Political Thought — 23

Part II.—Machiavelli: The Science of Power

1. Machiavelli's Practical Goal — 29
2. Machiavelli's Method — 40
3. Political Man — 49
4. Machiavelli's Conception of History — 62
5. Machiavelli's Reputation — 74

Part III.—Mosca: The Theory of the Ruling Class

1. The Machiavellian Tradition — 81
2. The Ruling Class — 87
3. Composition and Character of the Ruling Class — 95
4. Tendencies in the Ruling Class — 102
5. The Best and Worst Governments — 107

Part IV.—SOREL: A NOTE ON MYTH AND VIOLENCE

1. The Function of Myth 119
2. The Function of Violence 126

Part V.—MICHELS: THE LIMITS OF DEMOCRACY

1. Michels' Problem 135
2. The Fact of Leadership 141
3. The Autocracy of Leadership 152
4. The Iron Law of Oligarchy 163

Part VI.—PARETO: THE NATURE OF SOCIAL ACTION

1. Logical and Non-logical Conduct 171
2. Residues and Derivations 183
3. Social Utility 197
4. The Circulation of the Elites 205

Part VII.—POLITICS AND TRUTH

1. The Nature of the Present 223
2. The Meaning of Democracy 236
3. Can Politics Be Scientific? 255

Part I

DANTE: POLITICS AS WISH

1. The Formal Meaning of DE MONARCHIA

IN THE 1932 PLATFORM of the Democratic party we may read the following:

"Believing that a party platform is a covenant with the people to be faithfully kept by the party when entrusted with power, and that the people are entitled to know in plain words the terms of the contract to which they are asked to subscribe, we hereby declare this to be the platform of the Democratic party.

"The Democratic party solemnly promises by appropriate action to put into effect the principles, policies and reforms herein advocated and to eradicate the policies, methods and practices herein condemned.

"We advocate:

"1) An immediate and drastic reduction of governmental expenditures by abolishing useless commissions and offices, consolidating departments and bureaus and eliminating extravagance, to accomplish a saving of not less than 25% in the cost of the Federal government . . .

"2) Maintenance of the national credit by a Federal budget annually balanced on the basis of accurate executive estimates within revenues . . .

"3) A sound currency to be preserved at all hazards . . .

"We condemn: . . .

"4) The open and covert resistance of administrative officials to every effort made by Congressional committees to control the extravagant expenditures of the government . . .

"5) The extravagance of the Farm Board, its disastrous action which made the government a speculator in farm products . . .

"To accomplish these purposes and to recover economic liberty we pledge the nominees of the convention . . ."

That the nominees upheld the pledge was made clear by the candidate for the Presidency on July 2, 1932, when he spoke in public acceptance of the nomination:

"As an immediate program of action we must abolish useless offices. We must eliminate actual prefunctions of government—functions, in fact, that are not definitely essential to the continuance of government. We must merge, we must consolidate subdivisions of government, and like the private citizen, give up luxuries which we can no longer afford.

"I propose to you, my friends, and through you, that government of all kinds, big and little, be made solvent and that the example be set by the President of the United States and his cabinet."

He returned to these themes frequently throughout the campaign. In a radio address delivered July 30, 1932, for example, he summed up: "Any government, like any family, can for a year spend a little more than it earns. But you and I know that a continuation of that habit means the poorhouse."

What are we to make of the words in these several quotations? They would be easy enough to explain if we could assume that the men who wrote them were just liars, deliberately trying to deceive the people. There is, however, no convincing evidence that would permit us to draw so cynical a conclusion. Are we to believe, then, that they were utterly stupid, with no understanding of economics or politics or what was going on in the world? Taking the words as they stand, this would seem to be the only alternative conclusion. But this also does not seem very plausible. These men and their associates, though they doubtless knew less than everything and less than they thought they knew, were surely not so ignorant as to have believed literally what the words seem to indicate. There is some further puzzle here. Perhaps the words do not really have anything to do with cheap government and sound currency and balanced budgets and the rest of what appears to be their subject matter.

We are asking questions about the meaning of the words men use in connection with political and social affairs. In order to avoid bias from partisan feelings of the moment and to seek a greater generality in the answer, I shall briefly examine these same questions as they arise over words written more than six centuries ago.

* * *

Dante Alighieri, besides the most wonderful poem ever written, finished only one other major work. This was a treatise on politics, which he called *De Monarchia,* a title that may be translated as "On the Empire." *De Monarchia* is divided into three Books, each of these sub-divided into numerous chapters. The general subject stated by Dante is "the knowledge of the temporal monarchy . . . which is called empire," by which is meant "a unique princedom extending over all persons in time."* The topics for the three Books are explained as follows: "In the first place we may inquire and examine whether it [the unique empire] is needful for the well-being of the world; in the second, whether the Roman people rightfully assumed to itself the function of monarchy; and in the third, whether the authority of the monarchy depends immediately upon God, or upon some other minister or vicar of God." The "empire" that Dante has concretely in mind is the Holy Roman Empire of medieval times, which he mistakenly believed to be the continuation of the ancient Roman Empire.

In answer to his three main inquiries, he maintains: first, that

---

* All quotations and references are taken from Philip H. Wicksteed's translation in the Temple Classics Edition of *The Latin Works of Dante Alighieri,* published by J. M. Dent & Sons, London.

mankind should be governed by a single "empire" or state; second, that this sovereignty is properly exercised by the Holy Roman Emperor (conceived as the continuator of the ancient Roman Emperor); and third, that the temporal, the political authority exercised by the Emperor is independent of the authority of the Pope and the Church (as Dante puts it, "depends immediately on God").

To establish the first point, that there should be a single unified world-state,* Dante begins by stating certain "first principles," which, he believes, are the necessary foundation for all political reasoning. The ultimate goal for all mankind is the full development of man's potentialities, which means in the last analysis eternal salvation and the vision of God. The aim of temporal civilization is to provide the conditions for achieving this ultimate goal, chief among which is universal peace. A variety of subtle arguments, distinctions and analogies shows that this condition, and in general the organization of the collective life of mankind in such a way as to permit the reaching of the ultimate goal, can only be effectively carried out through "unity of direction." God, moreover, is Supreme Unity, and, it being His intention that mankind should resemble Him as much as possible, this can be done only when mankind is also unified under a single ruler. The motion of the heavens is regulated by the single uniform motion of the outermost sphere (the *primum mobile*), and man should strive, too, to imitate the heavens. Only a unified political administration can check tyrannical governments and thus give men freedom, can guard the freedom of others by itself being wholly free, can guarantee concord and harmony, which always presuppose unity. These arguments, which prove that there should be a single unified political administration for all

---

* The "world" that Dante had in mind was of course Europe and the littoral of the Mediterranean; but no such restriction is made in his argument, and his reasoning applies as well, or ill, to the entire world as to the world he knew.

mankind, led by a single ruler, are historically substantiated by the fact that the Incarnation of Christ took place under the temporal rule of the Emperor Augustus.

In the second Book, Dante considers and accepts the claim of the Roman people to the seat of the universal empire. It is justified by their nobility derived from their descent from the Trojan Aeneas, and by numerous miracles which God worked to give witness to the claim. The Roman public spirit showed that they were aiming at the right, and thus must have had right on their side. Furthermore, the legitimacy of their claim was proved by the fact that the Romans had the effective faculty of ruling, the power to rule, whereas all other peoples failed in effective rule, as noted in the Scriptures and other sacred writings. Finally, the sacrifice of Christ would not have been valid in erasing the stain of original sin from all mankind unless Pilate, as the representative of Rome, had had valid authority to pronounce judicial sentence upon all mankind.

Book III discusses the ever-recurring problem of the relations between Church and State, the question, as Dante's time saw it, whether the temporal, the political ruler had independent authority and sovereignty, or was subordinate to the spiritual authority of God's Vicar on earth, the Pope. The question must be judged, Dante argues, on the fundamental principle that whatever is repugnant to the intention of nature is contrary to the Will of God. The truth has been obscured by a factious spirit, and by a failure to recognize the primary authority of the Bible, the decrees of the councils and the writings of the Fathers. The argument for the subordination of the empire (that is, the state) to the Church on the basis of the analogy of the subordinate relation of the moon, representing the empire, to the sun, representing the Church, is without weight because the analogy is false, and, even if it were true, does not really establish the dependence. Nor are various often quoted instances in the Bible any more conclusive. Christ gave Peter, representing the Church, the power to loose and bind, but expressly limited this power to the things of Heaven, not of the earth.

The donation by which the Emperor Constantine, after his conversion and cure of leprosy, granted authority over the Empire to Pope Sylvester, was invalid, since it was contrary to nature for him to make the grant or for the Pope to receive it.* The argument that there cannot be two supreme individuals of the same kind, and, since the Pope cannot be regarded as inferior, he must be superior to the temporal ruler, does not hold. The spiritual and temporal authorities are of two different kinds, and the individual supreme in one order might well be inferior in the other. Positively indicating the independence of the temporal rule from the spiritual are such facts as that Christ, Paul, and even the angel who appeared to Paul acknowledged the temporal authority of the emperor. Finally, it is in harmonious accord with the two-fold nature of man, both body and spirit, that God should have established, directly dependent only on Himself, two supreme authorities, one temporal and one spiritual. The temporal ruler, then, is in no way subordinate, in temporal things, to the spiritual ruler, though it may be granted that he should properly give that reverence to the spiritual ruler which is due him as the representative of eternal life and immortal felicity.

* * *

Let us consider this outline of what may be called the *formal* argument of *De Monarchia*.

In the first place, we may note that the ultimate goal (eternal salvation in Heaven) by which Dante holds that all political

---

* The apologists for Papal supremacy made a strong point of the famed "donation of Constantine," and Dante was plainly troubled by it. The donation was proved a forgery by Lorenzo Valla in the 15th century.

DANTE: POLITICS AS WISH 9

questions must be judged is in the strictest sense impossible, since there is no such place as Heaven.

Second, the lesser goals derived from the ultimate goal—the development of the full potentialities of all men, universal peace, and a single unified world-state—though they are perhaps not inconceivable, are nevertheless altogether utopian and materially impossible.

Third, the many arguments that Dante uses in favor of his position are, from a purely formal point of view, both good and bad, mostly bad; but, from the point of view of actual political conditions in the actual world of space and time and history, they are almost without exception completely irrelevant. They consist of pointless metaphysical and logical distinctions, distorted analogies, garbled historical references, appeals to miracles and arbitrarily selected authorities. In the task of giving us information about how men behave, about the nature and laws of political life, about what steps may be taken in practice to achieve concrete political and social goals, they advance us not a single step.

Taking the treatise at face value and judging it as a study of politics, it is worthless, totally worthless. With this, it might seem that no more could, or ought to be, said about *De Monarchia*. Such a conclusion, however, would show a thorough failure to understand the nature of a work of this kind. So far we have been considering only the formal meaning of the treatise. But this formal meaning, the meaning which is explicitly stated, is the least important aspect of *De Monarchia*. The formal meaning, besides what it explicitly states when taken at face value, serves to express, in an indirect and disguised manner, what may be called the *real* meaning of the essay.

By "real meaning" I refer to the meaning not in terms of the fictional world of religion, metaphysics, miracles, and pseudo-history (which is the world of the formal meaning of *De Monarchia*), but in terms of the actual world of space, time, and events. To understand the real meaning, we cannot take the words at face value nor confine our attention to what they explicitly state; we must fit them into the specific context of Dante's times and his own life. It is characteristic of *De Monarchia,* and of all similar treatises, that there should be this divorce between formal and real meanings, that the formal meaning should not explicitly state but only indirectly express, and to one or another extent hide and distort, the real meaning. The real meaning is thereby rendered irresponsible, since it is not subject to open and deliberate intellectual control; but the real meaning is nonetheless there.*

What, then, is the real meaning of *De Monarchia?*

*I am arbitrarily defining the distinction between "formal meaning" and "real meaning" in the sense I have indicated, and I shall continue so to use it. The distinction has nothing to do with the psychological question whether Dante (or any other writer who may be in question) consciously attempts to deceive his audience by hiding the real meaning behind the façade of the formal meaning. The disguise is there, independently of any intention; and deception, including self-deception, does often occur. It is possible, of course, as we shall see further, that the formal meaning and the real meaning should be identical; and it is an object of science to see that, so far as possible, they are.

2. The Real Meaning of DE MONARCHIA

FROM THE 12th to the 14th centuries, many of the chief disputes and wars in feudal Europe focused around the prolonged struggle between Guelphs and Ghibellines. The exact origin of these two great international factions is not altogether clear. They first came into prominence in the year 1125, in a conflict over the succession to the Emperor Henry V, a member of the Hohenstaufen family. His son, Frederic, supported by the great nobles, claimed the Empire, which was not, however, a hereditary office. He was opposed by the Pope and by many of the lesser nobles, whose candidate was Lothair, the Duke of Saxony. Lothair was elected; but upon his death in 1137 was succeeded by the brother of Frederic, the Hohenstaufen Conrad, who was in turn (in 1152) followed by the great Hohenstaufen, Frederic Barbarossa.

The Guelph faction took its name from the party of Lothair; and the Ghibelline, from the party of the Hohenstaufen. The exact significance of the division varied from period to period, but in general line-up and most of the time, the Guelphs were the party of the Papacy; the Ghibellines, the party of the Empire. On the whole, the greater feudal nobles were Ghibellines, especially in the Germanic states and in Italy. As a counterweight to them, the Pope brought many of the Italian city-states into the Guelph camp, in particular the rising burgher class of the city-states, which was already in internal conflict with the great nobles at home. This distinction, however, holds only in general; often adherence to one or the other of the factions was a device to secure special and temporary advantages independent of the over-all division. For example, the House of France during the 13th century inclined toward the Guelphs in order to secure leverage against the Empire. Two of the junior members of the French royal family, Charles of Anjou and Charles of Valois, were among the leading champions of the Guelphs. The Italian cities, similarly, often chose sides in such a way as to aid them most in meeting local and immediate problems.

By the latter half of the 12th century, the Emperor ruled over most of the Germanic areas and the Kingdom of the Two Sicilies, which included most of southern Italy. The major expansive aim of the Empire was to secure control of the cities of northern Italy, the richest and most prosperous states of all Europe. The object of the Papacy and of the cities themselves, or at least of the burghers of the cities, was to block the advance of the Empire. The Papacy set out to destroy the Hohenstaufen family, which led the Empire, and which the Popes rightly understood to be the core of the Ghibelline faction. After a century of struggle, this was done; the hold of the Empire on the Kingdom of the Sicilies was broken by the Guelph, Charles of Anjou; and the last of the Hohenstaufen family, the romantic youth Conradin, was slaughtered after his defeat by Charles in the battle of Tagliacozzo—in 1268, three years after the birth of Dante. The struggle, however, continued, and the Empire still kept its dreams fixed on the Italian cities.

* * *

Now Florence, Dante's own seething, rich, dynamic city, the leader of Tuscany and one of the chief states of the late medieval world, became a great and uncompromising bulwark of the Guelph faction. Machiavelli, in his *History of Florence,* describes how internal conflicts within Florence broadened to join the international Guelph-Ghibelline division. In the course of a private quarrel, a group headed by the Uberti family assassinated a mem-

DANTE: POLITICS AS WISH 13

ber of the Buondelmonti family. "This Murder divided the whole City, part of it siding with the Buondelmonti, and part with the Uberti; and both the Families being powerful in Houses, Castles, and Men, the quarrel continued many years before either could be ejected; yet though the animosity could not be extinguished by a firm and stable peace, yet things were palliated and composed sometimes for the present, by certain Truces and Cessations, by which means (according to the variety of accidents) they were sometimes at quiet, and sometimes together by the Ears. In this Condition Florence continued till the Reign of Frederic II [of Hohenstaufen, Emperor from 1215-1250] who being King of Naples, and desirous to strengthen himself against the Church; to corroborate his interest in Tuscany, joined himself to the Uberti and their party, by whose assistance the Buondelmonti were driven out of Florence, and that City (as all Italy had done before) began to divide into the Factions of the Guelphs, and the Ghibellines." *

The triumph of the Ghibellines in Florence was, however, brief, as was only natural in a city which was beginning a great commercial and industrial expansion in terms of which the old-line nobility was a constant drain and obstacle. The death of Frederic II in 1250 gave the Florentine Guelphs their chance to overthrow the Ghibelline rule and exile the leaders of the Ghibelline faction. The Ghibellines returned temporarily to power after a victory in 1260, but were again and definitively driven out, with the help of Charles of Anjou, in 1266—a result which was a phase of the broader campaign of the Pope and Charles against the last of the Hohenstaufen.

After a number of experiments in internal administration, the

---

* All quotations from and references to Machiavelli are taken from the English translation: *"The Works of the famous Nicolas Machiavel,* London, Printed for J. S. and are to be sold by Robert Boulter at the Turks-Head in Cornhil, against the Royal Exchange, 1675." I have in some cases modernized the spelling.

government of the city, firmly Guelph, gravitated into the hands of the Merchant Guilds, now representing the chief social force in the town. Membership in a Guild became a prerequisite of political office. The executive power was held by a body of six Priors, elected every two months from each of the six wards into which Florence was divided. In 1293 the remarkable "Ordinances of Justice" placed heavy legal disabilities on the great nobles as individuals and as a class. Nobility, it was said, became a disgrace in the commercially based democracy of the Florentine Republic.

The hope that the suppression of the Ghibellines would end domestic turmoil in Florence quickly vanished. There was too much life there for tranquillity. In 1300 the dominant Florentine Guelphs themselves split into a new factional division: the Neri ("Blacks") and Bianchi ("Whites"). Here is Machiavelli's account:

"Never was this City in greater splendor, nor more happy in its condition than then, abounding both in men, riches, and reputation. They had 3,000 Citizens in the Town fit to bear Arms, and 70,000 more in their Territory. All Tuscany was at its devotion, partly as subjects, and partly as friends. And though there were still piques and suspicions betwixt the Nobility and the people, yet they did not break out into any ill effect, but all lived quietly and peaceably together; and had not this tranquillity been at length interrupted by dissension within, it had been in no danger from abroad; being in such terms at that time, it neither feared the Empire, nor its Exiles [e.g., the Ghibellines], and could have brought a force into the Field equivalent to all the rest of the States in Italy. But that disease from which *ab extra* it was secure, was engendered in its own bowels.

"There were two Families in Florence, the Cerchi, and the Donati, equally considerable, both in numbers, riches, and dignity; being Neighbors both in City and Country, there happened some exceptions and disgusts betwixt them, but not so great as to bring them to blows, and perhaps they would never have produced any considerable effects, had not their ill humors been agitated and fermented by new occasion. Among the chief Families in Pistoia, there was the Family of the Cancellieri: It happened that Lore, the Son of Gulielmo, and Geri, the son of Bertaccio, fell out by accident at play, and passing from words to blows, Geri received a slight wound. Gulielmo was much troubled at the business, and thinking by excess of humility to take off the scandal, he increased it and made it worse. He commanded his Son to go to Geri's Father's house, and demand his pardon; Lore obeyed, and went as his Father directed, but that act of humanity did not at all sweeten the acerbity of Bertaccio's mind, who causing Lore to be seized by his servants (to aggravate the indignity) he caused him to be led by them into the stable, and his hand cut off upon the Manger, with instruction to return to his Father, and to let him know, 'That wounds are not cured so properly by words, as amputation.' Gulielmo was so enraged at the cruelty of the fact, as he and his friends immediately took arms to revenge it; and Bertaccio and his friends doing as much to defend themselves, the whole city of Pistoia was engaged in the quarrel, and divided into two parties. These Cancellieri being both of them descended from one of the Cancellieri who had two Wives, one of them called Bianca: that party which descended from her, called itself Bianca; and the other in opposition [because the name "Bianca" has the same meaning as the word for "white"] was called Nera ["black"]. In a short time many conflicts happened betwixt them, many men killed, and many houses destroyed. Not being able to accommodate among themselves, though both sides were weary, they concluded to come to Florence, hoping some expedient would be found out there, or else to fortify their parties by the acquisition of new friends. The Neri having had familiarity with the Donati, were espoused by Corso, the head of that family. The Bianchi, to support themselves against the accession of the Donati, fell in with Veri, the chief of the Cerchi, a man not inferior to Corso in any quality whatever. . . .

"In the Month of May, several Holidays being publicly celebrated in Florence, certain young Gentlemen of the Donati, with their friends on Horseback, having stopped near St. Trinity, to see certain Women that were Dancing, it fell out that some of the Cerchi arrived there likewise with some of their friends, and being desirous to see as well as the rest, not knowing the Donati were before, they spurred on their horses, and jostled in among them. The Donati looking upon it as an affront, drew their Swords; the Cerchi were as ready to answer them, and after several cuts and slashes given and received, both sides retired. This accident was the occasion of great mischief; the whole City (as well People as Nobility) divided, and took part with the Bianchi and Neri, as their inclinations directed . . . Nor did this humor extend itself only in the City, but infected the whole Country [that is, all of Tuscany]. Insomuch that the Captains of the Arts [i.e., the Guilds], and such as favored the Guelphs, and were Lovers of the Commonwealth, very much apprehended lest this new distraction should prove the ruin of the City, and the restoration of the Ghibellines."

The last sentence gives the key to the meaning of the new division. The Neri faction, however it did in fact originate, was made up of the firm and unyielding ultra-Guelphs. The Bianchi were a centrist grouping, inclined to try to compromise and bridge the gulf between Guelphs and Ghibellines.

Dante, as an active citizen of Florence, had been brought up as a Guelph. He had enrolled in the Guild of Druggists and Physicians in order to be eligible for political office. When the new conflict broke out, he lined up with the Bianchi faction, though at first, apparently, he concealed his allegiance under a cover of impartiality. In 1300 he was elected one of the six Priors for the term June 15th to August 15th. The new conflict had by then

DANTE: POLITICS AS WISH 17

become threatening. Dante and his fellow Priors, as the chief magistrates of the City, made the mistake of trying to resolve it by banishing simultaneously several leaders of both factions. Probably this was a deceptive maneuver by the Bianchi, who thought thereby to get rid of the Neri leaders and then to readmit their own men at the first opportunity.

The Neri, however, were not so easily reconciled. They were determined, and they had a much firmer line than the Bianchi, who were in reality vacillating between the major camps of Guelphs and Ghibellines. The Neri made a clever move. They appealed to the Pope (Boniface VIII) to arbitrate the dispute. He sent as his delegate to Florence Cardinal Matteo d'Aquasparta. It was hard to make an open objection to this procedure. What more natural and fair than that the spiritual head of Christendom should intervene to compose the quarrels of his erring children? In truth, however, as we have seen, the Pope was the leader of the Guelphs. The object of his intervention would be to swing the decision to his firmest political supporters, the Neri. This the Bianchi well knew, and they therefore refused to accept the offices of Cardinal Matteo, who departed, leaving the city under an interdict.

The religious arm having failed, Boniface turned to the secular. He called upon his old allies of the House of France. At his request, Charles of Valois, brother of King Philip, came to Italy. On November 1, 1301, he entered Florence in great state, still nominally as arbitrator and pacifier. He quickly arranged a purge of the Bianchi. There was issued, on January 27, 1302, a decree of fines and two years' banishment against Dante and a number of his colleagues. When this was disregarded, a sterner decree was published on March 10th, calling for the death by burning of Dante and fourteen others if they should fall into the hands of the Republic. They were forced thus into exile.

There then occurred what had been sure from the beginning

of the Neri-Bianchi division. The Bianchi, routed within Florence, were too weak to recover power unaided. Their only possible allies were the remaining Ghibellines of Tuscany, with whom the Bianchi joined. Before long the Bianchi, toppled from their hopeless center position, were themselves full-fledged Ghibellines.

The united Bianchi-Ghibelline forces were, however, still not strong enough. Their attempts to re-enter Florence by force were repulsed. In a state of disintegration, the last and only hope seemed to be the ancient core of the Ghibelline faction, the Empire itself, and to the Empire their dreams turned. The Emperor would come, like an avenging leopard, to crush the pride and insolence of unbridled Florence. Since the Pope's success against the Hohenstaufen, however, the Empire, under the guidance for the first time of the cautious and remarkable Hapsburg family, had curbed its ambitions and stayed at home. But the new star of the House of Luxemburg was rising. To it the embittered Ghibellines of Tuscany chained their hopes. In 1308, Henry of Luxemburg was elected Emperor as Henry VII. Dante, in a series of bombastic public letters, called upon his Roman sword to smite the wicked of the Church and the cities, and restore Italy to its imperial grandeur.

"O Italy! henceforth rejoice; though now to be pitied by the very Saracens, yet soon to be envied throughout the world! because thy bridegroom, the solace of the world and the glory of thy people, the most clement Henry, Divus and Augustus and Caesar, is hastening to the bridal. Dry thy tears and remove the marks of grief, O thou fairest one; for nigh at hand is he who shall release thee from the prison of the impious, and, smiting the malicious, shall destroy them with the edge of the sword, and shall give out his vineyard to other husbandmen such as shall render the fruit of justice at time of harvest. . . .

"But you [Florentines], who transgress divine and human law, whom a dire rapaciousness hath found ready to be drawn into

DANTE: POLITICS AS WISH 19

every crime,—doth not the dread of the second death pursue you? For ye first and alone, shunning the yoke of liberty, have murmured against the glory of the Roman prince, the king of the world and the minister of God, and on the plea of prescriptive right have refused the duty of the submission which ye owed, and have rather risen up in the insanity of rebellion! . . ."

Henry did at last come down into Italy. But he could make up his mind to nothing; he dallied sluggishly with his army, undertaking and lifting half-hearted sieges of the towns. In 1313 he fell ill and died. The rhetorical balloons of the Ghibelline exiles thus ingloriously burst. Dante never re-entered Florence. The rest of his days were spent wandering among the households of the remaining Ghibelline princes in northern Italy. His revenge on his Guelph enemies had to be satisfied by thrusting them into the worst torments of his Inferno. For Boniface VIII, ultimate author of his defeats, though he was not yet dead in 1300—the date which Dante assigns to his journey throught Hell and Purgatory and Heaven—a particularly hideous spot in Hell is duly reserved and waiting.*

* * *

We are now in a position to understand the real meaning of *De Monarchia*.

Eternal salvation, the highest development of man's potentialities, everlasting peace, unity, and harmony, the delicate balance of abstract relations between Church and State, all these ghosts and myths evaporate, along with the whole elaborate structure of theology, metaphysics, allegory, miracle, and fable. The entire formal meaning, which has told us nothing and proved nothing, assumes its genuine role of merely expressing and disguising the

---

*Inferno, Canto XIX. Nicholas III, Boniface's predecessor, is already there, stuffed head first into a narrow hole, with flames moving eternally over both his feet. As Dante goes by, he stops to talk to the inverted Nicholas. With a marvelous sense of irony, Nicholas is made to mistake Dante for Boniface.

real meaning. This real meaning is simply an impassioned propagandistic defense of the point of view of the turncoat Bianchi exiles from Florence, specifically; and more generally of the broader Ghibelline point of view to which these Bianchi capitulated. *De Monarchia* is, we might say, a Ghibelline Party Platform.

It should not be imagined, however, that this point of view is argued rationally, that there is offered in its favor any proof or evidence, that any demonstration is attempted to show that its acceptance would contribute to human welfare. The proof and evidence and demonstration, such as they are, are all devoted to the mysteries of the formal meaning. The real meaning is expressed and projected indirectly through the formal meaning, and is supported by nothing more than emotion, prejudice, and confusion. The real aims are thus intellectually irresponsible, subject to no intellectual check or control. Even if they were justifiable, the case for them is in no degree established.

The ostensible goals of the formal argument are noble, highminded, what people often call "idealistic." This serves to create a favorable emotional response in the reader, to disarm him, to lead him to believe in the "good will" of the author. The unwary reader carries this attitude over to the practical aims of the real argument. But what of these latter aims, what do they concretely amount to? When we dig behind the formal façade, they emerge as vicious and reactionary.

They are the aims of an embittered and incompetent set of traitors. Dante and his friends had failed miserably in their political careers. They had been defeated in their attempt to take over the government of their country. Quite properly, in accordance with the customs of the time, and for the interests of internal security, they had been exiled. They then joined with the disintegrated forces of earlier exiles, whose only wish was to revenge themselves on Florence, and to destroy her power. The enlarged group also failed. They then crawled slavishly to the feet of the Republic's oldest and most thorough enemy—the Emperor—begging him to do what they were too weak and too stupid to have done. The aims of the Empire in northern Italy were very far indeed from eternal salvation, universal peace, and the highest development of man's potentialities. The Empire clutched greedily after the amazing wealth and resources of these remarkable cities, and dreamed of reducing their proud, fierce independence to the tyrannical rule of its *Gauleiters*.

In those days, by an odd conjuncture, the Papacy with the Guelph faction was supporting the most progressive developments in society. It was the newly rising class of burghers in the cities that was just beginning to break the now withering hand of feudalism. The burghers were expanding trade and industry— already the splendid woolens finished in Florence, and the gold-pieces ("florins," they were called) which its citizens had resolved to protect against the hitherto universal practice of debasement, were becoming known throughout the western world. The merchants were reopening among men links of social communication that involved more of life than war and pillage. Nor was it merely trade and industry that were advancing: the new riches were being transformed into an art that was perhaps the most magnificent the world has known (Giotto himself was Dante's contemporary), and were stimulating a renewed interest in the endless possibilities of a more truly human knowledge.

Naturally, the great nobles looked with alarm. They and their ways could have little place in this new world. The economic position of the nobles rested on the land, on an agriculture carried out by serfs and villeins tied to the soil. The burghers wanted men to work in the shops. The cities subordinated the countryside to themselves, exploiting it ruthlessly, it is true, to supply cheap food and raw materials. The nobles were trained only for war—war conducted as the personal combat of knights—and political intrigue. The burghers wanted less war, because it interfered with commercial prosperity; and, when it came, wanted it for valuable economic ends (a port or a source of supplies or a market). They wanted a politics and government by law instead of by personal privilege.

The great nobles, in short, and their party, the Ghibellines, wanted to stop history short; more, wanted to go back to their full day, which was already beginning to end, its twilight first seen in these Italian cities. Dante, whom commentators willing to judge from surfaces are so fond of calling "the first modern man," "the precursor of the Renaissance," was their spokesman. His practical political aims toward his country were traitorous; his sociological allegiance was reactionary, backward-looking. Without his exile, true enough, it may well be that he would never have written his poem. A rotten politics, which besides had no appreciable influence on the course of political events, was no doubt a small price to pay for so marvelous a human gain. But there is an intellectual advantage in separating the two, the poetry and the politics, for judgment.

3. The Typical Method of Political Thought

IT IS EASY to dismiss *De Monarchia* as having a solely historical, archaic, or biographical interest. Few now would consider it seriously as a study of the nature and laws of politics, of political behavior and principles. We seldom, now, talk about "eternal salvation" in political treatises; there is no more Holy Roman Empire; scholastic metaphysics is a mystery for all but the neo-Thomists; it is not fashionable to settle arguments by appeal to religious miracles and allegorical parables from the Bible or the Fathers.

All this is so, and yet it would be a great error to suppose that Dante's method, in *De Monarchia,* is outworn. His method is exactly that of the Democratic Platform with which we began our inquiry. It has been and continues to be the method of nine-tenths, yes, much more than nine-tenths, of all writing and speaking in the field of politics. The myths, the ghosts, the idealistic abstractions, change name and form, but the method persistently remains. It is, then, important to be entirely clear about the general features of this method. They may be summarized as follows:

1. There is a sharp divorce between what I have called the formal meaning, the formal aims and arguments, and the real meaning, the real aims and argument (if there is, as there is usually not, any real argument).

2. The formal aims and goals are for the most part or altogether either supernatural or metaphysical-transcendental—in both cases meaningless from the point of view of real actions in the real world of space and time and history; or, if they have some em-

pirical meaning, are impossible to achieve under the actual conditions of social life. In all three cases, the dependence of the whole structure of reasoning upon such goals makes it impossible for the writer (or speaker) to give a true descriptive account of the way men actually behave. A systematic distortion of the truth takes place. And, obviously, it cannot be shown how the goals might be reached, since, being unreal, they cannot be reached.

3. From a purely logical point of view, the arguments offered for the formal aims and goals may be valid or fallacious; but, except by accident, they are necessarily irrelevant to real political problems, since they are designed to prove the ostensible points of the formal structure—points of religion or metaphysics, or the abstract desirability of some utopian ideal.

4. The formal meaning serves as an indirect expression of the real meaning—that is, of the concrete meaning of the political treatise taken in its real context, in its relation to the actualities of the social and historical situation in which it functions. But at the same time that it expresses, it also disguises the real meaning. We think we are debating universal peace, salvation, a unified world government, and the relations between Church and State, when what is really at issue is whether the Florentine Republic is to be run by its own citizens or submitted to the exploitation of a reactionary foreign monarch. We think, with the delegates at the Council of Nicea, that the discussion is concerned with the definition of God's essence, when the real problem is whether the Mediterranean world is to be politically centralized under Rome, or divided. We believe we are disputing the merits of a balanced budget and a sound currency when the real conflict is deciding what group shall regulate the distribution of the currency. We imagine we are arguing over the moral and legal status of the principle of the freedom of the seas when the real question is who is to control the seas.

5. From this it follows that the real meaning, the real goal

DANTE: POLITICS AS WISH

and aims, are left irresponsible. In Dante's case the aims were also vicious and reactionary. This need not be the case, but, when this method is used, they are always irresponsible. Even if the real aims are such as to contribute to human welfare, no proof or evidence for this is offered. Proof and evidence, so far as they are present at all, remain at the formal level. The real aims are accepted, even if right, for the wrong reasons. The high-minded words of the formal meaning serve only to arouse passion and prejudice and sentimentality in favor of the disguised real aims.

This method, whose intellectual consequence is merely to confuse and hide, can teach us nothing of the truth, can in no way help us to solve the problems of our political life. In the hands of the powerful and their spokesmen, however, used by demagogues or hypocrites or simply the self-deluded, this method is well designed, and the best, to deceive us, and to lead us by easy routes to the sacrifice of our own interests and dignity in the service of the mighty.

* * *

The chief historical effects of the French Revolution were to break up the system of the older French monarchy, with its privileged financiers and courtiers, to remove a number of feudal restrictions on capitalist methods of production, and to put the French capitalists into a position of greater social power. It might well have been argued, prior to the Revolution, that these goals promised to contribute to the welfare of the French people and perhaps of mankind. Evidence for and against this expectation might have been assembled. However, this was not the procedure generally followed by the ideologists of the Revolution. They based their treatises not upon an examination of the facts, but upon supposedly fundamental and really quite mythical notions of a primitive "state of nature," the "natural goodness of man," the "social contract," and similar nonsense. They sloganized, as the aims of the Revolution, Liberty, Equality and Fraternity, and the utopian kingdom of the Goddess Reason. Naturally, the workers and peasants were disappointed by the outcome, after so much blood; but, oddly enough, most of France seemed to feel not many years later that the aims of the Revolution were well enough realized in the military dictatorship of Bonaparte.

No doubt a unification of Europe under Hitler is a bad thing for the European peoples and the world. But this is no more proved by complicated deductions to show the derivation of Nazi thought from Hegelian dialectic and the philosophic poetry of Nietzsche than is the contradictory by Hitler's own mystical pseudo-biology. "Freedom from want" is very nearly as meaningless, in terms of real politics, as "eternal salvation"—men are wanting beings; they are freed from want only by death. Whatever the book or article or speech on political matters that we turn to—those of a journalist like Pierre van Paassen, a demagogue like Hitler, a professor like Max Lerner, a chairman of a sociology department like Pitirim Sorokin, a revolutionist like Lenin, a trapped idealist like Henry Wallace, a bull-dozing rhetorician like Churchill, a preacher out of a church like Norman Thomas or one in like Bishop Manning, the Pope or the ministers of the Mikado—in the case of them all we find that, though there may be incidental passages which increase our fund of real information, the integrating method and the whole conception of politics is precisely that of Dante. Gods, whether of Progress or the Old Testament, ghosts of saintly, or revolutionary, ancestors, abstracted moral imperatives, ideals cut wholly off from mere earth and mankind, utopias beckoning from the marshes of their never-never-land—these, and not the facts of social life together with probable generalizations based on those facts, exercise the final controls over arguments and conclusions. Political analysis becomes, like other dreams, the expression of human wish or the admission of practical failure.

Part II

MACHIAVELLI: THE SCIENCE OF POWER

1. *Machiavelli's Practical Goal*

DANTE'S *De Monarchia* is in no respect a scientific study of politics. It is not, however, as is sometimes supposed, the mere fact that Dante has ethical aims or goals that makes his treatise, or any treatise making use of similar methods, unscientific. All human activities have goals, usually several of them, open or hidden, whether or not admitted by the actor. The activity of scientific investigation is no exception. Machiavelli, like Dante, has goals and practical aims that he pursues in his work. But they are very different from those that we have discovered in Dante.

There are certain goals which are peculiar and proper to science, without which science does not exist. These are: the accurate and systematic description of public facts; the attempt to correlate sets of these facts in laws; and, through these correlations, the attempt to predict, with some degree of probability, future facts. Many scientific investigations do not try to go beyond these special goals; nor is there any need for them to do so. In the field of historical, social, and political science, as in other sciences, these goals might be, and sometimes are, alone relevant. But without these goals, whether or not there are also others, an inquiry is not scientific.

These special goals of science are not present in *De Monarchia*. They could not be served by Dante's methods. In Machiavelli's writings, in contrast, they are always present, and they control the logic of his investigations.

If an inquiry is to remain scientific, but nevertheless pursue other goals than these that are peculiar to science, there are certain requirements which the additional goals must meet. In the first place, they must be non-transcendental—that is, they must be something formulated in terms of the actual world of space and time and history. Second, they must have at least a minimum probability of realization. For example, a scientist might have as his goal the development of a drug to cure tuberculosis or some other disease; or a new defensive weapon to counteract the offensive threat of bombers; or a new fertilizer that would also help plants resist blights and insects; or a new method of transmitting electric power without wires. All of these goals are located in the actual world, they are all sufficiently specific to permit us to know what we are talking about (and, what is not unimportant, to tell whether or not they are reached), and all would have at least a certain minimum chance of being achieved.

We noticed, however, that Dante's formal goals were either transcendental, as in the case of his religious and metaphysical ideals, or, as in the case of his plan for an eternally unified and peaceful world empire (in the 14th century), too wildly improbable to be worth debating. We noticed also that his real goals, hidden beneath the formal goals, were, though specific enough, vicious and reactionary.

There is a further strict requirement by which science limits the function of goals or aims. The goals themselves are not evidence; they cannot be allowed to distort facts or the correlations among facts. The goals express our wishes, hopes, or fears. They therefore prove nothing about the facts of the world. No matter how much we may wish to cure a patient, the wish has nothing to do with the objective analysis of his symptoms, or a correct prediction of the probable course of the disease, or an estimate of the probable effects of a medicine. If our aim is peace, this does not entitle us, from the point of view of science, to falsify human nature and the facts of social life in order to pretend to prove that "all men naturally desire peace," which, history so clearly tells us, they plainly do not. If we are interested in an equalitarian

MACHIAVELLI: SCIENCE OF POWER 31

democracy, this cannot be a scientific excuse for neglecting the uninterrupted record of social inequality and oppression.

In short, though our practical goals may dictate the direction that scientific activity takes, though they show us what we are trying to accomplish by the scientific investigation, what problem we are trying to solve; nevertheless, the logic of the scientific inquiry itself is not controlled by the practical aims but by science's own aims, by the effort to describe facts and to correlate them. In this respect, too, Dante violates the demand of science. His treatise is merely the elaborate projection of his wish. It tells us nothing.

* * *

Machiavelli's chief immediate practical goal is the national unification of Italy. There are other practical aims in his writings, some of them more general, and I shall discuss them later on. To make Italy a nation, a unified state, is, however, central and constant.

Compared to Dante's glittering ideals, this goal is doubtless humble, almost sordid. In any case, it is specific and meaningful. We all know what a national state, in the modern sense, means. Machiavelli, writing in the first quarter of the 16th century, and his contemporaries, with the example of France and England and Spain fresh before them, knew what the goal meant. Moreover, the goal was neither wild nor fantastic; it was accomplished elsewhere in Europe during those times, and there was no reason to think it too improbable of accomplishment in Italy.

In the case of Dante we had to distinguish carefully between the formal, presumed goals, and the hidden real goals. In Machiavelli, as in all scientific writing, there is no such distinction. Formal and real are one, open and explicit. The last chapter of *The Prince* is plainly entitled, "An Exhortation to Deliver Italy from the Barbarians [that is, foreigners]." In it Machiavelli calls for a champion to rally Italy for the task of unification:

"Having weighed, therefore, all that is said before, and considered seriously with myself whether in this juncture of affairs in Italy, the times were disposed for the advancement of a new Prince, and whether there was competent matter that could give occasion to a virtuous and wise person to introduce such a form as would bring reputation to him, and benefit to all his subjects; it seems to me that at this present so many things concur to the exaltation of a new Prince, that I do not know any time that has been more proper than this.... 'Tis manifest how prone and ready she is to follow the Banner that any man will take up; nor is it at present to be discerned where she can repose her hopes with more probability, than in your illustrious Family [of the Medici], which by its own courage and interest, and the favor of God and the Church, of which it is now chief [Leo X of the Medici family was Pope when Machiavelli was writing this passage], may be induced to make itself Head in her redemption: which will be no hard matter to be effected, if you lay before you the lives and actions of the persons above named; who though they were rare, and wonderful, were yet but men, and not accommodated with so fair circumstances as you. Their enterprise was not more just, nor easy, nor God Almighty more their friend than yours. You have Justice on your side; for that War is just which is necessary, and 'tis piety to fight, where no hope is left in anything else. The people are universally disposed, and where the disposition is so great, the opposition can be but small, especially you taking your rules from those persons which I have proposed to you for a Model . . ." (*The Prince,* Chap. 26.)

Machiavelli's careful treatise on *The Art of War* and the lengthy discussions of war in his *Discourses on Livy* have an ever-present aim of showing Italians how they can learn to fight in such a way as to beat back the forces of France and the Empire

MACHIAVELLI: SCIENCE OF POWER 33

and Spain, and thereby control their own destiny as an Italian nation. The *History of Florence* finds in the stories of the past a traditional spirit that can be linked with arms in the struggle. The examples of ancients and moderns, joined in the *Discourses on Livy,* show the direction along the political road.

There is nothing ambiguous about this goal of making Italy a nation. Anyone, reading Machiavelli, could accept it or reject it, and, doing so, would know exactly what he was accepting or rejecting. There are no dreams or ghosts in Machiavelli. He lives and writes in the daylight world.

* * *

Again unlike Dante's ideals, this goal of Machiavelli's is appropriate to the context of his times; and is, moreover, unquestionably progressive.

Italy, in his day, as it had been since the breakup of the Roman Empire, was divided into a number of turbulent, varying states, provinces, and half-states. Most of the South was included in the Kingdom of Naples. There, in the backward, unorganized, undeveloped countryside, feudal relations prevailed, with anarchic barons lording it over their fiefs of the moment. In the center were the changing Papal States, related through the Pope and his designs to the intrigues of all Europe. In the North, part of the country districts were still under feudal domination, but for the most part the territory was subordinated to the small city-states: Venice, Milan, and Florence the most powerful, and lesser cities like Genoa, Ferrara, and Bologna.

This fragmentation of Italy had left it open to an uninterrupted series of invasions, by adventurers, junior members of royal families, knights returning from the Crusades, kings, and emperors. Control over cities and territories shifted every decade, from Normans to Spaniards to Frenchmen to local bosses to Germans to Popes and back again. Nevertheless, the amazing city-states of the North had made Italy, during the 14th and 15th centuries, the center of Europe. It is hard for us today, thinking in terms of modern nations or of the great regional super-states now being built through the present war, to understand how important these cities were in those times.

We must remember that the cities had their period of chief influence and power against the background of a predominantly feudal, agricultural Europe. The feudal organization of society was centrifugal in tendency, each feudal lord claiming jurisdiction over his particular fiefs, vassals, and serfs, and acknowledging the authority only of his particular suzerain. Under feudalism there was no developed central state power. The sovereignty of the medieval kings, therefore, was largely fictional except as it held over their immediate feudal domain, or as it might suit the interests of their feudal peers to collaborate with them. Until the 15th century, the attempts of the kings to consolidate a firm governmental authority always met a strong and on the whole successful resistance from the lords.

Moreover, the primitive economy, the lack of manufacture for the market, of money-exchange, of extensive foreign trade, of easy transportation and communication, meant the absence of a socio-economic basis for lasting large-scale political units. In the first stages of the breakup of feudalism, those who were aiming toward the national political system, which was later to win out, were working at a disadvantage. They were ahead of their times, trying to erect too weighty a structure on an unfinished foundation.

It was in these stages that the city-states, such as those of northern Italy—as well as those, somewhat different in character, of the Lowlands and parts of Germany—had their great opportunity. They were not trying to do too much; they were small enough to be viable, and yet large enough, for those times, to hold

MACHIAVELLI: SCIENCE OF POWER 35

their own politically. They established control over the surrounding countryside, in order to assure their food supplies. They could put armies in the field, either of their own citizens or of hired mercenaries, able to meet the forces of feudal lords and princes, even if the princes called themselves King of France, or Emperor. And these cities were concentrating on industry, trade, commerce, banking. They did not manufacture only for use, or wait for an annual or quarterly market-day for exchange. They manufactured for the general market, and they traded, in money as well as goods, every day. They had their ships and their land convoys everywhere; they established trading posts or "factors" all over Europe and the Mediterranean basin. They were first-class powers, as powers then went. Their ambassadors and ministers were respected at any Court. Along with their economic and political prosperity went also their unequaled cultural expansion.

The cities, thus, had a head start. But the very factors that had brought their early advantage were, by the 16th century, when Machiavelli was writing, turning them toward ruin. As the new world began to take more definitive form, these first children of that world were already old and socially decadent. They were rich, easy, luxurious, "have" powers, for all their small number of acres. They were ready to let others do their fighting for them, to rely, as Machiavelli a thousand times upbraids them, on money and treaties, not on the strength and virtue of their own citizens.

Trade, which had so aided them in their climb to glory and which they had so notably furthered, was now pushing beyond their power to control. By the end of the 15th century, the ships were sailing around the Cape to the East and across the Atlantic. The market was becoming world-wide. The volume of goods was multiplying; gold and silver were pouring in; serfs were leaving the land to make commodities; manufacturing plants were becoming larger. The city-states, which had once nursed the new economy, were now beginning to strangle it. The guild restrictions which had kept up the quality of Florentine woolens or Venetian glass or Genoese weapons were now, in order to maintain the traditional privileges of their members, preventing an influx of new workers and new capital. The state power of the cities, and their armed forces, were not now strong enough to police transportation routes, guard the sea lanes, put down brigandage and the vagaries of barons who did not realize that their world was ending. Uniform systems of taxation and stable, standardized money for large areas were now required. For all such tasks only the modern nation-state could adequately provide.

Italy, then, in Machiavelli's day, faced a sharp, imperative choice, a choice that had already been pointed by the examples of Spain and especially of France and England. Italy could remain under the existing political structure. If so, if it continued in the old ways, it was sure to retrogress, to decline economically and culturally, to sink into the backyard of Europe. Or Italy could follow the example of France and England, unify itself, organize as a nation; and thereby continue in the front rank, be, perhaps, the chief state of the modern world.

This was the problem, and this problem Machiavelli, in its political aspects above all, fully understood. Machiavelli made his decision, explained it, advocated it. Unfortunately for Italy, his advice was not accepted. Italy paid her historical penalty. More than three centuries later she tried to catch up with Machiavelli; but by then, as we know today well enough, it was too late. A new style of barbarian, with new techniques, has once again swept over her from the North.

* * *

Machiavelli concluded that Italy could be unified only through a Prince, who would take the initiative in consolidating the country into a nation. Those who think sentimentally rather than

MACHIAVELLI: SCIENCE OF POWER 37

scientifically about politics are sure to misunderstand this conclusion. Machiavelli did not reach it because he preferred a monarchy or absolutist government—we shall see later what his own preferences were. He reached it because he found that it was dictated by the evidence.

Moreover, in this conclusion Machiavelli was undoubtedly correct. All of the European nations were consolidated through a Prince—or, rather, a succession of Princes—and it is hard to see how it could have been otherwise. So it was in France, so in England, so in Spain. The feudal lords did not want nation-states, which in the end were sure to bring the destruction of their power and privileges. The masses were too inarticulate, too ignorant, too weak, to function as a leading political force. The Church knew that its international overlordship was gravely threatened if the national system were successful.

The one great social group that required the national system was the new and spreading class of the burghers, the business men, the merchants, the early capitalists. This class, however, was too young, too untried, too unused to rule, to take on the job by itself. But the monarchy also—the King and those immediately associated with the King—was ready for the nation, through which the full political sovereignty of the monarch could be centralized and brought to bear against the centrifugal pull of feudalism. Therefore a *de facto* alliance was made, and around the monarchy the nation was pulled together. It was Machiavelli's own contemporary, Sir Thomas More, most successful lawyer in London, leading spokesman for the London merchants, who was the first commoner to become Chancellor of England. A younger contemporary and fellow-Florentine, Catherine, of the same Medici family to one of whose members *The Prince* is dedicated, daughter of a banker, became Queen and ruler of France.

If the path of the nation led through the monarchy in these other countries, Machiavelli indicated why this was even more necessarily so in Italy, where the political divisionalism was even more extreme. Only a Prince could rally around him the force and enthusiasm needed to smash and re-fuse the disparate units. In such a way only could Italy become a nation.

* * *

Almost all commentators on Machiavelli say that his principal innovation, and the essence of his method, was to "divorce politics from ethics." Thereby he broke sharply with the Aristotelian tradition which had dominated medieval political thought. His method, they grant, freed politics to become more scientific and objective in its study of human behavior; but it was most dangerous because, through it, politics was released from "control" by ethical conceptions of what is right and good.

We have already seen enough to realize that this opinion is confused. Machiavelli divorced politics from ethics only in the same sense that every science must divorce itself from ethics. Scientific descriptions and theories must be based upon the facts, the evidence, not upon the supposed demands of some ethical system. If this is what is meant by the statement that Machiavelli divorced politics from ethics, if the statement sums up his refusal to pervert and distort political science by doctoring its results in order to bring them into line with "moral principles"—his own or any others—then the charge is certainly true.

This very refusal, however, this allegiance to objective truth, is itself a moral ideal. Moreover, in another sense, Machiavelli undertook his studies of politics for the sake of very definite goals, one of which I have analyzed in this section. These goals, like all goals, have an ethical content: indeed, ethics is simply the consideration of human behavior from the point of view of goals, standards, norms, and ideals. Machiavelli divorced politics from a certain kind of ethics—namely, from a transcendental, otherworldly, and, it may be added, very rotten ethics. But he did so in order to bring politics and ethics more closely into line, and to locate both of them firmly in the real world of space and time and history, which is the only world about which we can know anything. Machiavelli is as ethical a political writer as Dante. The difference is that Machiavelli's ethics are much better.

2. Machiavelli's Method

MACHIAVELLI'S METHOD is the method of science applied to politics. Naturally, Machiavelli's conceptions often seem to us somewhat immature—we know so much more than Machiavelli knew. We must make our judgment in a proper historical perspective, remembering that he wrote more than four centuries ago. In those days, scientific method in our sense, deliberate, systematic, self-conscious, was only beginning. Leonardo da Vinci, the romantically brilliant prophet of science, was a contemporary of Machiavelli, and also a Florentine. Copernicus' great works on astronomy, the turning point for modern science, were only first published a short while after Machiavelli's death. In Machiavelli, as in Leonardo and Copernicus, the nature of scientific method is not fully understood; many pre-scientific notions, held over from medieval and ancient metaphysics and theology, are retained. Copernicus himself, after all, still thought that the planets must move in circular orbits around the sun, because a perfect God would have created none but perfect motion in a circle for the heavenly bodies.

In connection with Machiavelli's own subject-matter there were special difficulties. The critical study of historical texts and source-materials had only just begun, and was confined chiefly to Biblical and Church texts that were at issue in the religious controversies. (Luther, too, was a contemporary of Machiavelli's in that age when the world was at a crisis in another of its slow, great social revolutions.) Almost all writers on historical subjects, Machiavelli among them, tended to accept Greek and Roman authors much more literally than we would, nowadays. There was a readier trust of picturesque dramatic episodes than our colder sense of fact permits us.

Such qualifications as these to Machiavelli's use of the scientific method may, however, be taken for granted by those who do not expect the 16th century to be identical with the 20th.

Positively, then, in the first place, we find that Machiavelli uses language in a cognitive, scientific manner. That is, except where he is frankly urging his readers to action, he uses words not in order to express his emotions or attitudes, but in such a way that their meaning can be tested, can be understood in terms of the real world. We always know what he is talking about. This, a requirement for all scientific discourse, is in political and social discussion an achievement of the very first rank.

Second, Machiavelli delineates with sufficient clarity the field of politics. What are we talking about when we talk politics? Many, to judge by what they write, seem to think we are talking about man's search for the ideally good society, or his mutual organization for the maximum social welfare, or his natural aspiration for peace and harmony, or something equally removed from the world as it is and has been. Machiavelli understood politics as primarily the study of the struggles for power among men. By so marking its field, we are assured that there is being discussed something that exists, not something spun out of an idealist's dreams, or nightmares. If our interest is in man as he is on this earth, so far as we can learn from the facts of history and experience, we must conclude that he has no natural aspiration for peace or harmony, he does not form states in order to achieve an ideally good society, nor does he accept mutual organization to secure the maximum social welfare. But men, and groups of men, do, by various means, struggle among themselves for relative increases in power and privilege. In the course of these struggles and as part of them, governments are established and overthrown, laws passed and violated, wars fought and won and lost. A definition is arbitrary, true enough, but Machiavelli's implied definition of the field of politics as the struggle for power is at least insurance against nonsense.

Third, Machiavelli assembles, and with some measure of system, a large number of facts: facts drawn from his reading in the historical works available to him, from what others, prominent in the politics of his own day, have told him, and from what he has himself observed during his own active political career. In any field except politics, such a procedure might seem too obvious to deserve comment. But in writing about politics, the usual approach is that of Dante, starting not with observed facts, but with supposed general principles governing the nature of man, society, and the universe. Conclusions are reached by deductions from the principles; if facts disagree, so much the worse for the facts. For Machiavelli, the facts come first; questions are answered by appeal to them as final court. If they disclose that successful rulers lie frequently and break treaties, then such a generalization takes precedence over an opposite law drawn from some metaphysical dogma which states that all men have an innate love of the truth, or from an optimistic, unexamined hope that in the long run truth triumphs over lies. If the facts show that a government is more securely based on the confidence and support of the people than on the building of fortresses, then that must answer the argument over the merits of fortresses, widely debated in Machiavelli's time, even though many rulers doubtless preferred to believe otherwise. Florence, with plenty of money and little stomach for fighting, wanted to believe that it could maintain itself by hiring mercenary troops, but the facts, again, proved that only the citizenry in arms could really be trusted. For Machiavelli, when the facts decide, it is the principles that must be scrapped.

Fourth, Machiavelli is always attempting to correlate sets of facts into generalizations or laws. He is interested not alone or primarily in the individual, unique political event, but in laws relating events. He does not suppose that it will be possible for him to formulate, at that primitive stage of political science, universal laws covering the whole realm of politics. But he evidently thinks it possible to state approximate generalizations about many kinds of political event. He is always wondering whether something recorded in Livy or Thucydides, or observed in his own time, is an exception, a unique, peculiar action; or whether it may not be understood as an instance of a general pattern of political behavior. In the vigorous days of the Republic, the Romans elected consuls for a year only. Even if the consuls were leading armies in the field, they were recalled and replaced at the end of their year. This was often a military inconvenience, threatening, at times, military defeat or at least the prolongation of a campaign. But was it wise from the point of view of the preservation of the liberty of the Republic? Machiavelli finds that not only in that connection, but as a general rule, it was not only wise but essential; that the liberty of a Republic is secure only when its officials are elected for short, definite terms, which are never prolonged; and that the twilight of the Roman Republic, as of so many other republican states, was first plainly indicated by the practice of extending the terms of officials.

How should states proceed, if they are to prosper, in the treatment of enemies, internal or external, once the enemies have been defeated? Machiavelli is not interested in the single instance. By examples from Roman and Greek and Carthaginian and Italian and French history, he shows that the "middle way" in such cases almost invariably works out badly; that the enemy should be either completely crushed or completely conciliated, that a mixture of the two simply guarantees both the continuation of a cause for resentment and revenge and the possibility for later translating these into action.

"And because the sentence and judgment of the Senate at that time upon the Latins is more than ordinarily remarkable; that it may be readier for the imitation of Princes when occasion is offered, I shall set down the words which Livy makes Camillus speak, which confirm what we have said about the ways which the Romans observed in the enlargement of their Empire; and shows, that in their determinations in matters of State, they left the middle ways, and followed only the extremes. For Government is nothing but keeping subjects in such a posture as that they may have no will, or power to offend you. And this is done either by taking away all means from them of doing you any hurt; or by obliging and indulging them so, as they may not in reason hope to better their fortune; all which will appear, first by Camillus his Speech to the Senate, and then by their resolution upon it. His words were these: 'The Gods have put it into the power of this Reverend Counsel, to determine whether the Latins shall be a people, or not. As to them, your peace will be perpetual, which way soever you take. Are you disposed to severity, and will destroy those poor people that are conquered, and your prisoners? They are at your mercy, and you may extinguish their very name. Are you disposed according to the example of your ancestors to propagate your interest by receiving them into your City? You have an opportunity of doing it with the highest advantage and glory. Certainly no Empire is so firm, as where subjects exult in their obedience. It will be expedient, therefore, whilst they are in amazement and suspense, to settle their minds one way, either by punishment or pardon.' According to the Consul's proposal, the Senate came to an issue, and gave sentence Town by Town, according to the nature of their deserts; but all in extremes, without any mediocrity; for some they not only pardoned, but loaded them with benefits, made them free of their own City, and gave them many other privileges, and exemptions, and thereby secured them not only from rebelling, but from ever conspiring again. The rest whom they thought fit to make examples, were brought prisoners to Rome, punished with all kind of severity,

MACHIAVELLI: SCIENCE OF POWER 45

their houses destroyed, their lands confiscated, their persons dispersed, so as it was not possible for them any way to do any mischief for the future.

"This was the way the Romans took in the settlement of Latium, which ought to be observed and imitated by all wise Princes and States; and if the Florentines had followed it in the year 1502, when Arezzo and the whole Valley of Chiana rebelled, they had continued their authority, augmented their State, and supplied themselves with those fields which they wanted for their subsistence. But they took the middle way (betwixt the extremes of rigor and remission) which is always the most dangerous; they kept the City, removed the Magistrates, degraded the great men, banished some, and executed others. . . . And things being so, we conclude, according to our proposition in the beginning of our discourse: that upon any great Sentence to be given against a people or City that has been formerly free, the surest way is, to waive all moderation, and either to caress or extinguish them. . . ." (*Discourses,* Book II, Chap. 23.)

It may be further remarked that Machiavelli ordinarily tests his generalizations by examples drawn from several different periods of history. The reason for this is to guard against mistaking a type of behavior characteristic of some particular period for a more general historical law. This striving toward a more embracing political science is most evident in the *Discourses on Livy,* where he customarily links references to Roman and Greek history with references to Italian or European history comparatively close to his own times.

"Because it is easy to begin war as a man pleases, but harder to end it, every Prince before he undertakes an enterprise is obliged to consider his own strength well, and to regulate by it. But then he must be so wise, too, as not to make a wrong judgment, and that he will certainly do as often as he computes it by his Bags [*i.e.,* money-bags], by the situation of his Towns, or the affection of his Friends, rather than by his own proper Power and Arms. Money, and Towns, and Friends, are all good, when in conjunction with a strong Army of your own, but without it they do nothing: without Men, to what purpose is either Money or Towns? and the affection of your subjects will hold no longer than you are able to defend them. There is no mountain, no lake, no strait inaccessible, where there is no force to defend it. Vast sums of money are not only incapable of protecting you, but they expose you to more danger; nor can anything be more false than that old and common saying, 'That money is the sinews of war.' . . . Which saying is nowadays in every Prince's mouth, but improperly, in my judgment: for relying wholly upon that Maxim, they think their treasure is sufficient to defend them, not considering that, if that would have done it, Darius would have conquered Alexander; the Grecians, the Romans; Duke Charles, the Swiss; and of late the Pope and Florentines united, would not have found it so hard to have mastered Francesco Maria (Nephew to Julius II) at the Battle of Urbino. But these whom I have mentioned, presuming more upon the multitude of their bags than the goodness of their men, were all beaten and overcome. . . . Again, when after the death of Alexander the Great, a great Army of Gauls transplanted into Greece (from whence they passed afterwards into Asia) before they began their march, the Gauls sent Ambassadors to the King of Macedon to treat an accord; which being almost concluded, to make the Ambassadors more pliable, the said King shows them his treasure, which consisted of a vast quantity of silver and gold, which the Ambassadors had no sooner seen, but longing impatiently to be at it, they broke off the treaty, and brought their Army into his Country; so that that very thing in which he had reposed his great confidence and security proved his ruin and destruction. The Venetians not long since had their coffers well stored, yet they lost all, and their wealth was not able to defend them. So that I do affirm 'tis not money (as the common opinion will have it) but good soldiers that is the sinews of war: for money cannot find good soldiers, but good soldiers will be sure to find money. . . ." (*Discourses,* Book II, Chap. 10.)

Finally, though this is not strictly part of the logic of scientific method, we feel everywhere in Machiavelli, in every line and chapter, an intense and dominant passion for the truth. Whatever other interests and goals he may have, to this all the rest are, if need be, subordinated. No prejudice, no weighty tradition, no authority, no emotional twist is enough to lead him to temper his inquiry into the truth, so far as he can discover it. If we remember the established attitudes of his times, their provincial narrowness, their lack of scholarship and research and a critical sense, this passion for truth is wonderfully revealed, I think, in the sane, controlled, and balanced preface to the Second Book of the *Discourses on Livy:*

"It is the common practice of Mankind, to commend the ancient, and condemn the present times; but in my judgment not always with reason; for so studiously are they devoted to things of antiquity, that they do not only admire what is transmitted by old authors, but applaud and cry up when they are old, the passages and occurrences in their youth. But my opinion is, This their way of computation is many times false, and that upon several accounts. First, because of such very ancient things we can have no absolute knowledge; for most commonly in the narrative of affairs, what is infamous, or ill done, is pretermitted in silence, whilst what is well done, and honorable, is related with all the Arts, and amplifications of rhetoric; for so much are historians accustomed to attribute to the fortune of the conqueror, that to increase his praise, they do not only expatiate upon his conduct, and exploits, but they do likewise so magnify and illustrate the very actions of the Enemy, that they who come after, beholding things at a great distance, have reason to admire those times, and those men, and by consequence to love them. Besides it being envy or fear which disposes people to hatred; neither of those passions extending to what cannot possibly hurt them, two great causes are wanting of finding fault with Antiquity; for as things so long passed cannot any way prejudice, so they cannot provoke to envy or discontent: But present things which are obvious to our own sense, are universally known, and no circumstance that passes (whether good or bad) that can be totally concealed; from whence it proceeds, that observing with the excellence and virtue of our present affairs, whatever is concomitant of imprudence or vice, we are in a manner compelled to postpone them to things of antiquity, where the good only is displayed, and the bad passed by, though perhaps the present things are more worthily glorious. . . .

"To which it may be added, that the desires of mankind are immense, and insatiable; that naturally we are covetous of everything, whereas fortune allows us but little; that from thence it happens that no man is contented, every man despises what he is already possessed of, commends what is passed, condemns what is present, and longs for what is to come, though induced by no reasonable occasion. Things being thus, I cannot resolve myself whether ever I may not be of that number, who in these my discourses have so highly magnified the old times and exploits of the Romans, to the diminution of our own. . . ." (*Discourses,* Preface to Book II.)

In general summary of Machiavelli's method, we may recall the distinction between formal and real meaning which I defined in analyzing *De Monarchia*. It is a characteristic of Machiavelli's writing, as of all scientific discourse, that this distinction is inapplicable. Formal meaning and real meaning are one. There is no hidden meaning, no undisclosed purpose. This is why, where Machiavelli is wrong, it is easy to correct him; and why he cannot deceive us.

3. Political Man

THERE HAVE BEEN many critical discussions about Machiavelli's supposed views on "human nature." Some defend him, but he is usually charged with a libel upon mankind, with having a perverted, shocking, and detestable notion of what human beings are like. These discussions, however, are beside the point. Machiavelli has no views on human nature; or, at any rate, none is presented in his writings. Machiavelli is neither a psychologist nor a moral philosopher, but a political scientist.

It is clear from a study of Machiavelli that what he is trying to analyze is not "man" but "political man," in somewhat the same way that Adam Smith analyzed "economic man." Adam Smith did not suppose for a moment—though he, too, is often enough misunderstood—that he was exhaustively describing human nature when he said that economic man seeks a profit, that, when a man operates in the capitalist market, he seeks the greatest possible economic profit. Of course Adam Smith realized that men, in the course of their many and so various activities, are motivated by many other aims than the search for profit. But he was not interested in human nature as a whole. Man's nature was relevant to his studies only insofar as man functioned economically, in the market. Adam Smith was abstracting from human nature, and introducing the conception of an "economic agent," which he believed, with some justice, would aid him in formulating the laws of economics. Analogous procedures are followed in all sciences. Newton, when he introduced ideas of frictionless motion, bodies not acted upon by any forces, perfectly elastic bodies, and so on, did not imagine that such things existed; Newton, also, was abstracting for the sake of generalizing more adequately about certain types of phenomena, in his case physical phenomena.

Similarly with Machiavelli. He is interested in man in relation to political phenomena—that is, to the struggle for power; in man as he functions politically, not in man as he behaves toward his friends or family or god. It does not refute Machiavelli to point out that men do not always act as he says they act. He knows this. But many sides of man's nature he believes to be irrelevant to political behavior. If he is wrong, he is wrong because of a false theory of politics, not because of a false idea of man.

Most people think that politics is ultimately a question of psychology, because, they argue, it is after all human beings who carry on political actions. This belief lies back of the common attempt to explain politics in terms of the character and motives of political leaders, or even of the "common man," an attempt familiar not only from ordinary discussion but more prominently from the journalists' books on politics that have plagued us during recent years. It is the basis, as well, of more pretentious studies which claim to explain politics in terms of some contemporary psychological system such as psychoanalysis or behaviorism.

The relation between psychology and politics, is, however, by no means so direct. If we had at our disposal a completely developed and general science of psychology, presumably it would include politics and sociology, economics, and history besides. But we have nothing even promising such a psychology. As things are, the proper study of politics is quite plainly distinct from the study of psychology, and the laws of politics can in no way be deduced from the laws of psychology. To understand politics, we must get our evidence directly, from the record of political struggles themselves. Those minor details which psychology is now able to tell us about reaction-times, conditioned reflexes, and infant peculiarities teach us nothing at all about how forms of government change or a ruling class is wiped out.

From studying the facts of politics, then, Machiavelli reached certain conclusions, not about man but about "political man."

First, he implies everywhere a rather sharp distinction between two types of political man: a "ruler-type," we might call one, and a "ruled-type," the other. The first type would include not merely those who at any moment occupy leading positions in society, but those also who aspire to such positions or who might so aspire if opportunity offered; the second consists of those who neither lead nor are capable of becoming leaders. The second is the great majority. There is a certain arbitrariness in any such distinction as this, and obviously the exact line between the two groups is hazy. Nevertheless, it is clear that Machiavelli—and all those, moreover, who write in the tradition of Machiavelli—thinks that the distinction reflects a basic fact of political life, that active political struggle is confined for the most part to a small minority of men, that the majority is and remains, whatever else happens, the ruled.

The outstanding characteristic of the majority is, then, its political passivity. Unless driven by the most extreme provocation on the part of the rulers or by rare and exceptional circumstance, the ruled are not interested in power. They want a small minimum of security, and a chance to live their own lives and manage their own small affairs. "Whilst the generality of the world live quietly upon their estates, and unprejudiced in their honor, they live peaceably enough, and all [a ruler's] contention is only with the pride and ambition of some few persons who are many ways, and with great ease to be restrained." (*The Prince,* Chap. 19.)

"In the general," Machiavelli finds, "men are ungrateful, inconstant, hypocritical, fearful of danger, and covetous of gain; whilst they receive any benefit by you, and the danger is at distance, they are absolutely yours, their Blood, their Estates, their

Lives, and their Children (as I said before) are all at your Service, but when mischief is at hand, and you have present need of their help, they make no scruple to revolt." (*The Prince,* Chap. 17.) "The people," moody and changeable, "being deceived with a false imagination of good, do many times solicit their own ruin, and run the commonwealth upon infinite dangers and difficulties." (*Discourses,* Book I, Chap. 53.) At the same time, they have a great respect for firm authority. "There is nothing more certain to appease a popular tumult, and reduce the people to reason, than the interposition of some wise person of authority among them, as Vergil has told us with very good reason: 'If in their tumults, a grave man appears, All's whist, and nothing stirring but their ears.'" (*Discourses,* Book I, Chap. 54.)

The "multitude without a head is altogether unserviceable. . . . Upon the accident of Virginius, the people having taken arms, and retired to the holy Mount, the Senate sent to them to know upon what account they had abandoned their Officers, and betaken themselves to that Mount: and the authority of the Senate was so venerable among the people, that having no head among them, there was no body durst return an answer: Titus Livy tells us, 'They wanted not what to say, but who to deliver it.' For having no certain Commander, every private person was unwilling to expose himself to their displeasure. From whence we may understand how useless a thing the multitude is without a head. . . ." (*Discourses,* Book I, Chap. 44.)

"The Romans being overthrown, and their Country much wasted, upon the coming of the Gauls; many of them (contrary to an express Order and Edict of the Senate) transplanted to Veii, and left Rome. Whereupon, by a new Proclamation, the Senate commanded, that by a precise day, and upon a certain penalty, they should return to their old habitations: when the news of this Proclamation was first brought to Veii, it was despised and laughed at by everybody; but when the day appointed for their return arrived, there was not a man but packed up his goods, and came back as was required, and as Livy says in the case, 'Not one of them who were so contumacious together, but apart began to fear, and that fear made him obedient.' And certainly nothing can give us a more lively description of the nature of a multitude than this case. They are bold, and will speak liberally against the decrees of their Prince; and afterwards when they see their punishment before their faces, everyone grows fearful of his neighbor, slips his neck out of the collar, and returns to his obedience. So that it is not much to be considered what the people say, either of their Prince's good management or bad; so they be strong enough to keep them in their good humor when they are well disposed, and provide (when they are ill) that they do them no hurt. By this ill disposition of the people, I mean all dispositions but what arise either from the loss of their liberty, or the loss of some excellent Prince still living, upon whom they had settled their affections.

"For the evil dispositions proceeding from these causes are transcendentally dreadful, and strong remedies are to be applied to restrain them.

"In other cases, their anger is nothing, especially having nobody to head them; for as there is nothing so terrible as their fury in one case, so there is nothing so vain and inconsiderable in the other, because, though they have betaken themselves to their arms, they are easily reduced, if you can but avoid the first heat of their fury; for by degrees they will cool, and every man considering it is his duty to return, will begin to suspect himself, and think of his security, either by making his peace, or escape. Whenever, therefore, the multitude is in a mutiny, their best way is immediately to choose themselves a Head, who may correct, keep them united, and contrive for their defense, as the Romans did when leaving Rome upon the death of Virginia; for their protection and security, they created twenty Tribunes from among themselves: and if this course be neglected, it happens to them as Livy presaged in the foregoing sentence, 'That as nothing is more courageous than the multitude united, so nothing is more abject when they are separate and divided.'" (*Discourses,* Book I, Chap 57.)

Nevertheless—and this observation applies to rulers and ruled alike—no man is perfectly good or bad. "Wise men who were then about his Holiness [Pope Julius II] . . . could not imagine how it should come to pass, that Pagolo having his Enemy [Julius] as it were naked in his hands, and by consequence an opportunity (with perpetual glory to himself) to have secured him, and pillaged his equipage . . . should so strangely neglect it; especially when they considered that it was neither conscience nor good nature which restrained him; for neither of those were to be supposed in a man who had been nought with his own sister, and murdered several of his relations, to make his way to the Government; wherefore it was concluded to happen, because it is so provided by Providence, that no man can be exquisitely wicked, no more than good in perfection. . . ." (*Discourses,* Book I, Chap. 27.)

When Machiavelli concludes that no man is perfectly good or bad, he is not making a primarily moral judgment. He means, more generally, that all men make mistakes at least sometimes, that there are no super-men, that no man is always intelligent and judicious, that even the stupid have occasional moments of brilliance, that men are not always consistent, that they are variable and variously motivated. Obvious as such reflections may seem, they are easily forgotten in the realm of political action, which is alone in question. The tendency, in political judgments, is toward black and white: the leader, or the proletariat, or the people, or the party, or the great captain is always right; the bosses or the crowd or the government, always wrong. From such reasoning flow not a few shocks and dismays at turns of events that might readily have been anticipated.

MACHIAVELLI: SCIENCE OF POWER

The ruled majority, changeable, weak, short-sighted, selfish, is not at all, for Machiavelli, the black to the rulers' white. Indeed, for him, the ruler-type is even less constant, less loyal, and on many occasions less intelligent.

"That nothing is more vain and inconstant than the multitude, Titus Livy and all other historians do agree. . . . He says, 'The nature of the multitude is, to be servilely obedient, or insolently tyrannical.'

"Things being thus, I know not whether I shall not seem too bold, to undertake the defense of a thing, which all the world opposes; and run myself upon a necessity of either quitting it with disgrace, or pursuing it with scandal; yet methinks, being to maintain it with arguments, not force, it should not be so criminal. I say then in behalf of the multitude; that what they are charged withal by most authors, may be charged upon all private persons in the world, and especially upon Princes; for whoever lives irregularly, and is not restrained by the Law, is subject to the same exorbitancies, and will commit as bad faults as the most dissolute multitude in the world: and this may be easily known, if it be considered how many Princes there have been, and how few of them good. . . . I conclude, therefore, against the common opinion, that the people are no more light, ungrateful, nor changeable than Princes; but that both of them are equally faulty, and he that should go about to excuse the Princes, would be in a very great error. . . ." (*Discourses*, Book I, Chap. 58.)

A Note on Machiavelli's Terminology

In understanding Machiavelli, there are confusions that may result from his use of certain words.

In *The Prince,* Machiavelli divides all governments, with respect to their form, into "monarchies" (principalities) and "commonwealths" (republics). A monarchy means a government where sovereignty rests, formally, in a single man; a commonwealth means a government where sovereignty rests, formally, in more than one man. A commonwealth, therefore, need not be "democratic" in any usual sense; nor a monarchy, tyrannical.

At the beginning of the *Discourses on Livy*, Machiavelli distinguishes three kinds of government: monarchy, aristocracy, and democracy. Through this distinction, which is taken from Aristotle, he is referring not only to differences in governmental form, but also to differing social relations in the state. In particular, by the terms "aristocracy" and "democracy" he is taking account of the relative power of "nobility" and "people."

When Machiavelli discusses the nobility and the people, he has in mind the distinction between "patricians" and "plebs" in Rome, and between the feudal nobility and the burghers in the Italian cities. Originally, in Rome, the patricians were the heads of the families belonging to the ancient tribes. Their class included, in a subordinate status, the rest of their families, their clients, servants, slaves, and so on. At first, the patricians alone were eligible to the senate and the consulship.

The class of the "plebs," or "people," was sub-divided primarily according to wealth. Its articulate and politically active members, who gradually won citizenship in Rome, the creation of the office of tribune, and eligibility to the senate and consulship, were for a long time only a small minority of the entire plebs—just as the patricians proper, who were the descendants of the early family heads in the eldest male line, were only a minority of the entire patrician class. In speaking of the "people," therefore, in connection with Rome, the reference is not to everyone, or even to "the masses" in an indiscriminate sense, but ordinarily to the upper stratum of the plebs.

Analogously in the case of the Italian cities. "People" meant in the first instance the burghers and the leading members of the

MACHIAVELLI: SCIENCE OF POWER 57

guilds. These were opposed to the class of the nobility, dominated by the heads of the noble houses. In the course of time, the class of "people" expanded. It became necessary to distinguish between the richer burghers and chiefs of the major guilds *(popolo grasso)*, and the lesser people *(popolo minuto)*, whom Machiavelli sometimes calls "people of the meaner sort." But when Machiavelli wants to refer to the lower strata of "the masses," to the apprentices and workmen and those not regularly employed, he ordinarily calls them, not "people," but "rabble," or sometimes "multitude."

There are two important consequences of this terminology: The form of government—monarchy or commonwealth—is independent of the social ascendancy or subordination of the "people," since the people could set up a monarchy or tyranny as well as a commonwealth, and the nobility could rule through a republic or commonwealth, as it did during much of the history of Rome, in Venice, and typically in a long period of the history of the ancient cities. Second, the distinction between "ruler-type" and "ruled-type" is also independent: specifically, both types are to be found among the "people" as well as in other classes.

* * *

The ruler-type, then, is not distinguished by Machiavelli from the ruled by any moral standard, nor by intelligence or consistency, nor by any capacity to avoid mistakes. There are, however, certain common characteristics that mark the rulers and potential rulers, and divide them from the majority that is fated always to be ruled.

In the first place, the ruler-type has what Machiavelli calls *virtù*, what is so improperly translated as "virtue." *Virtù* is a word, in Machiavelli's language, that has no English equivalent. It includes in its meaning part of what we refer to as "ambition," "drive," "spirit" in the sense of Plato's θυμός, the "will to power." Those who are capable of rule are above all those who want to rule. They drive themselves as well as others; they have that quality which makes them keep going, endure amid difficulties, persist against dangers. They are those whom Marlowe's Tamburlaine is talking of:

> "Our souls, whose faculties can comprehend
> The wondrous architecture of the world,
> And measure every wandering planet's course,
> Still climbing after knowledge infinite,
> And always moving as the restless spheres,
> Will us to wear ourselves, and never rest,
> Until we reach the ripest fruit of all,
> That perfect bliss and sole felicity,
> The sweet fruition of an earthly crown."

The ruler-type has, usually, strength, especially martial strength. War and fighting are the great training ground of rule, Machiavelli believes, and power is secure only on the basis of force.

Even more universal a quality of the ruler-type, however, is fraud. Machiavelli's writings contain numerous discussions of the indispensable role of fraud in political affairs, ranging from analyses of deceptions and stratagems in war to the breaking of treaties to the varied types of fraud met with daily in civil life. In the *Discourses,* Book II, Chapter 13, he generalizes "that from mean to great fortune, people rise rather by fraud, than by force."

"I have found it always true, that men do seldom or never advance themselves from a small beginning, to any great height, but by fraud, or by force (unless they come by it by donation, or right of inheritance). I do not think any instance is to be found where force alone brought any man to that grandeur, but fraud and artifice have done it many times, as is clear in the lives of Philip of Macedon, Agathocles the Sicilian, and several others, who from mean and inconsiderable extraction, came at length to be Kings. Xenophon in his History of Cyrus insinuates the necessity of fraud when he represents (in his first Expedition against the King of Armenia) how all Cyrus' actions and negotiations were full of fallacy and deceit, and that it was that way he conquered his Kingdom, and not by bravery and force, by which he implies that no Prince can do any great matters without that art of dissembling . . . and indeed I am of opinion that from a mean and base fortune never any man came to be very great by downright generosity and force; but by fraud alone there have been many, as particularly Gian Galeazzo, who by that alone wrested the Government of Lombardy out of the hands of Messer Bernardo, his uncle. And the same courses which Princes are forced to in the beginning of their authority, the same courses are taken by commonwealths at first, till they be settled in their government, and have force sufficient to defend themselves. Rome (which either by chance or election took all ways to make itself great) was not without this: and what greater cunning or artifice could it use in the beginning of its greatness, than what it did take, and is mentioned before . . . ? Which things being so, it is manifest the Romans wanted not at the beginning of their rise, that dexterity of cheating that is so necessary to all people that are ambitious of raising themselves to a great height, from an inconsiderable beginning; which artifice is always the less scandalous, by how much he that does practice it, understands better how to disguise it by some honorable pretense, as the Romans did very well."

The combination of force and fraud is picturesquely referred to in the famous passages of *The Prince* which describe the successful ruler as both Lion and Fox.

"You must understand that there are two ways of contending, by Law, and by force: The first is proper to men; the second to beasts; but because many times the first is insufficient, recourse must be had to the second. It belongs, therefore, to a Prince to understand both, when to make use of the rational, and when of the brutal way; and this is recommended to Princes (though abstrusely) by ancient writers, who tell them how Achilles and several other Princes were committed to the education of Chiron, the Centaur, who was to keep them under his discipline, choosing them a Master, half man and half beast, for no other reason but to show how necessary it is for a Prince to be acquainted with both, for that one without the other will be of little duration. Seeing, therefore, it is of such importance to a Prince to take upon him the nature and disposition of a beast, of all the whole flock, he ought to imitate the Lion and the Fox; for the Lion is in danger of toils and snares, and the Fox of the Wolf: so that he must be a Fox to find out the snares, and a Lion to fright away the Wolves, but they who keep wholly to the Lion, have no true notion of themselves . . ." (*The Prince,* Chap. 18.)

Finally, political man of the ruler-type is skilled at adapting himself to the times. In passage after passage, Machiavelli returns to this essential ability: neither cruelty nor humaneness, neither rashness nor caution, neither liberality nor avarice avails in the struggle for power unless the times are suited.

"I believe again that Prince may be happy whose manner of proceeding concerts with the times, and he unhappy who cannot accommodate to them: For in things leading to the end of their designs (which every man has in his eye, and they are riches and honor) we see men have various methods of proceeding. Some with circumspection, others with heat; some with violence, others with cunning; some with patience, and others with fury, and everyone (notwithstanding the diversity of their ways) may possibly attain them. Again we see two persons equally cautious, one of them prospers, and the other miscarries, and on the other side, two equally happy by different measures, one being deliberate, and the other as hasty; and this proceeds from nothing but the condition of the times which suits, or does not suit, with the manner of their proceedings. From hence arises what I have said, that two persons by different operations do attain the same end, whilst two others steer the same course, and one of them succeeds, and the other is ruined. From hence likewise may be deduced the vicissitudes of good; for if to one who manages with deliberation and patience, the times and conjuncture of affairs come about so favorably that his conduct be in fashion, he must needs be happy; but if the face of affairs, and the times change, and he changes not with them, he is certainly ruined." (*The Prince,* Chap. 25.)

4. Machiavelli's Conception of History

MACHIAVELLI DOES NOT have a systematically worked out theory of history. The many generalizations which he states are for the most part limited, dealing with some special phase of political action, and a list of them would be a summary of most of his writings. There are, however, in addition to those that I have already analyzed, a few wider principles of great influence in the later development of Machiavellism.

1. Political life, according to Machiavelli, is never static, but in continual change. There is no way of avoiding this change. Any idea of a perfect state, or even of a reasonably good state, much short of perfection, that could last indefinitely, is an illusion.

The process of change is repetitive, and roughly cyclical. That is to say, the pattern of change occurs again and again in history (so that, by studying the past, we learn also about the present and future); and this pattern comprises a more or less recognizable cycle. A good, flourishing, prosperous state becomes corrupt, evil, degenerate; from the corrupt, evil state again arises one that is strong and flourishing. The degeneration can, perhaps, be delayed; but Machiavelli has no confidence that it could be avoided. The very virtues of the good state contain the seeds of its own destruction. The strong and flourishing state is feared by all neighbors, and is therefore left in peace. War and the ways of force are neglected. The peace and prosperity breed idleness, luxury, and license; these, political corruption, tyranny, and weakness. The state is overcome by the force of uncorrupted neighbors, or itself enters a new cycle, where hard days and arms purge the corruption, and bring a new strength, a new virtue and prosperity. But once again, the degeneration sets in.

"Governments in the variations which most commonly happen to them, do proceed from order to confusion, and that confusion afterwards turns to order again. For Nature having fixed no sublunary things, as soon as they arrive at their acme and perfection, being capable of no farther ascent, of necessity they decline. So, on the other side, when they are reduced to the lowest pitch of disorder, having no farther to descend, they recoil again to their former perfection: good Laws degenerating into bad customs, and bad customs engendering good Laws. For, virtue begets peace; peace begets idleness; idleness, mutiny; and mutiny, destruction: and then, *vice versa;* that ruin begets laws; those laws, virtue; and virtue begets honor and good success." (*History of Florence,* Book V.)

2. The recurring pattern of change expresses the more or less permanent core of human nature as it functions politically. The instability of all governments and political forms follows in part from the limitless human appetite for power.

"Wise men were wont to say (and perhaps not unworthily) that he who would know what will be, must consider what has been already, because there is nothing in the world now, nor will be hereafter, but what has, and will have conformity with the productions of former times; and the reason is, because proceeding from men who have, and have had always the same passions, they must necessarily have the same effects." (*Discourses,* Book III, Chap. 43.)

"It is observed by most ancient Writers, that as men are afflicted in adversity, so they are satiated in prosperity; and that joy and grief have the same effects: For when men are not necessitated to fight, they fight for ambition, which is so powerful in our minds, that let us arrive at what height of good fortune we can, we are never contented, but are still laboring for more; and this happens to us, because we are naturally capable of desiring many things, which we are unable to compass; and therefore our desire being greater than our power to acquire, our minds are never at rest with what we enjoy. And this is the occasion of all our varieties of fortune." (*Discourses,* Book I, Chap. 37.)

3. Machiavelli assigns a major function in political affairs to what he calls "Fortune." Sometimes he seems almost to personify Fortune, and, in the manner that lingered on through the Middle Ages from ancient times, to write about her as a goddess. He discusses Fortune not merely in occasional references, but in a number of lengthy passages scattered throughout his works.

From these passages it becomes clear what Machiavelli means by "Fortune." Fortune is all those causes of historical change that are beyond the deliberate, rational control of men. In the case both of individuals and of states, Machiavelli believes that those causes are many, often primary, and in the long run probably dominant. He does not altogether exclude from history the influence of deliberate human control, but he reduces it to a strictly limited range.

"I am not ignorant that it is, and has been of old the opinion of many people, that the affairs of the world are so governed by Fortune and Divine Providence, that Man cannot by his Wisdom correct them, or apply any remedy at all; from whence they would infer that we are not to labor and sweat, but to leave everything to its own tendency and event. This opinion has obtained more in our days, by the many and frequent revolutions, which have been, and are still seen beyond all human conjecture. And when I think of it seriously sometimes, I am in some measure inclined to it myself; nevertheless that our own free will may not utterly be exploded, I conceive it may be true that fortune may have the arbitrament of one half of our actions, but that she leaves the other half (or little less) to be governed by ourselves. Fortune, I do resemble to a rapid and impetuous River, which when swelled, and enraged, overwhelms the Plains, subverts the Trees, and the Houses, forces away the Earth from one place, and carries it to another, everybody fears, everybody shuns, but nobody knows how to resist it; Yet though it be thus furious sometimes, it does not follow but when it is quiet and calm, men may by banks, and fences, and other provisions correct it in such manner, that when it swells again, it may be carried off by some Canal, or the violence thereof rendered less licentious and destructive. So it is with Fortune, which shows her power where there is no predisposed virtue to resist it, and turns all her force and impetuosity, where she knows there are no banks, no fences to restrain her . . ." (*The Prince,* Chap. 25.)

"Wherefore men are not so much to be blamed or commended for their adversity or prosperity; for it is frequently seen, some are hurried to ruin, and others advanced to great honor by the swing and impulse of their fate, wisdom availing little against the misfortunes of the one, and folly as little against the felicity of the other. When fortune designs any great matter, she makes choice of some man of such courage and parts, as is able to discern when she presents him with an occasion: and so on the other side, when she intends any great destruction, she has her Instruments ready to push on the wheel, and assist to her designs; and if there be any man capable of obstructing them in the least, she either rids him out of the way, or deprives him of all authority, and leaves him without any faculty to do good." (*Discourses,* Book II, Chap. 29.)

This conception of Fortune fits in closely with the idea, which we have already noted, that the ruler-type of political man is one who knows how to accommodate to the times. Fortune cannot be overcome, but advantage may be taken of her.

"Yet this I shall assert again (and by the occurrences in all

History there is nothing more true) that men may second their fortune, not resist it; and follow the order of her designs, but by no means defeat them: Nevertheless men are not wholly to abandon themselves, because they know not her end; for her ways being unknown and irregular, may possibly be at last for our good; so that we are always to hope the best, and that hope is to preserve us in whatever troubles or distresses we shall fall." (*Discourses,* Book II, Chap. 29.)

Beyond such accommodation ("opportunism," we might nowadays call it), men and states will make the most of fortune when they display *virtù,* when they are firm, bold, quick in decision, not irresolute, cowardly, and timid.

"In all consultations, it is best to come immediately to the point in question, and bring things to a result, without too tedious a hesitation and suspense . . . and it is a fault peculiar to all weak and improvident Princes and Governments to be slow and tedious, as well as uncertain in their Councils, which is as dangerous as the other . . ." (*Discourses,* Book II, Chap. 15.)

4. Machiavelli believes that religion is essential to the well-being of a state. In discussing religion, as in discussing human nature, Machiavelli confines himself to political function. He is not engaged in theological dispute, nor inquiring whether religion, or some particular religion, is true or false, but trying to estimate the role that religious belief and ritual perform in politics. He is analyzing, we might say in a general sense, "myth," and myth he finds to be politically indispensable.

"Though Rome should have been founded by Romulus, and owe him (as his Daughter) for her Birth, and Education; yet the Heavens foreseeing that the Constitutions of Romulus would not be sufficient for so great an Empire, put it into the heart of the Roman Senate, to create Numa Pompilius for his Successor, to the end that what was left defective by the first, might be com-

MACHIAVELLI: SCIENCE OF POWER 67

pleted by the latter. Numa finding the people martial and fierce, and being desirous by the Arts of Peace to reduce them to civil obedience, he betook himself to Religion, as a thing absolutely necessary to the maintenance of civil policy; and he ordered things, so that for many ages together never was the fear of God so eminently conspicuous as in that Commonwealth, which was a great promotion to whatever was designed either by the Senate or Princes." *

"And surely it will be found by whoever considers the Roman History, how useful a thing Religion was to the governing of Armies, to the uniting of the people, to the keeping of men good, and to the deterring them from being bad; so that should it fall into dispute whether Rome was most obliged to Romulus or Numa, I am of opinion, Numa would have the pre-eminence ... Take away Religion, and take away the foundation of Government ... Those Princes and Commonwealths who would keep their Governments entire and incorrupt, are above all things to have a care of Religion and its Ceremonies, and preserve them in due veneration...." (*Discourses,* Book I, Chapters 11 and 12.)

5. We have already seen that Machiavelli's chief immediate practical goal was the national unification of Italy. In the review of his descriptive conclusions about the nature of political activity, no reference has been made to any more general goals or ideals to which Machiavelli adhered. I return now to this problem of goal, in order to answer the question: What kind of government did Machiavelli think best?

Machiavelli's writings, taken in their entirety, leave no doubt about the answer. Machiavelli thinks that the best kind of govern-

---

* *Discourses,* Book I, Chap. 11. Livy—whom Machiavelli is following—was wrong in attributing the Roman religion to the deliberate plan of Numa; but this error in no way affects Machiavelli's analysis of the political function of religion.

ment is a republic, what he called a "commonwealth." Not only does he prefer a republican government; other things being equal, he considers a republic stronger, more enduring, wiser and more flexible than any form of monarchy. This opinion is above all clarified by Machiavelli's most important work, the *Discourses on Livy,* but it is at least implicit in everything that he wrote. When, in his Letter to Zenobius, he replies to the accusation that in all his writings he "insinuates" his "great affection to the Democratical Government," he accepts frankly the justice of the accusation:

"Why should I be condemned of heresy or indiscretion for preferring a Commonwealth before a Monarchy? was I not born, bred, and employed in a City, which being at the time I write, under that form of Government, did owe all wealth and greatness, and all prosperity to it? If I had not very designedly avoided all dogmaticalness in my observations (being not willing to imitate young Scholars in their Declamations) I might easily have concluded from the premises I lay down, that a Democracy founded upon good orders is the best and most excellent Government, and this without the least fear of confutation; for I firmly believe, that there are none but Flatterers and Sophisters would oppose me, such as will wrest Aristotle, and even Plato himself, to make them write for Monarchy, by misapplying some loose passages in those great Authors, nay, they will tell their Readers, that what is most like the Government of the world by God is the best, which wholly depends upon his absolute power [this could be a reference to Dante]; to make this Comparison run with four feet, these Sycophants must give the poor Prince they intend to deify, a better and superior Nature to humanity, must create a necessary dependence of all Creatures upon him, must endow him with infinite wisdom and goodness, and even with omnipotency itself."

Nor does this preference for a republic contradict his conclusion that the leadership of a prince was required for the national uni-

MACHIAVELLI: SCIENCE OF POWER

fication of Italy. If a republic is the best form of government, it does not follow that a republic is possible at every moment and for all things. Machiavelli's preferences are always disciplined by the truth. The truth here, as he correctly saw it, was that Italy could not then be unified except, in the initial stages at least, through a prince.

But in preferring a republican form of government, Machiavelli paints no utopia. He states the defects of his ideals as honestly as their virtues. It is true, moreover, that he does not attach quite the ultimate importance to the choice of form of government that would be attributed to that choice by utopians who believe that all human problems can be solved if only their own private ideal can be realized. There is no way, Machiavelli believes, to solve all or even most human problems.

Beyond and superior to his preference among the forms of government, Machiavelli projects his ideal of "liberty." For any given group of people, "liberty," as Machiavelli uses the word, means: independence—that is, no external subjection to another group; and, internally, a government by law, not by the arbitrary will of any individual men, princes or commoners.

Independence, the first condition of liberty, can be secured in the last analysis only by the armed strength of the citizenry itself, never by mercenaries or allies or money; consequently arms are the first foundation of liberty. There is no lasting safeguard for liberty in anything but one's own strength.

Internally, also, liberty rests on force—on the public force of the state, however, never on force exercised by private individuals or groups, which is invariably a direct threat to liberty. Guaranteed by force, then, internal liberty means government by law, with strict adherence to due legal process.

As protectors of liberty, Machiavelli has no confidence in individual men as such; driven by unlimited ambition, deceiving even themselves, they are always corrupted by power. But individuals can, to some extent at least and for a while, be disciplined within the established framework of wise laws. A great deal of the *Discourses* is a commentary on this problem. In chapter after chapter, Machiavelli insists that if liberty is to be preserved: no person and no magistrate may be permitted to be above the law; there must be legal means for any citizen to bring accusations against any other citizen or any official; terms of office must be short, and must never, no matter what the inconvenience, be lengthened; punishment must be firm and impartial; the ambitions of citizens must never be allowed to build up private power, but must be directed into public channels.

Machiavelli is not so naïve as to imagine that the law can support itself. The law is founded upon force, but the force in turn will destroy the law unless it also is bridled; but force can be bridled only by opposing force. Sociologically, therefore, the foundation of liberty is a balancing of forces, what Machiavelli calls a "mixed" government. Since Machiavelli is neither a propagandist nor an apologist, since he is not the demagogue of any party or sect or group, he knows and says how hypocritical are the calls for a "unity" that is a mask for the suppression of all opposition, how fatally lying or wrong are all beliefs that liberty is the peculiar attribute of any single individual or group—prince or democrat, nobles or people or "multitude." Only out of the continuing clash of opposing groups can liberty flow.

"All cities . . . do some time or other alter their government, yet not (as many think) by means of Liberty and Subjection; but by occasion of servitude, and licentiousness: for only the name of Liberty is pretended by popular persons, such as are the instruments of licentiousness; and servitude is sought for by those that are Noble, neither of them both desiring to be restrained either by Laws or anything else." (*History of Florence,* Book IV.)

"I cannot in silence pass over the tumults and commotions which happened in Rome betwixt the death of the Tarquins, and the creation of those Tribunes. Nor can I forbear saying something against the opinion of many who will needs have Rome to have been a tumultuous Republic, so full of mutiny and confusion, that had not its good fortune and valor supplied for its defects, it would have been inferior to any other commonwealth whatsoever . . . I say, those who object against the tumults betwixt the Nobles and the People, do in my opinion condemn those very things which were the first occasion of its freedom, regarding the noise and clamors which do usually follow such commotions, more than the good effects they do commonly produce, not considering that in all commonwealths there are two opposite humors, one of the people, the other of the Noblesse; and that all Laws which are made in favor of liberty, proceed from the differences betwixt them . . ." (*Discourses,* Book I, Chap. 4.)

This balancing clash of opposed interests will the more surely preserve liberty when the state guards against too great inequality in privilege and wealth.

"The other reason [for the integrity and justice of certain states] is, because those commonwealths who have preserved their liberties, and kept themselves incorrupt, do not suffer any of their citizens to live high . . . but they live all in an equality and parity." (*Discourses,* Book I, Chap. 55.)

Liberty, then—not the rhetorical liberty of an impossible and misconceived utopia, but such concrete liberty as is, when they are fortunate, within the grasp of real men, with their real limitations —is the dominant ideal of Machiavelli, and his final norm of judgment. Tyranny is liberty's opposite, and no man has been a clearer foe of tyranny. No man clearer, and few more eloquent. In the 14th century, the Florentine people, threatened by external danger and by internal dissension, decided to turn their government over to a foreigner, the Duke of Athens. Machiavelli, in his *History of Florence,* narrating the events just before the Duke took over full power, puts this address into the mouth of one of the Signori, to whom were entrusted the ancient liberties of the Republic:

"My Lord . . ., your endeavor is to bring this City into servitude (which has always lived free). . . . Have you considered how important and dear the name of Liberty is to us? A thing, no force can extirpate, no time can extinguish, nor no merit preponderate. Think, Sir, I beseech you, what Power will be necessary to keep such a City in subjection. All the strangers you can entertain will not be sufficient; those which are inhabitants you cannot prudently trust; for though at present they are friends, and have pushed you forward upon this resolution, yet, as soon as they have glutted themselves upon their enemies, their next plot will be to expel you. . . . The People, in whom your greatest confidence is placed, will turn, upon every slight accident, against you, so that in a short time you will run a hazard of having the whole City your enemies, which will infallibly be the ruin both of it and yourself; because those Princes only can be secure, whose enemies are but few, and they easily removed either by banishment or death; but against universal hatred there is no security, because the spring and fountain is not known, and he that fears every Man, can be safe against no Man. If yet you persist, and take all possible care to preserve yourself, you do but encumber yourself with more danger, by exciting their hatred and making them more intent and serious in their revenge. That time is not able to eradicate our desire of Liberty, is most certain. We could mention many good Cities in which it has been reassumed by those who never tasted the sweetness of it, yet upon the bare character and tradition of their Fathers, they have not only valued, but fought and contended to recover it, and maintained it afterwards against all difficulties and dangers. Nay, should their Fathers have neglected, or forgot to recommend it, the public Palaces, the Courts for the Magistrates, the ensigns of their freedom (which are of necessity to be known by all Citizens) would certainly proclaim it. What action of yours can counterpoise against the sweetness of Liberty? For what can you do to expunge the desire of it out of the Hearts of the People? Nothing at all, no, though you should add all Tuscany to this State, and return every day into this City with new victory over your Enemies. The Honor would be yours, not ours; and the Citizens have gained fellow-servants rather than subjects. Nor is it in the power of your deportment to establish you. Let your Life be never so exact, your conversation affable, your judgments just, your liberality never so conspicuous, all will not do, all will not gain you the affections of the People; if you think otherwise, you deceive yourself, for to People that have lived free, every link is a load, and every bond a burden."

5. *Machiavelli's Reputation*

MEN ARE FOND of believing that, even though they may for a while be mistaken, yet in the long run they do suitable honor, if not to the persons then at least to the memories, of those who have brought some measure of truth and enlightenment to the world. We may burn an occasional Bruno, imprison a Galileo, denounce a Darwin, exile an Einstein; but time, we imagine, restores judgment, and a new generation recognizes the brave captains of the mind who have dared to advance through the dark barriers of ignorance, superstition, and illusion. Machiavelli was so plainly one of these. His weapons, his methods—the methods of truth and science—he shared with Galileo and Darwin and Einstein; and he fought in a field of much greater concern to mankind. He tried to tell us not about stars or atoms, but about ourselves and our own common life. If his detailed conclusions were sometimes wrong, his own method, as the method of science always does, provides the way to correct them. He would be the first to insist on changing any of his views that were refuted by the evidence.

Though this is so, Machiavelli's name does not rank in this noble company. In the common opinion of men, his name itself has become a term of reproach and dishonor. He is thought of as Marlowe, not so long after his death, has him speak of himself in the prologue to *The Jew of Malta:*

"To some perhaps my name is odious,
But such as love me guard me from their tongues;

MACHIAVELLI: SCIENCE OF POWER

And let them know that I am Machiavel,
And weigh not men, and therefore not men's words.
Admired I am of those that hate me most.
Though some speak openly against my books,
Yet they will read me, and thereby attain
To Peter's chair: and when they cast me off,
Are poisoned by my climbing followers.
I count religion but a childish toy,
And hold there is no sin but ignorance.
Birds of the air will tell of murders past!
I am ashamed to hear such fooleries.
Many will talk of title to a crown:
What right had Caesar to the empery?
Might first made kings, and laws were then most sure
When like the Draco's they were writ in blood."

Why should this be? If our reference is to the views that Machiavelli in fact held, that he stated plainly, openly and clearly in his writings, there is in the common opinion no truth at all. We face here what can hardly be, after all these centuries, a mere accident of misunderstanding. There must be some substantial reason why Machiavelli is so consistently distorted.

It might be argued that there have indeed been oppressors and tyrants who learned from Machiavelli how to act more effectively in the furtherance of their designs, and that this justifies the common judgment of his views. It is true that he has taught tyrants, from almost his own days—Thomas Cromwell, for example, the low-born Chancellor whom Henry VIII brought in to replace Thomas More when More refused to make his conscience a tool of his master's interests, was said to have a copy of Machiavelli always in his pocket; and in our own time Mussolini wrote a college thesis on Machiavelli. But knowledge has a disturbing neutrality in this respect. We do not blame the research analyst who has solved the chemical mysteries of a poison because a murderer made use of his treatise, nor a student of the nature of alloys because a safe is cracked with the help of his formulas, nor chemists and physical scientists because bombs explode when they drop on Warsaw or Chungking. Perhaps we should do so; perhaps, as the story in *Genesis* almost suggests, all knowledge is evil. But the mere fact that the knowledge made explicit by Machiavelli has been put to bad uses, which is a potential fate of all knowledge, cannot explain why he is singled out for infamy.

It may be remarked that the harsh opinion of Machiavelli has been more widespread in England and the United States than in the nations of Continental Europe. This is no doubt natural, because the distinguishing quality of Anglo-Saxon politics has always been hypocrisy, and hypocrisy must always be at pains to shy away from the truth. It is also the case that judgments of Machiavelli are usually based upon acquaintance with *The Prince* alone, an essay which, though plain enough, can be honestly misinterpreted when read out of the context of the rest of his writings. However, something more fundamental than these minor difficulties is at stake.

We are, I think, and not only from the fate of Machiavelli's reputation, forced to conclude that men do not really want to know about themselves. When we allow ourselves to be taken in by reasoning after the manner of Dante, we find it easy to believe such remarks as Aristotle made at the beginning of his *Metaphysics:* "All men naturally desire knowledge"; and to imagine that it is self-evident that knowledge will always be welcomed. But if we examine not what follows from some abstract metaphysical principle but how men behave, some doubts arise. Even in the case of the physical world, knowledge must often hammer long at the door. Where they are themselves the subject-matter, men still keep the door resolutely shut. It may even be that they are right in this resistance. Perhaps the full disclosure of what we really are and how we act is too violent a medicine.

In any case, whatever may be the desires of most men, it is most certainly against the interests of the powerful that the truth should be known about political behavior. If the political truths stated or approximated by Machiavelli were widely known by men, the success of tyranny and all the other forms of oppressive political rule would become much less likely. A deeper freedom would be possible in society than Machiavelli himself believed attainable. If men generally understood as much of the mechanism of rule and privilege as Machiavelli understood, they would no longer be deceived into accepting that rule and privilege, and they would know what steps to take to overcome them.

Therefore the powerful and their spokesmen—all the "official" thinkers, the lawyers and philosophers and preachers and demagogues and moralists and editors—must defame Machiavelli. Machiavelli says that rulers lie and break faith: this proves, they say, that he libels human nature. Machiavelli says that ambitious men struggle for power: he is apologizing for the opposition, the enemy, and trying to confuse you about us, who wish to lead you for your own good and welfare. Machiavelli says that you must keep strict watch over officials and subordinate them to the law: he is encouraging subversion and the loss of national unity. Machiavelli says that no man with power is to be trusted: you see that his aim is to smash all your faith and ideals.

Small wonder that the powerful—in public—denounce Machiavelli. The powerful have long practice and much skill in sizing up their opponents. They can recognize an enemy who will never compromise, even when that enemy is so abstract as a body of ideas.

Part III

MOSCA: THE THEORY OF THE RULING CLASS

1. The Machiavellian Tradition

MACHIAVELLI LIVED and wrote during a great social revolution, through which feudal society, its economy, political arrangement, and culture, were being replaced by the first stage of capitalist society. This revolution occupied a long period of time, and its boundaries cannot be given exact dates. Nevertheless, we may consider that it reached a decisive turning point during Machiavelli's own life, with the discovery of the New World, the rise of the first international stock exchanges, the Protestant religious revolution, the consolidation of the English national state under the Tudors, and the first appointment of bourgeois representatives—by Henry VIII—to the chief political offices of a great kingdom.

We also live during a great social revolution, a revolution through which capitalist society is being replaced by what I have elsewhere defined as "managerial society."* It is, perhaps, the close analogy between our age and Machiavelli's that explains why the Machiavellian tradition, after centuries during which it was either neglected or misunderstood or merely repeated, has, in recent decades, been notably revived. Through the thought and research of a number of brilliant writers, Machiavellism has undergone a profound and extensive development.

The crisis of capitalist society was made plain by the first World War. With a far from accidental anticipation, much of the chief work of the modern Machiavellians was done in the period immediately preceding that war. Gaetano Mosca, it is true, had formu-

---

* In *The Managerial Revolution,* published by the John Day Co. in 1941.

81

lated many of his ideas as early as 1883, when he finished his first book, *Teorica dei governi e governo parlamentare*. However, his mature and finished thought is presented, with the war experiences close at hand, in the revised and expanded 1923 edition of *Elementi di scienza politica,* which is the basis of what has been translated into English as *The Ruling Class*.* Georges Sorel's active career went on through the war, and ended with his death in 1922. Robert Michels and Vilfredo Pareto were writing their major books when the war began.

In a revolutionary transition, the struggle for power, which, during years of social stability, is often hidden or expressed through indirect and undramatic forms, becomes open and imperious. Machiavellism is concerned with politics, that is, with the struggle for power. It seems natural, therefore, that its first appearance as well as its revival should be correlated with social revolution. The revolutionary crisis makes men, or at least a certain number of men, discontent with what in normal times passes for political thought and science—namely, disguised apologies for the status quo or utopian dreams of the future; and compels them to face more frankly the real issues of power: some because they wish to understand more clearly the nature of the world of which they are a part, others because they wish also to discover whether and in what way they might be able to control that world in the furtherance of their own ideals.

Modern Machiavellism has, needless to say, weighty advantages over Machiavelli himself. Mosca, Michels, and Pareto, heirs—as all of us are who wish to be—of 400 years of scientific tradition, have an altogether clear understanding of scientific method. Machiavelli wrote at the beginnings of science; he was scientific,

* Edited and Revised, with an Introduction, by Arthur Livingston. Translated by Hannah D. Kahn. Published, 1939, by McGraw-Hill Book Co., New York and London. In this Part, all quotations are, with the kind permission of the publishers, from this edition. Page numbers are given alone, without repeating the title. (Mosca was born in 1858, and died in 1941.)

often, by instinct and impulse rather than design. Many of Machiavelli's insights are only implicit in his writings—indeed, I have done him perhaps more than justice in making explicit much that was probably not fully so to himself. Machiavelli mixed together an art and a science of politics; his scientific conclusions are frequently the by-products of an attempt to lay down a rule for securing some particular kind of political result. The modern Machiavellians are fully conscious of what they are doing and of the distinctions between an art and a science. They have, moreover, the incalculable advantage of that great treasury of historical facts which the patient and accumulating research of post-Renaissance scholars has put at our disposal.

* * *

Gaetano Mosca, like all Machiavellians, rejects any monistic view of history—that is, any theory of history which holds that there is one single cause that accounts for everything that happens in society. From the days, in the early centuries of Christianity, when the first philosophies of history attributed all that happened to the Will of God as sole causal principle, there have been dozens of examples of such monistic theories. Mosca examines three of them in some detail: the "climatic theory," the "racial theory," and the "economic materialist theory," which maintain, respectively, that differences in climate, in race, or in methods of economic production, are able to explain the course of history. He rejects all of these theories, not because of any prejudice against monism, but for that simple and final reason that seems to have no attraction for monists: because these theories do not accord with the facts.

Mosca is acquainted with the history of the nations not only of Europe but of the world. He has no difficulty in showing that the supposed invariable influences of hot or cold or dry or rainy climate on the fate of peoples and nations do not operate; that huge empires or democracy or courage or sluggishness or art or slavery have arisen in North and South, in the cold and the hot, in dry and in humid territories. So, too, in the case of different races, besides the initial difficulty in all racial theories to be found in the fact that the concept of "race" has no biological precision.

Both the racial and the climatic theories were popular when Mosca first was writing, in the last years of the 19th century. Nowadays they have few adherents, outside of the Nazi racial school, but theories of "economic materialism" or "economic determinism" are still influential. However, these, also, are unable to meet the test of the facts. Social and political events of the very greatest scope and order—the collapse of the Roman Empire, the rise of Christianity, the advance of Islam—have occurred without any important correlated change in the mode of economic production; consequently the mode of production cannot be the sole cause of social change.

The critique of these monistic views does not mean that Mosca wishes to substitute some similar view of his own, or, on the other hand, to deny that such factors as climate, race, or mode of production have causal influences in history. Climate, obviously, can change the course of events: some regions of the earth are literally uninhabitable, others so unhealthy or so arid that a high level of civilization cannot be supported by them (though a vigorous society learns to conquer unfavorable natural conditions); a drop in rainfall might lead to a migration. Changes in the mode of economic production must unquestionably be recognized as one of the chief factors entering into the historical process: the invention of new tools or machines, new ways of organizing work, new relationships of economic ownership, may have vast repercussions throughout the social order. Even racial differences may conceivably affect political and social organization. For that matter, still other circumstances can influence history—new types of armaments or ways of fighting, to take an important example, or shifts in religion and social beliefs.

Mosca himself holds what is sometimes called an "interdependence" theory of historical causation: the view that there are a number of important factors that determine historical change, that no one of these can be considered solely decisive, that they interact upon each other, with changes in one field affecting and in turn being affected by changes in others. He makes his critique of historical monism in order to break down abstract approaches to history, to do away with preconceptions of how things ought to be, and to force a concrete examination of the facts in each specific problem rather than an adjustment of the facts to fit the requirements of some schematic theory. Monistic theories of history, he believes, are a great obstacle to a recognition of the facts.

His particular field is politics. He thinks that by a comparative and historical approach to the facts of political life it is possible to have a science of politics, though he is very modest in his hopes about what political science can at the present time accomplish, either in reaching general conclusions or in providing guides for action:

"Man neither creates nor destroys any of the forces of nature, but he can study their manner of acting and their interplay and turn them to his advantage. That is the procedure in agriculture, in navigation, in mechanics. By following it modern science has been able to achieve almost miraculous results in those fields of activity. The method surely cannot be different when the social sciences are involved, and in fact it is the very method that has already yielded fair results in political economy. Yet we must not disguise the fact that in the social sciences in general the difficulties to be overcome are enormously greater. Not only does the greater complexity of psychological laws (or constant tendencies) that are common to all human groups make it harder to determine their operation, but it is easier to observe the things that go on about us than it is to observe the things we ourselves do. Man can much more easily study the phenomena of physics, chemistry or botany than he can his own instincts and his own passions. . . . But then, even granting that . . . individuals can attain scientific results, it is highly problematical whether they can succeed in using them to modify the political conduct of the great human societies." (*The Ruling Class,* pp. 40-41.)

Since the primary purpose of Machiavellians is to discover the truth, they do not feel required to make demagogic claims even about their own accomplishments.

2. *The Ruling Class*

IT IS CHARACTERISTIC of Machiavellian political analysis to be "anti-formal," using "formal" in the sense which I have defined in the discussion of Dante's *De Monarchia*. That is, Machiavellians, in their investigations of political behavior, do not accept at face value what men say, think, believe, or write. Whether it is the speech or letter or book of an individual, or a public document such as a constitution or set of laws or a party platform, Machiavellians treat it as only one fact among the larger set of social facts, and interpret its meaning always in relation to these other facts. In some cases, examination shows that the words can be accepted just as they stand; more often, as we found with *De Monarchia,* a divorce between formal and real meaning is discovered, with the words distorting and disguising the real political behavior which they indirectly express.

This anti-formal approach leads Mosca to note as a primary and universal social fact the existence of two "political classes," a ruling class—always a minority—and the ruled.

"Among the constant facts and tendencies that are to be found in all political organisms, one is so obvious that it is apparent to the most casual eye. In all societies—from societies that are very meagerly developed and have barely attained the dawnings of civilization, down to the most advanced and powerful societies—two classes of people appear—a class that rules and a class that is ruled. The first class, always the less numerous, performs all political functions, monopolizes power and enjoys the advantages that power brings, whereas the second, the more numerous class, is directed and controlled by the first, in a manner that is now more or less legal, now more or less arbitrary and violent, and supplies the first, in appearance at least, with material means of subsistence and with the instrumentalities that are essential to the vitality of the political organism.

"In practical life we all recognize the existence of this ruling class. . . . We all know that, in our own country, whichever it may be, the management of public affairs is in the hands of a minority of influential persons, to which management, willingly or unwillingly, the majority defer. We know that the same thing goes on in neighboring countries, and in fact we should be put to it to conceive of a real world otherwise organized—a world in which all men would be directly subject to a single person without relationships of superiority or subordination, or in which all men would share equally in the direction of political affairs. If we reason otherwise in theory, that is due partly to inveterate habits that we follow in our thinking. . . ." (P. 50.)

The existence of a minority ruling class is, it must be stressed, a universal feature of all organized societies of which we have any record. It holds no matter what the social and political forms—whether the society is feudal or capitalist or slave or collectivist, monarchical or oligarchical or democratic, no matter what the constitutions and laws, no matter what the professions and beliefs. Mosca furthermore believes that we are fully entitled to conclude that this not only has been and is always the case, but that also it always will be. That it will be, follows, in the first place, from the univocal experience of the past: since, under all conditions, it has always been true of political organization, it must be presumed that it is a constant attribute of political life and will continue to hold for the future. However, the conclusion that there will always be a minority ruling class can be further demonstrated in another way.

By the theory of the ruling class Mosca is refuting two widespread errors which, though the opposite of each other, are oddly

MOSCA: THEORY OF RULING CLASS 89

enough often both believed by the same person. The first, which comes up in discussions of tyranny and dictatorship and is familiar in today's popular attacks on contemporary tyrants, is that society can be ruled by a single individual. "But," Mosca observes, "the man who is at the head of the state would certainly not be able to govern without the support of a numerous class to enforce respect for his orders and to have them carried out; and granting that he can make one individual, or indeed many individuals, in the ruling class feel the weight of his power, he certainly cannot be at odds with the class as a whole or do away with it. Even if that were possible, he would at once be forced to create another class, without the support of which action on his part would be completely paralyzed." (P. 51.)

The other error, typical of democratic theory, is that the masses, the majority, can rule themselves.

"If it is easy to understand that a single individual cannot command a group without finding within the group a minority to support him, it is rather difficult to grant, as a constant and natural fact, that minorities rule majorities, rather than majorities minorities. But that is one of the points—so numerous in all the other sciences—where the first impression one has of things is contrary to what they are in reality. In reality the dominion of an organized minority, obeying a single impulse, over the unorganized majority is inevitable. The power of any minority is irresistible as against each single individual in the majority, who stands alone before the totality of the organized minority. At the same time, the minority is organized for the very reason that it is a minority. A hundred men acting uniformly in concert, with a common understanding, will triumph over a thousand men who are not in accord and can therefore be dealt with one by one. Meanwhile it will be easier for the former to act in concert and have a mutual understanding simply because they are a hundred and not a thousand. It follows that the larger the political community, the smaller will the proportion of the governing minority to the governed majority be, and the more difficult will it be for the majority to organize for reaction against the minority." (P. 53.)

Nor is this rule at all suspended in the case of governments resting in form upon universal suffrage.

"What happens in other forms of government—namely, that an organized minority imposes its will on the disorganized majority—happens also and to perfection, whatever the appearances to the contrary, under the representative system. When we say that the voters 'choose' their representative, we are using a language that is very inexact. The truth is that the representative *has himself elected* by the voters, and, if that phrase should seem too inflexible and too harsh to fit some cases, we might qualify it by saying that his friends *have him elected*. In elections, as in all other manifestations of social life, those who have the will and, especially, the moral, intellectual and material *means* to force their will upon others take the lead over the others and command them.

"The political mandate has been likened to the power of attorney that is familiar in private law. But in private relationships, delegations of powers and capacities always presuppose that the principal has the broadest freedom in choosing his representative. Now in practice, in popular elections, that freedom of choice, though complete theoretically, necessarily becomes null, not to say ludicrous. If each voter gave his vote to the candidate of his heart, we may be sure that in almost all cases the only result would be a wide scattering of votes. When very many wills are involved, choice is determined by the most various criteria, almost all of them subjective, and if such wills were not co-ordinated and organized it would be virtually impossible for them to coincide in the spontaneous choice of one individual. If his vote is to have any efficacy at all, therefore, each voter is forced to limit his choice

MOSCA: THEORY OF RULING CLASS

to a very narrow field, in other words to a choice among the two or three persons who have some chance of succeeding; and the only ones who have any chance of succeeding are those whose candidacies are championed by groups, by committees, by *organized minorities*." (P. 154.)

Few who have paid attention to the political facts, rather than to theories about these facts, in the United States, will disagree with the account as it applies to this country.

Within the ruling class, it is usually possible to distinguish roughly two layers: a very small group of "top leaders," who among themselves occupy the highest and key positions of the society; and a much larger group of secondary figures—a "middle class," as it could properly be called—who, though not so prominent nor so much in the limelight, constitute the day-by-day active directors of the community life. Just as Mosca believes that the individual supreme leader is unimportant to the fate of a society, compared to the ruling class, so does he believe that this secondary level of the ruling class is, in the long run at least, more decisive than the top.

"Below the highest stratum in the ruling class, there is always, even in autocratic systems, another that is much more numerous and comprises all the capacities for leadership in the country. Without such a class any sort of social organization would be impossible. The higher stratum would not in itself be sufficient for leading and directing the activities of the masses. In the last analysis, therefore, the stability of any political organism depends on the level of morality, intelligence and activity that this second stratum has attained. . . . Any intellectual or moral deficiencies in this second stratum, accordingly, represent a graver danger to the political structure, and one that is harder to repair, than the presence of similar deficiencies in the few dozen persons who control the workings of the state machine. . . ." (Pp. 404-5.)

From the point of view of the theory of the ruling class, a

society is the society of its ruling class. A nation's strength or weakness, its culture, its powers of endurance, its prosperity, its decadence, depend in the first instance upon the nature of its ruling class. More particularly, the way in which to study a nation, to understand it, to predict what will happen to it, requires first of all and primarily an analysis of the ruling class. Political history and political science are thus predominantly the history and science of ruling classes, their origin, development, composition, structure, and changes. The theory of the ruling class in this way provides a principle with the help of which the innumerable and otherwise amorphous and meaningless facts of political life can be systematically assembled and made intelligible.

However arbitrary this idea of history as the history of ruling classes may seem to be, the truth is that all historians, in practice —even such historians as Tolstoy or Trotsky, whose general theories directly contradict it—are compelled to write in terms of it. If for no other reason, this must be because the great mass of mankind leaves no record of itself except insofar as it is expressed or led by outstanding and noteworthy persons. Nor does this method result in any falsification of the historical development. The account of a war cannot nor need not cover what all or a most part of the soldiers did, nor need the accounts of a school of art or the formation of a constitution or the growth of a religion or the progress of a revolution tell everything about everyone. Even if theory were to decide that ultimately the movements of the masses are the cause of what happens in history, yet these movements attain historical significance only when they alter major institutions and result in shifts in the character and composition of the ruling class. Thus, the analysis of the ruling class, if not directly, then indirectly, will produce an adequate history and an adequate political science.

There is an ambiguity, which is noted by Professor Livingston, in Mosca's concept of the "ruling class." Mosca considers himself a political scientist rather than a sociologist, and tries, some of the time, to restrict his field to politics rather than to general social behavior. If literally translated from the Italian, his phrase would usually be "political class," or "governing class," rather than "ruling class." In his writings his meaning seems to shuttle between the narrower concept of a "governing class"—that is, the class directly or indirectly concerned with the specific business of government—and the more general concept of a "social élite"—that is, the class of all those in a society who are differentiated from the masses by the possession of some kind of power or privilege, many of whom may have no specific relation to government.

However, this ambiguity does not affect Mosca's argument to any considerable degree; and if we judge by the context, the general concept of an "élite" is usually more appropriate to his meaning. What seems to have happened is that Mosca began his work in the narrower field of politics, with the narrower concept in mind. His political inquiries then led him outward into the wider field of social action, since the political field could not be understood apart from the background of the whole social field. The idea of the political class expanded its meaning into the idea of a social élite without an explicit discussion of the change. In later Machiavellian thought—in Pareto, particularly—the wider meaning of "élite" is consistently employed.

We should further note that in stating the theory of the ruling class, Mosca is not making a moral judgment, is not arguing that it is good, or bad, that mankind should be divided into rulers and ruled. I recently read, in a review by a well-known journalist, that "this country will never accept a theory of the élite"—as if it is wicked to talk about such things, and noble to denounce them. The scientific problem, however, is not whether this country or any other will accept such theories, but whether the theories are true. Mosca believes that the stratification of society into rulers and ruled is universal and permanent, a general form of political life. As such it would be absurd to call it good or bad; it is simply the way things are. Moral values, goodness and badness, justice and injustice, are indeed to be found, and Mosca does not try to avoid making moral judgments; but they are meaningful only within the permanent structure of society. Granted that there are always rulers and ruled, then we may judge that the societies of some ruling classes are good, or more good, just, or less unjust, than others.

3. Composition and Character of the Ruling Class

MOSCA REJECTS the many theories which have tried to apply the Darwinian theory of evolution directly to social life. He finds, however, a social tendency that is indirectly analogous to the process of biological evolution:

"The struggle for *existence* has been confused with the struggle for *pre-eminence,* which is really a constant phenomenon that arises in all human societies, from the most highly civilized down to such as have barely issued from savagery. . . .

"If we consider . . . the inner ferment that goes on within the body of every society, we see at once that the struggle for pre-eminence is far more conspicuous there than the struggle for existence. Competition between individuals of every social unit is focused upon higher position, wealth, authority, control of the means and instruments that enable a person to direct many human activities, many human wills, as he sees fit. The losers, who are of course the majority in that sort of struggle, are not devoured, destroyed or even kept from reproducing their kind, as is basically characteristic of the struggle for life. They merely enjoy fewer material satisfactions and, especially, less freedom and independence. On the whole, indeed, in civilized societies, far from being gradually eliminated by a process of natural selection so-called, the lower classes are more prolific than the higher, and even in the lower classes every individual in the long run gets a loaf of bread and a mate, though the bread be more or less dark and hard-earned and the mate more or less unattractive or undesirable." (Pp. 29-30.)

The outcome of this "struggle for pre-eminence" is the decision who shall be, or continue to be, members of the ruling class.

What makes for success in the struggle? or, in other words, what qualities must be possessed by individuals in order that they may secure or maintain membership in the ruling class? In answering a question like this, it is above all necessary to avoid the merely formal. Spokesmen for various ruling classes have numerous self-satisfying explanations of how superior morality or intelligence or blood or racial inheritance confer membership. But Mosca, like all Machiavellians, looks beyond the verbal explanations to the relevant facts.

He finds that the possession of certain qualities is useful in all societies for gaining admittance to the ruling class, or for staying within it. Deep wisdom, altruism, readiness at self-sacrifice, are not among these qualities, but, on the contrary, are usually hindrances.

"To rise in the social scale, even in calm and normal times, the prime requisite, beyond any question, is a capacity for hard work; but the requisite next in importance is ambition, a firm resolve to get on in the world, to outstrip one's fellows. Now those traits hardly go with extreme sensitiveness or, to be quite frank, with 'goodness' either. For 'goodness' cannot remain indifferent to the hurts of those who must be thrust behind if one is to step ahead of them. . . . If one is to govern men, more useful than a sense of justice—and much more useful than altruism, or even than extent of knowledge or broadness of view—are perspicacity, a ready intuition of individual and mass psychology, strength of will and, especially, confidence in oneself. With good reason did Machiavelli put into the mouth of Cosimo dei Medici the much quoted remark, that states are not ruled with prayer-books." (Pp. 449-450.)

The best means of all for entering the ruling class is to be born into it—though, it may be observed, inheritance alone will not suffice to keep a family permanently among the rulers. Like Machiavelli here also, Mosca attributes not a little to "fortune."

"A certain amount of work is almost always necessary to achieve success—work that corresponds to a real and actual service to society. But work always has to be reinforced to a certain extent by 'ability,' that is to say, by the art of winning recognition. And of course a little of what is commonly called 'luck' will not come amiss—those unforeseeable circumstances which help or seriously harm a man, especially at certain moments. One might add that in all places at all times the best luck, or the worst, is often to be born the child of one's father and one's mother." (P. 456.)

These qualities—a capacity for hard work, ambition (Machiavelli's *virtù*), a certain callousness, luck in birth and circumstances—are those that help toward membership in any ruling class at any time in history. In addition, however, there is another group of qualities that are variable, dependent upon the particular society in question. "Members of a ruling minority regularly have some attribute, real or apparent, which is highly esteemed and very influential in the society in which they live." (P. 53.) To mention simple examples: in a society which lives primarily by fishing, the expert fisherman has an advantage; the skilled warrior, in a predominantly military society; the able priest, in a profoundly religious group; and so on. Considered as keys to rule, such qualities as these are variable; if the conditions of life change, they change, for when religion declines, the priest is no longer so important, or when fishing changes to agriculture, the fisherman naturally drops in the social scale. Thus, changes in the general conditions of life are correlated with far-reaching changes in the composition of the ruling class.

The various sections of the ruling class express or represent or control or lead what Mosca calls *social forces,* which are continually varying in number and importance. By "social force"

Mosca means any human activity which has significant social and political influence. In primitive societies, the chief forces are ordinarily war and religion. "As civilization grows, the number of the moral and material influences which are capable of becoming social forces increases. For example, property in money, as the fruit of industry and commerce, comes into being alongside of real property. Education progresses. Occupations based on scientific knowledge gain in importance." (Pp. 144-5.) All of these—war, religion, land, labor, money, education, science, technological skill—can function as social forces if a society is organized in terms of them.

From this point of view, it may be seen that the relation of a ruling class to the society which it rules need not be at all arbitrary; in fact, in the long run cannot be. A given ruling class rules over a given society precisely because it is able to control the major social forces that are active within that society. If a social force—religion, let us say—declines in importance, then the section of the ruling class whose position was dependent upon control of religion likewise, over a period, declines. If the entire ruling class had been based primarily upon religion, then the entire ruling class would change its character (if it were able to adapt itself to the new conditions) or would (if it could not adapt itself) be overthrown. Similarly, if a new major social force develops—commerce, for example, in a previously agricultural society, or applied science—then either the existing ruling class proves itself flexible enough to gain leadership over this new force (in part, no doubt, by absorbing new members into its ranks); or, if it does not, the leadership of the new force grows up outside of the old class, and in time constitutes a revolutionary threat against the old ruling class, challenging it for supreme social and political power. Thus, the growth of new social forces and the decline of old forces is in general correlated with the constant process of change and dislocation in the ruling class.

MOSCA: THEORY OF RULING CLASS 99

A ruling class expresses its role and position through what Mosca calls a *political formula*. This formula rationalizes and justifies its rule and the structure of the society over which it rules. The formula may be a "racial myth," as in Germany at the present time or in this country in relation to the Negroes or the yellow races: rule is then explained as the natural prerogative of the superior race. Or it may be a "divine right" doctrine, as in the theories elaborated in connection with the absolutist monarchies of the 16th and 17th centuries, or in Japan at the present day: then rule is explained as following from a peculiar relationship to divinity, very often in fact from direct blood descent (such formulas were very common in ancient times, and have by no means lost all efficacy). Or, to cite the formula most familiar to us, and functioning now in this country, it is a belief in the "will of the people": rule is then said to follow legitimately from the will or choice of the people expressed through some type of suffrage.

"According to the level of civilization in the peoples among whom they are current, the various political formulas may be based either upon supernatural beliefs or upon concepts which, if they do not correspond to positive realities, at least appear to be rational. We shall not say that they correspond in either case to scientific truths. A conscientious observer would be obliged to confess that, if no one has ever seen the authentic document by which the Lord empowered certain privileged persons or families to rule his people on his behalf, neither can it be maintained that a popular election, however liberal the suffrage may be, is ordinarily the expression of the will of a people, or even of the will of the majority of a people.

"And yet that does not mean that political formulas are mere quackeries aptly invented to trick the masses into obedience. Anyone who viewed them in that light would fall into grave error.

The truth is that they answer a real need in man's social nature; and this need, so universally felt, of governing and knowing that one is governed not on the basis of mere material or intellectual force, but on the basis of a moral principle, has beyond any doubt a practical and real importance." (P. 71.)

Since the problem of such formulas (ideologies, myths) will occupy us at length later on, I shall note here only two further facts concerning them. First, the special political formula employed within a given nation is often related to wider myths that are shared by a number of nations, so that several political formulas appear as variations on similar basic themes. Conspicuous among these wider myths are the great world religions—Christianity, Buddhism, Mohammedanism—which, unlike most earlier religions or still-continuing religions of the type of Japanese Shintoism, are not specifically bound up with a single nation or people; the myth, probably best expressed by Rousseau, which is built out of such ideas as the innate goodness of man, the will of the people, humanitarianism, and progress; and the contemporary myth of collectivism, which, in Mosca's opinion, is the logical extension of the democratic Rousseau myth.

Second, it may be seen from historical experience that the integrity of the political formula is essential for the survival of a given social structure. Changes in the formula, if they are not to destroy the society, must be gradual, not abrupt. The formula is indispensable for holding the social structure together. A widespread skepticism about the formula will in time corrode and disintegrate the social order. It is perhaps for this reason, half-consciously understood, that all strong and long-lived societies have cherished their "traditions," even when, as is usually the case, these traditions have little relation to fact, and even after they can hardly be believed literally by educated men. Rome, Japan, Venice, all such long-enduring states, have been very slow to change the old formulas, the time-honored ways and stories and rituals; and they have been harsh against rationalists who debunk them. This, after all, was the crime for which Athens put Socrates to death. From the point of view of survival, she was probably right in doing so.

4. Tendencies in the Ruling Class

WITHIN ALL RULING CLASSES, Mosca shows that it is possible to distinguish two "principles," as he calls them, and two "tendencies." These are, it might be said, the developmental laws of ruling classes. Their relative strength establishes the most important difference among various ruling classes.

The "autocratic" principle may be distinguished from the "liberal" principle. These two principles regulate, primarily, the method by which governmental officials and social leaders are chosen. "In any form of political organization, authority is either transmitted from above downward in the political or social scale [the autocratic principle], or from below upward [the liberal principle]." (P. 394.) Neither principle violates the general law that society is divided into a ruling minority and a majority that is ruled; the liberal principle does not mean, no matter how extended, that the masses in fact rule, but simply gives a particular form to the selection of leadership. Moreover, it is seldom, probably never, that one of the two principles operates alone within a ruling class. They are usually mixed, with one or the other dominant. Certain absolute monarchies or tyrannies show the closest approximation to a purely autocratic principle, with all positions formally dependent upon appointment by the despot. Some small city-states, such as Athens at certain times in its history, have come very close to a purely liberal principle, with all officials chosen from below—though the voters were at the same time a restricted group. In the United States, as in most representative governments of the modern kind, both principles are actively at work. The greater part of the bureaucracy and much of the judiciary, especially the Federal judiciary, is an expression of the autocratic principle; the President himself, as well as the members of Congress, are selected according to the liberal mode.

Each principle in practice displays typical advantages and defects. Autocracy has been by far the more common of the two, and of it Mosca remarks: "A political system that has been so widely recurring and so long enduring among peoples of the most widely various civilizations, who often have had no contacts material or intellectual with one another, must somehow correspond to the political nature of man. . . . Autocracy supplies a justification of power that is simple, clear and readily comprehensible to everybody. There can be no human organization without rankings and subordinations. Any sort of hierarchy necessarily requires that some should command and others obey. And since it is in the nature of the human being that many men should love to command and that almost all men can be brought to obey, an institution that gives those who are at the top a way of justifying their authority and at the same time helps to persuade those who are at the bottom to submit is likely to be a useful institution." (P. 397.) Autocracy, moreover, seems to endow societies over which it operates with greater stability and longer life than does the liberal principle. When autocracy is functioning well, it can bring about the deliberate selection of the ablest leadership from all strata of society to perform the various tasks of the state.

However, in compensation, autocracy seems unable to permit a free and full development of all social activities and forces—no autocracy has ever stimulated so intense a cultural and intellectual life as have developed under some of the shorter-lived liberal systems, such as those of Greece and western Europe. And in the selection of leaders by the autocrat and his immediate clique, favoritism and personal prejudice easily take the place of objective judgment of merit, while the method encourages sycophancy and slavishness on the part of the candidates.

The liberal principle, conversely, stimulates more than the autocratic the development of varied social potentialities. At the same time, it by no means avoids the formation of closed cliques at the top, such as are usually found in autocracies; the mode of formation of such cliques is merely different. "In order to reach high station in an autocracy it is sufficient to have the support of one or more persons, and that is secured by exploiting all their passions, good and bad. In liberal systems one has to steer the inclinations of at least the whole second stratum of the ruling class, which, if it does not in itself constitute the electorate, at least supplies the general staffs of leaders who form the opinions and determine the conduct of the electing body." (P. 410.) When the liberal system is broadly based (that is, where suffrage is widely extended or universal), the candidates for high office must proceed by exploiting the backward sentiments of the masses:

"Whatever their origins, the methods that are used by the people who aim to monopolize and exploit the sympathy of the masses always have been the same. They come down to pointing out, with exaggerations, of course, the selfishness, the stupidity, the material enjoyments of the rich and the powerful; to denouncing their vices and wrongdoings, real and imaginary; and to promising to satisfy a common and widespread sense of rough-hewn justice which would like to see abolished every social distinction based upon advantage of birth and at the same time would like to see an absolutely equal distribution of pleasures and pains.

"Often enough the parties against which this demagogic propaganda is directed use exactly the same means to combat it. Whenever they think they can profit by doing so, they too make promises which they will never be able to keep. They too flatter the masses, play to their crudest instincts and exploit and foment all their prejudices and greeds." (P. 412.)

* * *

The distinction which Mosca makes between the "aristocratic" and "democratic" tendencies is independent of his distinction between the autocratic and liberal principles. Aristocratic and democratic, as Mosca uses the terms, refer to the sources from which new members of the ruling class are drawn. "The term 'democratic' seems more suitable for the tendency which aims to replenish the ruling class with elements deriving from the lower classes, and which is always at work, openly or latently and with greater or lesser intensity, in all political organisms. 'Aristocratic' we would call the opposite tendency, which also is constant and varies in intensity, and which aims to stabilize social control and political power in the descendants of the class that happens to hold possession of it at the given historical moment." (P. 395.)

In terms of this definition, there can be, as there have often been, in spite of common opinion to the contrary, autocracies which are primarily democratic in tendency, and liberal systems which are largely aristocratic. The most remarkable example of the former is the Catholic Church, which is almost perfectly autocratic, but at the same time is always recruiting new members of its hierarchy from the masses. Hitler, in *Mein Kampf,* observes that the rule of celibacy compels the Church to remain thus democratic in its policy of recruitment, and he concludes that this is a principal source of the Church's strength and power of endurance. On the other hand, modern England, during many generations, was in many respects liberal, but, by various devices, preserved an aristocratic continuity in the membership of its ruling class. This was also the case in many of the ancient city-states which had liberal extensions of the suffrage to all citizens, but restrictions on eligibility to office which kept rule in the hands of a small group of families.

Since all of us in the United States have been educated under democratic formulas, the advantages of the democratic tendency are too familiar to need statement. We less often discuss certain of its disadvantages, or some possible advantages of aristocracy. To begin with, so long as the family remains, and in some form it is likely to remain as long as we can foresee, the aristocratic tendency will always be asserting itself to some degree at least; it too accords with ineradicable human traits, with the fact that, since a man cannot help all other men equally and since all cannot prosper equally, he will prefer as a rule that those should be favored toward whom he feels some special attachment. A revolutionary movement ordinarily proclaims that its aim is to do away with all privileges of birth, but invariably, once it is in power, the aristocratic tendency reasserts itself, and a new ruling group crystallizes out from the revolution.

"It is not so certain, meantime," Mosca adds, "that it would be altogether beneficial to the collectivity to have every advantage of birth eliminated in the struggle for membership in the ruling class and for high position in the social hierarchy. If all individuals could participate in the scramble on an equal footing, struggle would be intensified to the point of frenzy. This would entail an enormous expenditure of energy for strictly personal ends, with no corresponding benefit to the social organism, at least in the majority of cases. On the other hand, it may very well be that certain intellectual and, especially, moral qualities, which are necessary to a ruling class if it is to maintain its prestige and function properly, are useful also to society, yet require, if they are to develop and exert their influence, that the same families should hold fairly high social positions for a number of generations." (P. 419.)

The fact of the matter, however, is that both of these tendencies, aristocratic and democratic, are always operative within every society. The heavy predominance of one of them is usually the occasion or the aftermath of a period of rapid and often revolutionary social change.

5. The Best and Worst Governments

MOSCA, like Machiavelli, does not stop with the descriptive analysis of political life. He states plainly his own preferences, his opinions about what types of government are best, what worst. Naturally, as is the case with all Machiavellians, his goal is not anything supernatural or utopian; to be the best, a government must be first of all possible. He does no dreaming about a "perfect state" or "absolute justice." In fact, Mosca suggests what I had occasion to mention in connection with Dante: namely, that political doctrines which promise utopias and absolute justice are very likely to lead to much worse social effects than doctrines less entrancing in appearance; that utopian programs may even be the most convenient of cloaks for those whose real aims are most rightly suspect. The impossibility of attaining absolute justice, however, does not render useless an effort after what measure of approximate justice is possible in the actual social world that we inhabit.

"Human sentiments being what they are, to set out to erect a type of political organization that will correspond in all respects to the ideal of justice, which a man can conceive but can never attain, is a utopia, and the utopia becomes frankly dangerous when it succeeds in bringing a large mass of intellectual and moral energies to bear upon the achievement of an end that will never be achieved and that, on the day of its purported achievement, can mean nothing more than triumph for the worst people and distress and disappointment for the good. Burke remarked more than a century ago that any political system that assumes the existence of superhuman or heroic virtues can result only in vice and corruption." (P. 288.)

"But even if there is never to be an absolute justice in this world until humanity comes really to be molded to the image and likeness of God, there has been, there is and there will always be a relative justice in societies that are fairly well organized. There will always be, in other words, a sum of laws, habits, norms, all varying according to times and peoples, which are laid down and enforced by public opinion, and in accordance with which what we have called the struggle for pre-eminence—the effort of every individual to better and to conserve his own social position—will be regulated." (P. 456.)

Again following Machiavelli, the dominant element in Mosca's conception of that "relative justice" which he thinks possible as well as desirable is liberty. The meaning of "liberty" he makes more precise by defining it in terms of what he calls "juridical defense."

"The social mechanisms that regulate this disciplining of the moral sense constitute what we call 'juridical defense' (respect for law, government by law). . . . It will further be noted that our view is contrary to the doctrine of Rousseau, that man is good by nature but that society makes him wicked and perverse. We believe that social organization provides for the reciprocal restraint of human individuals by one another and so makes them better, not by destroying their wicked instincts, but by accustoming them to controlling their wicked instincts." (Pp. 126-7.)

"Guicciardini defines political liberty as 'a prevalence of law and public decrees over the appetites of particular men.' If we take 'particular men' in the sense of 'individuals,' meaning 'single individuals,' and including individuals who have power in their hands, it would be difficult to find a more rigorously scientific definition. . . . A corrupt government, in which the person who commands 'makes his will licit in his law'—whether in the name of God or in the name of the people does not matter—will obviously be inadequate to fulfilling its mission in regard to juridical defense." (Pp. 130-1.) "The freest country is the country where the rights of the governed are best protected against arbitrary caprice and tyranny on the part of rulers." (P. 13.)

Juridical defense, then, means government by law and due process—not merely formally, in the words of constitutions or statutes, but in fact; it means a set of impersonal restrictions on those who hold power, and correlatively a set of protections for the individuals against the state and those who have power. The specific forms of juridical defense include the familiar "democratic rights": "In countries that have so far rightly been reputed free, private property cannot be violated arbitrarily. A citizen cannot be arrested and condemned unless specified rules are observed. Each person can follow the religion of his choice without forfeiture of his civil and political rights. The press cannot be subjected to censorship and is free to discuss and criticize acts of government. Finally, if they conform with certain rules, citizens can meet to engage in discussions of a political character, and they can form associations for the attainment of moral, political or professional ends." (Pp. 469-70.) Of all these rights, Mosca considers the right of public discussion—of free speech, as we usually call it—the most important, and the strongest foundation of juridical defense as a whole.

A firm juridical defense is required for the attainment and maintenance of a relatively high "level of civilization." Level of civilization is measured, according to Mosca's definition, by the degree of development and number of social forces: that is, the more social forces there are and the more fully each is developed, the higher the level of a given civilization. A civilization that has an active art, an active literature and commerce and science and industry, a strong army, and a progressive agriculture, is higher than one that concentrates on only one or two of these, or one that is mediocre in most or all of them. Thus, the conception of "level of civilization" can serve as a rough standard for evaluating different cultures.

But what is it that makes possible a high level of juridical defense and of civilization? With the answer to this question we come to what is perhaps the most profound and most important of all Mosca's ideas, though it, also, has its source in Machiavelli. Mosca's answer, moreover, is sharply at variance with many accepted theories, and particularly opposed to the arguments of almost all the spokesmen of the ruling class.

The mere formal structure of laws and constitutions, or of institutional arrangements, cannot guarantee juridical defense. Constitutions and laws, as we certainly should know by now, need have no relation to what happens—Hitler never repealed the Weimar Constitution, and Stalin ordered the adoption of "the most democratic constitution in the history of the world." Nor can the most formally perfect organizational setup: one-house or two- or three-house legislatures, independent or responsible executives, kings or presidents, written or unwritten constitutions, judges appointed or elected—decisions on these formalities will never settle the problem. Nor will any doctrine, nor any reliance on the good will of whatever men, give a guarantee: the men who want and are able to get power never have the necessary kind of good will, but always seek, for themselves and their group, still more power.

In real social life, only power can control power. Juridical defense can be secure only where there are at work various and opposing tendencies and forces, and where these mutually check and restrain each other. Tyranny, the worst of all governments, means the loss of juridical defense; and juridical defense invariably disappears whenever one tendency or force in society succeeds in absorbing or suppressing all the others. Those who control the supreme force rule then without restraint. The individual has no protection against them.

From one point of view, the protective balance must be established between the autocratic and liberal principles, and between the aristocratic and democratic tendencies. Monopoly by the aristocratic tendency produces a closed and inflexible caste system, and fossilization; the extreme of democracy brings an unbridled anarchy under which the whole social order flies to pieces.

More fundamentally, there must be an approximate balance among the major social forces, or at the least a shifting equilibrium in which no one of these forces can overpower all the rest. "Even granted that such a world [the world of so many utopians, where conflicts and rivalries among different forces, religions, and parties will have ended] could be realized, it does not seem to us a desirable sort of world. So far in history, freedom to think, to observe, to judge men and things serenely and dispassionately, has been possible—always, be it understood, for a few individuals —only in those societies in which numbers of different religious and political currents have been struggling for dominion. That same condition . . . is almost indispensable for the attainment of what is commonly called 'political liberty'—in other words, the highest possible degree of justice in the relations between governors and governed that is compatible with our imperfect human nature." (P. 196.) "History teaches that whenever, in the course of the ages, a social organization has exerted such an influence [to raise the level of civilization] in a beneficial way, it has done so because the individual and collective will of the men who have held power in their hands has been curbed and balanced by other men, who have occupied positions of absolute independence and have had no common interests with those whom they have had to curb and balance. It has been necessary, nay indispensable, that there should be a multiplicity of political forces, that there should be many different roads by which social importance could be acquired . . ." (pp. 291-2.)

Freedom, in the world as it is, is thus the product of conflict and difference, not of unity and harmony. In these terms we see again the danger of "idealism," utopianism, and demagogy. The idealists, utopians, and demagogues always tell us that justice and the good society will be achieved by the absolute triumph of their doctrine and their side. The facts show us that the absolute triumph of any side and any doctrine whatsoever can only mean tyranny. "The absolute preponderance of a single political force, the predominance of any over-simplified concept in the organization of the state, the strictly logical application of any single principle in all public law are the essential elements in any type of despotism, whether it be a despotism based upon divine right or a despotism based ostensibly on popular sovereignty; for they enable anyone who is in power to exploit the advantages of a superior position more thoroughly for the benefit of his own interests and passions. When the leaders of the governing class are the exclusive interpreters of the will of God or of the will of the people and exercise sovereignty in the name of those abstractions in societies that are deeply imbued with religious beliefs or with democratic fanaticism, and when no other organized social forces exist apart from those which represent the principle on which sovereignty over the nation is based, then there can be no resistance, no effective control, to restrain a natural tendency in those who stand at the head of the social order to abuse their powers." (P. 134.)

By 1923, when Mosca revised his major book (the English translation is made from this revised version), he had come to the conclusion that the great parliamentary-representative governments of the 19th century had reached the highest level of civilization and juridical defense so far known in history. In many ways, this was a remarkable opinion for Mosca to have held. The chief theme of his entire work is a devastating attack on the entire

MOSCA: THEORY OF RULING CLASS 113

theoretical basis of democratic and parliamentary doctrine. He gives not a little space to a withering exposure of concrete abuses under modern parliamentary government. In his critique of collectivism, he states: "The strength of the socialist and anarchist doctrines lies not so much in their positive as in their negative aspects—in their minute, pointed, merciless criticism of our present organization of society" (p. 286), and he holds that the criticism is largely justified.

Nevertheless, Mosca does not expect utopia or absolute justice. Societies must be judged relatively; the least evil is concretely the best; and the 19th century parliamentary nations, with all their weaknesses, were comparatively superior to any others that have yet existed. In their governmental structures, the autocratic principle, functioning through the bureaucracy, balanced the liberal principle, expressed in the parliaments. The aristocratic tendencies of birth and inheritance were checked by a perhaps unprecedented ease with which vigorous new members were able to enter the ruling class. Above all, under these governments there occurred an astounding expansion not of one or a restricted few social forces, but of a great and rich variety, with no one force able to gain exclusive predominance over the rest. Commerce as well as the arts, education and science, technology and literature, all were able to flourish. His judgment on these governments thus follows from his general principles; he does not praise parliamentary government for its own sake, but because, under the specific circumstances of the 19th century, it was accompanied by this relatively high level of civilization and juridical defense.

From his favorable judgment, however, Mosca did not conclude that the 19th century form of parliamentary government was necessarily going to last. It is the habit of utopians, of those who, like Dante, interpret politics as wish, not of scientists, to confuse their desires with what is going to happen. Mosca, on the contrary, believed that it was almost certain that parliamentary governments, as the 19th century had known them, were not going to last very much longer.

The War of 1914, he believed, marked the end of an age that could be considered as having begun with the French Revolution, in 1789. The parliamentary governments were the great social achievement of that age; but the age was ending. In the new age, just beginning, these governments would be displaced. It was conceivable, he thought, that the new organization of society should be superior to the parliamentary-representative system: "If Europe is able to overcome the difficulties with which she is struggling at present, it is altogether probable that in the course of another century, or even within half that time, new ideas, new sentiments, new needs will automatically prepare the ground for other political systems that may be far preferable to any now existing." (P. 490.) But the depth of the crisis into which he understood that Europe had, with the first World War, irrevocably entered, suggested the probability of attempts at extreme and catastrophic solutions. These, he believed, could lead only toward the destruction of liberty and a decline in the level of civilization. Though a small reserve of optimism was permissible, pessimism was on the whole called for by the facts.

"The feeling that springs spontaneously from an unprejudiced judgment of the history of humanity is compassion for the contradictory qualities of this poor human race of ours, so rich in abnegation, so ready at times for personal sacrifice, yet whose every attempt, whether more or less successful or not at all successful, to attain moral and material betterment, is coupled with an unleashing of hates, rancors and the basest passions. A tragic destiny is that of men! Aspiring ever to pursue and achieve what they think is the good, they ever find pretexts for slaughtering and persecuting each other. Once they slaughtered and persecuted over the interpretation of a dogma, or of a passage in the Bible. Then they slaughtered and persecuted in order to inaugurate the kingdom of liberty, equality and fraternity. Today they are slaughtering and persecuting and fiendishly torturing each other in the name of other creeds. Perhaps tomorrow they will slaughter and torment each other in an effort to banish the last trace of violence and injustice from the earth!" (P. 198.)

Part IV

SOREL: A NOTE ON MYTH AND VIOLENCE

1. *The Function of Myth*

GEORGES SOREL cannot be considered in all respects a Machiavellian. For one thing, he was a political extremist. Though Machiavellian principles are not committed to any single political program, they do not seem to accord naturally with extremism. Further, Sorel partly repudiates, or seems to repudiate, scientific method, and to grant, in certain connections, the legitimacy of intuition and of a metaphysics derived from the French philosopher, Henri Bergson. To the extent that he rejects science, Sorel is certainly outside the Machiavellian tradition.

However, Sorel's repudiation of scientific method is largely appearance. In reality, he attacks not science, but academic pseudoscience, which he calls the "little science," that pretends to tell us about the nature of society and politics, but in truth is merely seeking to justify this or that group of power-seekers. Sorel does indeed contend that genuine scientific doctrines are not enough to motivate mass political action; but this conclusion, far from being anti-scientific, is reached by a careful scientific analysis. Moreover, Sorel shares fully what I have called the "anti-formalism" of the Machiavellians, their refusal to take at face value the words and beliefs and ideals of men. In common with other Machiavellians he defines the subject-matter of politics as the struggle for social power; and he makes the same general analysis of the behavior of "political man," of men, that is to say, as they act in relation to the struggle for power.

Sorel also requires mention because of his influence on the other Machiavellian writers, Robert Michels and Vilfredo Pareto, with whom we shall be concerned. Pareto more than once gives tribute to Sorel. He writes, for example: "It was the surpassing merit of Georges Sorel that in *Réflexions sur la violence* he threw all such fatuities overboard to ascend to the altitudes of science. He was not adequately understood by people who went looking for derivations and were given logico-experimental reasonings instead. As for certain university professors who habitually mistake pedantry for science, and, given a theory, focus their microscopes on insignificant errors and other trifles, they are completely destitute of the intellectual capacities required for understanding the work of a scientist of Sorel's stature." * Sorel, both through his writings and through personal acquaintance, played a considerable part in the transformation of Michels into a Machiavellian, which occurred when Michels took up residence in Switzerland after an earlier career at a German university.

I propose to deal only with two points discussed by Sorel in his most famous work, *Reflections on Violence*.† However, to understand the treatment of these points, it is necessary to summarize briefly the context in which the book was written.

Sorel was at that time active, chiefly as a journalist and theoretician, in the French and to some extent the international revolutionary labor movement. The greater part of the politically organized labor movement adhered in those days to the various social-democratic parties of the Second International. The activities of these parties were reformist. The parties were large in size and institutional strength, and devoted themselves to winning economic concessions (higher wages, social insurance, and so on) for the workers, and parliamentary or governmental posts for the party leaders. Ostensibly, however, the party programs still pro-

---

* *Mind and Society,* footnote 2 to § 2193, p. 1535, Vol. IV.

† The English translation, by T. E. Hulme, of *Réflexions sur la violence.* Originally issued in New York by B. W. Huebsch, this was re-published by Peter Smith, in 1941. The French text first appeared in 1906. Georges Sorel lived from 1847-1922.

fessed the goals of revolutionary socialism: the overthrow of capitalism and the institution of a free, classless society.

Sorel spoke for the dissident revolutionary *syndicalist* wing of the labor movement. The syndicalists were opposed both to the state—not only to the existing state but to all states and governments—and to all political parties, including the professedly labor parties. They advocated the economic "self-organization" of the workers, in revolutionary syndicates (that is, unions), with no professional officials and absolute independence from the state and all political parties. The state, whether the existing state or any other, they considered to be merely a political instrument for the oppression of the masses. Political parties, socialist as well as all the rest, have as their object the attainment of state power. Consequently, political parties are part of the machinery of oppression. If the socialist party took over governmental power, this would not at all mean the introduction of socialism, of a free and classless society, but simply the substitution of a new élite as ruler over the masses.

This analysis, we may remark, coincides exactly with that made by the other Machiavellians. In the later discussion of Robert Michels, we shall see in detail how it applies to the parties of socialism.

In contradistinction to the allegedly "scientific socialism" of the official parties, to their elaborate programs of "immediate demands" and desired reforms, to their lengthy treatises on how socialism will be brought about and what it will be like and how it will work, Sorel insists that the entire revolutionary program must be expressed integrally as a single catastrophic *myth:* the myth, he maintains, of the "general strike." The myth of the general strike is formulated in absolute terms: the entire body of workers, of proletarians, ceases work; society is divided into two irrevocably marked camps—the strikers on one side, and all the rest of society on the other; all production wholly ceases; the entire structure of the existing society, and all its institutions, collapse; the workers march back to begin production again, no longer as proletarians, but as free and un-ruled producers; a completely new era of history begins.

Only such an all-embracing myth, Sorel believes, can arouse the masses to uncompromising revolutionary action. No detailed rationalistic program, no careful calculation of pros and cons, no estimate of results and consequences, can possibly be efficacious. Indeed, the effect of such programs is to paralyze the independent action of the workers and to place power in the hands of the leaders who devise and manipulate the programs.

It is not the specific myth of the general strike, as treated by Sorel, that particularly concerns us, but rather the more general problem of the positive role of myth in political action. What kind of construction is such a political myth? If we interpret it as a scientific hypothesis, as a prediction about the future, it must be regarded as absurd, fantastic, false. But this interpretation, Sorel thinks, would be irrelevant. Nor is the myth in the least like a Utopia, though at first there might seem to be a close resemblance. Like a scientific hypothesis, a Utopia is an "intellectual product; it is the work of theorists who, after observing and discussing the known facts, seek to establish a model to which they can compare existing society in order to estimate the amount of good and evil it contains. It is a combination of imaginary institutions having sufficient analogies to real institutions for the jurist to be able to reason about them. . . . Whilst contemporary myths lead men to prepare themselves for a combat which will destroy the existing state of things, the effect of Utopias has always been to direct men's minds towards reforms which can be brought about by patching up the existing system . . ." (*Reflections on Violence*, pp. 32-3.)

A myth, in contrast to hypotheses or utopias, is not either true or false. The facts can never prove it wrong. "A myth cannot be refuted, since it is, at bottom, identical with the convictions of a group, being the expression of these convictions in the language of movement; and it is, in consequence, unanalyzable into parts which could be placed on the plane of historical descriptions." (P. 33.) "In the course of this study one thing has always been present in my mind, which seemed to me so evident that I did not think it worth while to lay much stress on it—that men who are participating in a great social movement always picture their coming action as a battle in which their cause is certain to triumph. These constructions, knowledge of which is so important for historians, I propose to call myths; the syndicalist 'general strike' and Marx's catastrophic revolution are such myths. As remarkable examples of such myths, I have given those which were constructed by primitive Christianity, by the Reformation, by the [French] Revolution and by the followers of Mazzini. I now wish to show that we should not attempt to analyze such groups of images in the way that we analyze a thing into its elements, but that they must be taken as a whole, as historical forces, and that we should be especially careful not to make any comparison between accomplished fact and the picture people had formed for themselves before action." (P. 22.)

"The myths," summing up, "are not descriptions of things, but expressions of a determination to act." (P. 32.)

"People who are living in this world of 'myths,' are secure from all refutation. . . . No failure proves anything against Socialism since the latter has become a work of preparation (for revolution); if they are checked, it merely proves that the apprenticeship has been insufficient; they must set to work again with more courage, persistence, and confidence than before . . ." (Pp. 35, 36.)

Though the myth is not a scientific theory and is therefore not required to conform to the facts, it is nevertheless not at all arbitrary. Not just any myth will do. A myth that serves to weld together a social group—nation, people, or class—must be capable of arousing their most profound sentiments and must at the same time direct energies toward the solution of the real problems which the group faces in its actual environment. "Use must be made of a body of images which, *by intuition alone,* and before any considered analyses are made, is capable of evoking as an undivided whole the mass of sentiments which corresponds to the different manifestations of the war undertaken by Socialism against modern society." (Pp. 130-1.) "It is a question of knowing what are the ideas which most powerfully move [active revolutionists] and their comrades, which most appeal to them as being identical with their socialistic conceptions, and thanks to which their reason, their hopes, and their way of looking at particular facts seem to make but one indivisible unity." (P. 137.)

The myth, though it is not fundamentally a utopia—that is, the picture of an ideal world to come in the future—does ordinarily contain utopian elements which suggest such an ideal world. Is there any probability that the ideal will be achieved? "The myth," Sorel replies, "must be judged as a means of acting on the present; any attempt to discuss how far it can be taken literally as future history is devoid of sense." (Pp. 135-6.) If we should nevertheless put the question, it is plain that the ideal will in truth never be achieved or even approximated. This in no way detracts from the power of the myth, nor does it alter the fact that only these myths can inspire social groups to actions which, though they never gain the formal ideal, yet do bring about great social transformations. "Without leaving the present, without reasoning about this future, which seems for ever condemned to escape our reason, we should be unable to act at all. . . . The first Christians expected the return of Christ and the total ruin of the pagan world, with the inauguration of the kingdom of the saints, at the end of the first generation. The catastrophe did not come to pass, but the Christian thought profited so greatly from the apocalyptic myth that certain contemporary scholars maintain that the whole preaching of Christ referred solely to this one point. The hopes which Luther and Calvin had formed of the religious exaltation of Europe were by no means realized. . . . Must we for that reason deny the immense result which came from the dreams of Christian renovation? It must be admitted that the real developments of the [French] Revolution did not in any way resemble the enchanting pictures which created the enthusiasm of its first adepts; but without those pictures would the Revolution have been victorious? . . . These Utopias came to nothing; but it may be asked whether the Revolution was not a much more profound transformation than those dreamed of by the people who in the eighteenth century had invented social Utopias." (Pp. 133-5.)

2. *The Function of Violence*

A GREAT MYTH makes a social movement serious, formidable, and heroic. But this it would not do unless the myth inspired, and was in turn sustained by, violence. In his analysis of violence—the most notorious and attacked part of Sorel's work—Sorel begins, as in the case of myth, with the narrowed problem of violence as related to the proletarian revolutionary movement. He is, however, seeking conclusions that will hold generally for all great social movements.

Sorel was writing, some years prior to the first World War, at a time when humanitarian and pacifist ideas were almost universally professed by the leaders of official opinion. International war was going to be stopped by treaties and arbitration; class war, by reforms and the internal policy of "social peace"; violence was a relic of barbarism, soon to disappear altogether. Ironically enough, in spite of the two world wars, these notions retain their hold in many quarters, and are always prominent in the dreams of what the world is going to be like after the current war. In the face of these official opinions, Sorel presents a defense of violence. However, we must exercise care in determining just what he is defending, and why.

Sorel does not take the ideas of humanitarianism and pacifism at face value. As in the case of any other ideas, he relates them to the historical environment in which they function. Their prominence does not mean that force has been eliminated from social relations: force is always a main factor regulating society. But, under advanced capitalism, much of the force is exercised as it were automatically and impersonally. The whole weight of the capitalist mode of production bears down upon the workers, keeping them in economic, political, and social subjection. From one point of view, the humanitarian chatter serves to obscure the social realities. Still more important, the moral denunciation of violence helps to keep the workers quiet and to prevent them from using their own violent methods in strikes and for the revolution.

It is true that overt acts of violence have become less frequent than in many former ages. Is this in all respects an improvement? It is, to the extent that "brutality"—such as used by robbers and brigands in earlier times, or by the state in the punishment of criminals—has become rarer. Sorel is careful to explain that by "violence" he does not mean brutality of this sort. From another point of view, the lessening of overt acts of violence in social relations is merely the correlative of an increase in fraud and corruption. Fraud, rather than violence, has become the more usual road to success and privilege. Naturally, therefore, those who are more adept at fraud than at force take kindly to humanitarian ideals. Crimes of fraud excite no such moral horror as acts of violence: "We have finally come to believe that it would be extremely unjust to condemn bankrupt merchants and lawyers who retire ruined after moderate catastrophes, while the princes of financial swindling continue to lead gay lives. Gradually the new industrial system has created a new and extraordinary indulgence for all crimes of fraud in the great capitalist countries." (P. 222.)

Similarly in the case of the modern working class when under the control of reformists and politicians. The frank acceptance of the method of proletarian violence would threaten all the existing institutions of society. Consequently, violence is deplored by all those who have a stake in existing society. Cunning, in the form of doctrines of "social peace," "co-operation," and "arbitration," is in favor. An occasional act of violence by the workers is comfortably overlooked, because it can be used by the labor bureaucrats—or a government allied with the bureaucrats—to scare the employers, to win concessions for themselves, and to prove their indispensable role in controlling proletarian violence. "In order that this system may work properly, a certain moderation in the conduct of the workmen is necessary. . . . If financiers are almost always obliged to have recourse to the services of specialists, there is all the more reason why the workmen, who are quite unaccustomed to the customs of this world, must need intermediaries to fix the sum which they can exact from their employers without exceeding reasonable limits.

"We are thus led to consider arbitration in an entirely new light and to understand it in a really scientific manner. . . . It would be evidently absurd to go into a pork butcher's shop, order him to sell us a ham at less than the marked price, and then ask him to submit the question to arbitration; but it is not absurd to promise to a group of employers the advantages to be derived from the fixity of wages for several years, and to ask the *specialists* what remuneration this guarantee is worth; this remuneration may be considerable if business is expected to be good during that time. Instead of bribing some influential person, the employers raise their workmen's wages; from their point of view there is no difference. As for the Government, it becomes the benefactor of the people, and hopes that it will do well in the elections . . ." (Pp. 235-6.)

"In the opinion of many well-informed people, the transition from violence to cunning which shows itself in contemporary strikes in England cannot be too much admired. The great object of the Trades Unions is to obtain a recognition of the right to employ threats disguised in diplomatic formulas; they desire that their delegates should not be interfered with when going the round of the workshops charged with the mission of bringing those workmen who wish to work to understand that it would be to their interests to follow the *directions* of the Trades Unions." (Pp. 247-8.)

Furthermore, the growth of the humanitarian and pacifist ideologies, this effort to hide the force that nevertheless continues operating in vicious and distorted ways, to place reliance for rule upon cunning and fraud and bribery and corruption, rather than frankly used violence, is the mark of a social degeneration. It is not only the masses who are lulled and degraded. The rulers, too, decay. The rulers rule hypocritically, by cheating, without facing the meaning of rule, and a general economic and cultural decline, a social softening, is indicated. "When the governing classes, no longer daring to govern, are ashamed of their privileged situation, are eager to make advances to their enemies, and proclaim their horror of all cleavage in society" (p. 213), they are acting like cowards and humbugs, not saints. "Let us therefore do more and more every day for the disinherited, say these [worthy liberals]; let us show ourselves more Christian, more philanthropic, or more democratic (according to the temperament of each); let us unite for the accomplishment of *social duty*. We shall thus get the better of these dreadful Socialists, who think it possible to destroy the prestige of the Intellectuals now that the Intellectuals have destroyed that of the Church. As a matter of fact, these cunning moral combinations have failed; it is not difficult to see why. The specious reasoning of these gentlemen—the pontiffs of 'social duty' —supposes that violence cannot increase, and may even diminish in proportion as the Intellectuals unbend to the masses and make platitudes and grimaces in honor of the union of the classes. Unfortunately for these great thinkers, things do not happen in this way; violence does not diminish in the proportion that it should diminish according to the principles of advanced sociology." (Pp. 213-4.)

An open recognition of the necessity of violence can reverse the social degeneration. Violence, however, can serve this function, can be kept free from brutality and from mere vengeful force, only if it is linked to a great myth. Myth and violence, reciprocally acting on each other, produce not senseless cruelty and suffering, but sacrifice and heroism.*

But, by what is only superficially a paradox, the open acceptance of violence, when linked with a great myth, in practice decreases the total amount of actual violence in society. As in the case of the early Christian martyrdoms, which research has shown to have been surprisingly few and minor, the absolute quality of the myth gives a heightened significance to what violence does take place, and at the same time guards against an endless repetition of vulgar brutalities. "It is possible, therefore, to conceive Socialism as being perfectly revolutionary, although there may only be a few short conflicts, provided that these have strength enough to evoke the idea of the general strike: all the events of the conflict will then appear under a magnified form, and the idea of catastrophe being maintained, the cleavage will be perfect. Thus one objection often urged against revolutionary Socialism may be set aside—there is no danger of civilization succumbing under the consequences of a development of brutality, since the idea of the general strike may foster the notion of the class war by means of incidents which would appear to middle-class historians as of small importance." (Pp. 212-3.)

This seeming paradox, that the frank recognition of the function of violence in social conflicts may have as a consequence a reduction in the actual amount of violence, is a great mystery to all those whose approach to society is formalistic. If men believe and say that they are against violence, if they express humanitarian and pacifist ideals, it must follow, so formalists think, that there will be less violence in the world than when men openly admit the necessity of violence. Historical experience does not, however,

---

* By the romantic moral overtone of this view, Sorel steps abruptly away from Machiavellism—though he is probably quite conscious of what he is doing.

bear out this hope, as all the Machiavellians understand. The humanitarian ideals of much of the French aristocracy in the 18th century did not in the least mitigate the enormous bloodshed of the Revolution and may indeed have greatly contributed to its excess. It cannot be shown that humanitarian conceptions of criminal punishment, such as have flourished during the past century or more, have decreased crimes of violence. Pacifist, "anti-war" movements are a prominent feature of modern life. They have not at all served to stop the most gigantic wars of history. They have, rather, in those countries where they were most influential, brought about a situation in which many more men have been killed than would have been if political policy had based itself on the fact that wars are a natural phase of the historical process. Countless experiences have proved that a firm blow now may forestall a thousand given and suffered tomorrow. A doctor who denied the reality of germs would not thereby lessen the destructive effect of germs on the human body. In politics those magical attitudes which medicine has left behind still prevail. It is still firmly believed that by denying the social role of violence, violence is thus somehow overcome.

Sorel's attitude toward violence is part of a more general social attitude which he does not hesitate to call "pessimism." He is quite prepared to defend the ethics of pessimism. "The optimist in politics," he writes, "is an inconstant and even dangerous man, because he takes no account of the great difficulties presented by his projects. . . . If he possesses an exalted temperament, and if unhappily he finds himself armed with great power, permitting him to realize the ideal he has fashioned, the optimist may lead his country into the worst disasters. He is not long in finding out that social transformations are not brought about with the ease that he had counted; he then supposes that this is the fault of his contemporaries, instead of explaining what actually happens by historical necessities; he is tempted to get rid of people whose obstinacy seems to him to be so dangerous to the happiness of all. During the Terror, the men who spilt most blood were precisely those who had the greatest desire to let their equals enjoy the golden age they had dreamt of, and who had the most sympathy with human wretchedness: optimists, idealists, and sensitive men, the greater desire they had for universal happiness the more inexorable they showed themselves.

"Pessimism . . . considers the *march towards deliverance* as narrowly conditioned, on the one hand, by the experimental knowledge that we have acquired from the obstacles which oppose themselves to the satisfaction of our imaginations (or, if we like, by the feeling of social determinism), and, on the other, by a profound conviction of our natural weakness. . . . If this theory is admitted, it then becomes absurd to make certain wicked men responsible for the evils from which society suffers; the pessimist is not subject to the sanguinary follies of the optimist, infatuated by the unexpected obstacles that his projects meet with; he does not dream of bringing about the happiness of future generations by slaughtering existing egoists." (Pp. 9-11.)

Part V

MICHELS: THE LIMITS OF DEMOCRACY

1. Michels' Problem

WHEN SOMEONE WRITES a book on democracy, we are accustomed to share with him the assumption, as a rule not even mentioned, that democracy is both desirable and possible. The book will sing the praises of democracy. Its ostensible problem will often be "how to make democracy work"—because even the most ardent democrats, when they get down to the concrete, discover that it has not been and is not working quite as well as democratic theory would lead us to expect. A similar approach is made to such goals as peace, employment, justice, and so on. It is assumed that these are desirable and possible. A writer then devotes his energy to stating his personal scheme for securing them, and thus saving mankind from the ills that somehow in the past have always beset it.

No Machiavellian, however, makes such an approach to social and political subjects. A Machiavellian does not *assume,* without examination, the desirability of democracy or peace or even of "justice" or any other ideal goal. Before declaring his allegiance, he makes sure that he understands what is being talked about, together with the probable consequences for social welfare and well-being. Above all, no Machiavellian assumes without inquiry that the various goals are possible. A goal must be possible before there is any point in considering it desirable. It is not possible merely because it sounds pleasant or because men want it badly. Before asking, for instance, how democracy can be made to work, we must ask whether in fact it can work, or how far it can work. In general, Machiavellians are very careful to separate scientific questions concerning the truth about society from moral disputes over what type of society is most desirable. "The present study," Robert Michels writes in the Preface to the English translation of his masterpiece, *Political Parties*,* "makes no attempt to offer a 'new system.' It is not the principal aim of science to create systems, but rather to promote understanding. It is not the purpose of sociological science to discover, or rediscover, solutions, since numerous problems of the individual life and the life of social groups are not capable of 'solution' at all, but must ever remain 'open.'"

The subject-matter of *Political Parties* seems, at first, both narrow and pedestrian. The entire book is an analysis of the nature of *organization* in relation to democracy. This is at the usual Machiavellian distance from those hymns to an earthly heaven which are so regularly turned out by utopian writers. The central question, which Michels asks and answers, might be put as follows: In what ways is the realization of democracy affected by the tendencies inherent in social organization?

When Michels wrote, the Marxist critique of capitalism had for many decades been stressing the point that political democracy was necessarily incomplete so long as there was economic inequality. The social power of the capitalist class rested upon its ownership of the chief means of production. This ownership was not affected by the outcome of the democratic political processes. Therefore, democracy under capitalism, as under any society where there was an inequality in economic rights and privileges, was largely an illusion. From these facts the Marxists concluded that the elimination of economic inequalities, through the building of an economically classless society in which no one should

---

* The first edition of this book was published in Germany, in 1911, with the title, *Zur Soziologie des Parteiwesens in der modernen Demokratie*. A new edition, somewhat revised, with a chapter on the war added, was published in Italy in late 1914. The English translation, by Eden and Cedar Paul, was made from the Italian edition, and published in 1915 by Hearst's International Library Co., New York. All the quotations in this Part are from this translation. (Michels lived from 1876 to 1936.)

have special rights of ownership over the means of production, was a prerequisite for the attainment of genuine democracy.

The reasoning of the Marxists was correct so far as it went. They failed, however, to demonstrate that it is possible to eliminate economic inequality and to organize a classless society. The Machiavellians, agreeing with the negative critique of the Marxists, at the same time show that their goals, on the basis of the evidence from historical experience, are in fact impossible, that the suppression of the specifically capitalist form of differential property rights would not at all guarantee a classless social structure but would be followed by the consolidation of new kinds of property rights and a new class division. Thus, from the point of view of the effect of economic factors on political and social relations, it is shown that the democratic goal cannot be reached.

Michels' analysis, however, is still more fundamental than this approach to the problem of democracy through the effects of economic structure. The economic field, after all, is only one among many phases of social life. It may be disputed just how decisively this economic phase affects the others. On the other hand, *organization* into groups and sub-groups—families, totems, tribes, cities, nations, empires, churches, economic classes, clubs, parties—is an altogether universal feature of human life. The general laws or tendencies of organization, then, are part of the very conditions of social existence. There will be no escape from them no matter what alterations occur in economic or political structure; all attainable social goals, good or evil, will lie within the limits set by them. It is these general laws or tendencies of organization that Michels sets out to discover, in particular those tendencies that bear upon the possibility of achieving democracy.

In this task, Michels does not, of course, proceed by abstract demonstration from "first principles"; he makes no appeal to metaphysics or theology or the "eternal nature of things" or to what "must be." Nor does he accept at face value what men say or think or believe they are doing or want to do. He follows, in short, not Dante's method, but Machiavelli's. He examines the facts about organizations, what actually happens in real and existing human organizations, past and present. His generalizations are derived solely from these facts.

In the course of his study, he draws upon the facts relating to many hundreds of human organizations, from the modern nation-states to ordinary clubs. However, he gives special and prolonged attention to the European mass labor organizations; and of these, particularly to the German Social Democratic Party and the larger German trade unions. It is necessary to understand his motivation for this emphasis.

Though Michels by no means neglects evidence from the operations of the state, considered as an organization, and of the reactionary or conservative political parties, he considers it already proved by others, and indeed sufficiently obvious, that the modern capitalist-parliamentary state and the conservative political parties are not genuinely democratic. The spokesmen of both, no doubt, express themselves usually in terms of a democratic ideology—since such an ideology is the accepted form of modern political thinking; but this must be regarded as no more than what Michels calls an "ethical embellishment" of their social struggle. "In an era of democracy, ethics constitute a weapon which everyone can employ. In the old regime, the members of the ruling class and those who desired to become rulers continually spoke of their own personal rights. Democracy adopts a more diplomatic, a more prudent course. It has rejected such claims as unethical. Today, all the factors of public life speak and struggle in the name of the people, of the community at large. The government and rebels against the government, kings and party-leaders, tyrants by the grace of God and usurpers, rabid idealists and calculating self-seekers, all are 'the people,' and all declare that in their actions they merely fulfil the will of the nation." (Pp. 14-5.)

"Even conservatism assumes [in our age] at times a democratic form. Before the assaults of the democratic masses it has long since abandoned its primitive aspect, and loves to change its disguise. Today we find it absolutist, tomorrow constitutional, the next day parliamentary. . . . Democracy must be eliminated by the democratic way of the popular will. . . . A conservative candidate who should present himself to his electors by declaring to them that he did not regard them as capable of playing an active part in influencing the destinies of the country, and should tell them that for this reason they ought to be deprived of the suffrage, would be a man of incomparable sincerity, but politically insane. . . . Nor does the theory of liberalism primarily base its aspirations upon the masses. It appeals for support to certain definite classes, which in other fields of activity have already ripened for mastery, but which do not yet possess political privileges—appeals, that is to say, to the cultured and possessing classes. For the liberals also, the masses pure and simple are no more than a necessary evil, whose only use is to help others to the attainment of ends to which they themselves are strangers." (Pp. 2-7.)

"In the society of today, the state of dependence that results from the existing economic and social conditions renders an ideal democracy impossible. This must be admitted without reserve." (P. 11.) In the government itself, therefore, and in all political parties which accept, in general, the existing economic and social conditions, we do not, and should not expect to, find democracy in practice. "But the further question ensues, whether, and if so how far, within the contemporary social order, among the elements which are endeavoring to overthrow that order and to replace it by a new one, there may exist in the germ energies tending to approximate towards ideal democracy, to find outlet in that direction, or at least to work towards it as a necessary issue." (P. 11.) Among these elements the first place, when Michels was writing, was clearly held by the Marxist, socialist parties, and by the mass trade unions. Among these, the German Social Democratic Party and the German trade unions had attained the greatest numbers, influence, and development.

Moreover, these working-class movements did arise historically for the sake of democratic struggle against oligarchy in all of its forms throughout social life; their official doctrine was and remains uncompromisingly democratic; their founders, who began the organizations and established the doctrine, were for the most part men of unquestionable and remarkable sincerity. Their membership is based primarily upon and comprises great numbers of the working mass of mankind. Upon all of these grounds, therefore, if democracy is possible, we may properly expect to find it, or the strong tendency toward it, in these organizations.

If, on the contrary, we discover in these organizations, also, not democracy nor a tendency toward democracy but rather oligarchy and powerful tendencies toward oligarchy, this will be a decisive test in establishing the fact that democracy, as theoretically conceived, is impossible. It will, together with the corroborative testimony from the study of other organizations, demonstrate that oligarchy or a tendency toward oligarchy is inherent in organization itself, and is thus a necessary condition of social life.*

* I shall not, in the following sections, stress the detailed facts which Michels draws from the experiences of the German Social Democratic Party, since it is rather the analysis that holds for all organizations that concerns me. I shall omit altogether any reference to his very brilliant analysis of the "social composition" of the socialist leadership. The general principle he arrives at is included in Pareto's discussion of the "circulation of the élites," and will be covered in Part VI, on Pareto.

2. *The Fact of Leadership*

DEMOCRATIC THEORY is based upon the principle of "self-government"; the persons belonging to a social group are, according to democratic theory, able to, and properly ought to, govern themselves.* It is possible to imagine, and even to discover, social groups in which this theory is fully realized. Such would be a small company of adults (half a dozen or so), united for some jointly held purpose (business or recreation or crime, whatever it might be), who shared the same interests and level of culture, and who reached decisions unanimously, after an adequate discussion, by what we call "a meeting of minds." Certainly such groups, which are not unknown, can be intelligibly said to be practicing, with respect to their organized purpose, "self-government": their members are, plainly enough, "governing themselves."

However, as soon as the group becomes at all large (and the politically important groups of modern civilized society are very large) it is necessary, still retaining the democratic intention, to introduce arbitrary rules that are not wholly in accord with democratic theory. For example, the "group" has to be re-defined in such a way as to exclude certain individuals who are nevertheless subject to its decisions: children up to a certain arbitrarily determined age, criminals, insane persons, and so on. Usually, it may be added, additional restrictions apply in practice even when not

* I must note that it is only with democracy in this traditional sense that I am here dealing. It is possible to define "democracy" in another way—roughly in the sense that the Machiavellians give to "liberty." If that is done, Michels' analysis is largely irrelevant, and his conclusions inapplicable. I shall return at some length, in Part VII, to this other definition of "democracy."

in theory—property and racial and educational restrictions, to mention some of the most prominent. Secondly, since in larger groups we seldom get opinions that are both freely given and unanimous, it is necessary to accept the decision of a numerical majority as the decision of the entire group.

Both of these qualifications are obviously unavoidable, and no sensible person could object to them. Nevertheless, it should not be overlooked that they do contradict strict democratic theory, even though it is easy enough for a clever philosopher to patch up the theory in order to allow for them. They are enough to show that strict and full democracy is not possible in practice. However, having noted this, we shall accept them as a legitimate emendation of democratic theory, and go on to inquire whether democracy thus circumscribed is compatible with the facts of organization.

Even if we accept majority opinion as democratically valid for the entire group, it is at once plain that, in the case of large groups, strict or "direct" democracy is impossible for *mechanical* and *technical* reasons. A large group cannot itself directly decide about its own affairs because there is no place big enough to permit a large group to assemble for discussion and decision. Even if the group is sufficiently small to be contained within one place, the study of crowd psychology shows that the decisions voted by a large crowd seldom reflect the considered opinions of the constituent members of the crowd. Choices have to be limited to a few simple alternatives, whereas a great number of divergent views may actually be held by various individuals. Only a few speakers can be heard, not all who think they have something to say. The devices of oratory, appeals to irrelevant sentiment, enthusiasm, boredom, and weariness sway the crowd while it remains together. In a large assembly, votes are very often unanimous, by "acclamation," when a survey of the individuals either before or shortly after the meeting would show large minorities or even a majority against the voted policy.

All of these characteristics of the crowd are well known. Even if they could be overcome or should be disregarded, the simple fact remains that the operating political groups that function in developed societies—the state itself or mass political parties—are far too large and too scattered in residence to be brought together in one place at one time. In reaching group decisions, there is no technical means to bring the will of the group—even if this could somehow be determined—*directly* to bear upon the problem at hand.

Furthermore, many of the group's decisions must be made quickly if the organized group is not to be severely weakened or destroyed. If the armed force of the enemy strikes, the nation must strike back at once. A political party unable to react quickly to the important events of the day, to meet or forestall sudden moves of rival parties or of the state, to "take a position" on wars and strikes and revolutions, would soon go under. Sometimes it is said that the events which require quick decision are "exceptional" and therefore do not count in the general history of the organizations. But it is just these events demanding quick action that are the great and crucial events, settling the fate of organizations. Again from a merely mechanical and technical standpoint, it is impossible for a large group as a whole to make a quick decision; there is just no way for all the members to participate.

When an organization grows to a certain size and when its aims have a certain scope and importance, the conduct of the organizational affairs becomes itself a considerable activity. There are innumerable bureaucratic details that must be seen to if the organization is to be kept alive. There are financial, administrative, diplomatic problems to be settled. With organizations such as political parties or trade unions, the facts of the economic and political situation must be at hand, campaigns must be planned and carried out, negotiations entered into with other organizations, speeches prepared and delivered, articles written and published. To be effectively performed, some of these tasks require special talents; all of them need training; and all take a great amount of time. The special talents are not possessed by all; and the great bulk of the membership, even if it had the inclination—which it does not—cannot acquire the training or give the time. The principle of the division of labor operates. Certain individuals specialize in the tasks peculiar to the organization and its operational life; they devote all or a considerable portion of their time and intelligence to the organization; they perfect themselves in the organizational duties. Once the organization is fairly large and its tasks of even a minimum importance—from those of a country club to those of an imperial state—this development, too, is unavoidable. Except through such a division of labor and specialization, there is no way for the organization to continue in active existence.

To sum up: All of these causes work alike, and inescapably, to create within the organization a *leadership*. The leadership, a minority and in a large organization always a relatively small minority, is distinguished from the mass of the organization. The organization is able to keep alive and to function only through its leaders.*

Democratic theory is compelled to try to adapt itself to the fact of leadership. This it does through the subsidiary theory of "representation." The group or organization is still "self-governing"; but its self-government works through "representatives." These

---

* I am referring, here and throughout this analysis, to the *de facto* leaders, who often are not the same as the nominal leaders. As everyone knows, the party "boss" does not necessarily occupy high position; the party chairman may be an unimportant person in the organization. Nor need the member of Parliament or Congress or even a Prime Minister or President be as much a leader as the man or group that gets them elected. It is the fact, not the form, of leadership that is under discussion. Equalitarian revolutionists—communards or anarchists or syndicalists or jacobins—can eliminate titles, but they cannot eliminate leaders.

have no independent status; what they do or decide merely represents the will of the organization as a whole; the principle of democracy is left intact.

This theory of representation is suspiciously simple, and those who are not bewitched by word-magic will guess at the outset that it is brought off by a verbal juggle. Indeed, the basic theorists of modern democracy were themselves more than a little troubled by "representation." The truth is that *sovereignty,* which is what —according to democratic principle—ought to be possessed by the mass, cannot be delegated. In making a decision, no one can represent the sovereign, because to be sovereign means to make one's own decisions. The one thing that the sovereign cannot possibly delegate is its own sovereignty; that would be self-contradictory, and would simply mean that sovereignty has shifted hands. At most, the sovereign could employ someone to carry out decisions which the sovereign itself had already made. But this is not what is involved in the fact of leadership: as we have already seen, there must be leaders because there must be a way of *deciding* questions which the membership of the group is not in a position to decide. Thus the fact of leadership, obscured by the theory of representation, negates the principle of democracy.

"For democracy, however, the first appearance of professional leadership marks the beginning of the end, and this, above all, on account of the logical impossibility of the 'representative' system, whether in parliamentary life or in party delegation. Jean Jacques Rousseau may be considered as the founder of this aspect of the criticism of democracy. He defines popular government as 'the exercise of the general will,' and draws from this the logical inference, 'it can never be alienated, and the sovereign, which is simply a collective being, can be represented only by itself.' Consequently, 'at the moment when a people sets up representatives, it is no longer free, it no longer exists.' A mass which delegates its sovereignty, that is to say transfers its sovereignty to the hands of a few individuals, abdicates its sovereign functions. For the will of the people is not transferable, nor even the will of the single individual." (Pp. 36-7. I have translated the quotations from Rousseau, which are left in French in the text.)

There is no need, however, to leave the matter with this somewhat abstract demonstration. The facts already cited indicate not merely how a leadership necessarily arises in an organization, but how favorably the leadership is placed for acting independently of and, when occasion arises, counter to the will of the mass of the membership. Let us, granting the fact of leadership, inquire further into the problem: who controls whom, the mass or the leaders? The leaders will always *say* that they are only expressing the will of the members (or "the people"), but we are prepared to pay very little attention to what they say.

We may observe that there are profound psychological causes not merely for the existence of the leadership (which rests in the first place, as we have seen, on mechanical and technical causes), but for the consolidation of the leadership as a special group, largely independent of control by the mass of the membership. For example, in nearly all organizations that have left the tempests of their birth, there comes to be accepted on all sides what might be called a customary right to office. Formally, a new election for an office may be held every year or two. But in practice, the mere fact that an individual has held the office in the past is thought by him and by the members to give him a moral claim on it for the future; or, if not on the same office, then on some other leadership post in the organization. It becomes almost unthinkable that those who have served the organization so well, or even not so well, in the past should be thrown aside. A duty to the leader is created in the sentiment of the members; the officeholder gains a right. If the vagaries of elections by chance turn out wrong, then a niche is found in an embassy or bureau or post-office, or, at the end, in the pension list.

The strength of this customary right to office is well shown by the history of the trade-union movement in this country. During the violent early days of many unions, administrations come and go in a series of overturns. But as soon as the union is established, with a substantial, regular list of dues-paying members, and a few signed contracts, the custom asserts itself. Hardly ever is the administration overthrown in a solid union. So long as the leaders have the necessary skill in the specialized task of guiding and controlling organizations, they may be criminals or saints, socialists or Republicans; depression or boom may come; wages may go up or down; strikes may be won or betrayed; but the administration rides through all. This very natural phenomenon is puzzling to those who reason formally. How, they wonder, can this convicted criminal, that grafter, this man who sold out his members to the bosses, or that one whose incompetence lost the chance to organize a whole new branch of the industry, be retained still in office? They can answer such questions, if they are not union members, by looking only a little closer at whatever organization is nearer to them—lodge or chamber of commerce or club or governmental bureaucracy.

The customary right to office makes possible an interesting device, frequent in many political organizations: the device of resignation. The leader, threatened with an adverse vote from a convention or a parliament (or, in a smaller group, an assembly of the entire membership), offers his resignation. The very heart, it would seem, of democracy! The leader no longer represents the group will, so he is ready to step aside as leader; and this is no doubt the way he puts it. But this is not the real meaning of the act. In truth, it is a powerful stroke whereby the leader forces his will upon the group. In the issue, the resignation is not accepted; it is the convention that gives up its opposition to the leader's proposals, the parliament that votes "confidence." Winston

Churchill has proved himself a master of this device, which is aided by the English system of a "responsible executive."

More fundamental than the right to office is the psychological need felt by the masses for leadership. This sentiment is a compound of numerous elements. Except in most unusual dramatic circumstances, and seldom even then, the bulk of the membership of any large organization is passive with respect to the organizational activities. Only a small percentage of a union's membership comes regularly to meetings. A still smaller part of the membership of a political party provides the active party workers: consider how difficult it is to get 20,000 party members from among New York City's millions to a Democratic or Republican campaign meeting—and attendance at a meeting is a minor enough activity. In a referendum, only a minority bothers to mail back the ballots. Unless voting is compulsory, only a fraction of the voting population can even be got to the polls. How much smaller is the fraction that participates in the constant, active, decisive work of the organization. "Though it grumbles occasionally, the majority is really delighted to find persons who will take the trouble to look after its affairs. In the mass, and even in the organized mass of the labor parties, there is an immense need for direction and guidance. This need is accompanied by a genuine cult for the leaders, who are regarded as heroes." (P. 53.) Whatever the causes of this indifference and passivity, and this willingness to let others do the active work of deciding, their existence is plain enough.

Moreover, as Machiavelli had also noted, "the most striking proof of the organic weakness of the mass is furnished by the way in which, when deprived of their leaders in time of action, they abandon the field of battle in disordered flight; they seem to have no power of instinctive reorganization, and are useless until new captains arise capable of replacing those that have been lost. The failure of innumerable strikes and political agitations is explained very simply by the opportune action of the authorities, who have placed the leaders under lock and key." (P. 56.) Nor is this phenomenon confined to labor organizations.

It may be added that this need for leadership brings it about that the leaders of such organizations as mass political parties—or the state—are kept extremely busy. "Their positions are anything but sinecures, and they have acquired their supremacy at the cost of extremely hard work. Their life is one of incessant effort. . . . In democratic organizations the activity of the professional leader is extremely fatiguing, often destructive to health, and in general (despite the division of labor) highly complex." (P. 57.)

The masses have deep feelings of political gratitude toward those who, seemingly, speak and write in their behalf, and who on occasion suffer, or have suffered, persecution, imprisonment, or exile in the name of their ideals. This gratitude finds ready expression in re-election to office, even where the events which gave occasion for the gratitude lie in a distant and out-lived past. Machiavelli was aware, also, of this natural sentiment of gratitude. In his zeal for the protection of liberty, he warned against it, and praised the Romans for not taking into account past services when they were judging a present fault.

There are certain qualities, some innate and some acquired by training, but none spread widely and evenly, that make for leadership and are accepted by the mass as doing so. Oratorical talent and the prestige of celebrity—in almost any field, however irrelevant—are prominent among them. In addition, "Numerous and varied are the personal qualities thanks to which certain individuals succeed in ruling the masses. These qualities, which may be considered as specific qualities of leadership, are not necessarily all assembled in every leader. Among them, the chief is the force of will which reduces to obedience less powerful wills. [Again, Machiavelli's *virtù*.] Next in importance come the following: a wider extent of knowledge which impresses the members of the leaders' environment; a catonian strength of conviction, a force of ideas often verging on fanaticism, and which arouses the respect of the masses by its very intensity; self-sufficiency, even if accompanied by arrogant pride, so long as the leader knows how to make the crowd share his own pride in himself; in exceptional cases, finally, goodness of heart and disinterestedness, qualities which recall in the minds of the crowd the figure of Christ, and reawaken religious sentiments which are decayed but not extinct." (P. 72.)

In the case of great organizations with important activities—the state, political parties, mass trade unions, and for that matter large industrial and commercial corporations—the mass, both as a body and in terms of most of the individuals composing it, is incompetent to carry on the work. This follows not only from the psychological qualities already mentioned, but because of the lack of the required knowledge, skill, and training. The work, even the routine through which the work is carried on—the intricacies of parliamentary procedure, for example—is exceedingly complex; even with native ability, time is required to become effective at it. With respect to the organizational tasks, the leaders possess a genuine superiority over the mass, and of this they are well aware. "Here, as elsewhere, the saying is true that no undertaking can succeed without leaders, without managers. In parallelism with the corresponding phenomena in industrial and commercial life, it is evident that with the growth of working-class [or any other] organization there must be an accompanying growth in the value, the importance, and the authority of the leaders." (P. 89.)

In short, the leaders—not every individual leader, but the leadership as a group, and a group with at least a considerable measure of stability and permanence—are *indispensable* to every important organization. Their genuine indispensability is the strongest lever whereby the position of the leadership is consolidated, whereby the leaders control and are not controlled by the mass, whereby, therefore, democracy succumbs. The power of the leadership, organized as an informal sub-group independent of the mass of the membership, follows as a necessary consequence of its indispensability.

3. The Autocracy of Leadership

CULTURAL AND PSYCHOLOGICAL causes, thus, combine with the technical conditions of organization to bring about a division between the leaders, on the one hand, and the mass of the organization's membership on the other. The leadership is consolidated as a group, relatively independent of the mass. The leaders are indispensable to the organization's life and activities. In practice, in spite of the forms and doctrines of democracy, the leaders are in a position to control and dominate the mass. Let us study further how the autocracy of the leadership expresses and maintains itself.

The leaders—mere "representatives," according to democratic theory—have effective control of the organization's finances. The funds are for the most part supplied by the mass. In theory and to some extent in fact, the mass can impose certain restrictions on what is done with the funds. But in practice the use and distribution of funds is under the direct control of the leaders.

This control is often very crudely expressed by the tendency of leaders to assign relatively large amounts of money to themselves, a tendency of particular interest as it operates in labor organization.* In the early days of trade unions or labor political parties, the leaders are usually non-professional, serving perhaps part-time with little or no pay. The indispensable need for full-time and professional leaders is soon apparent. There is usually a stage when the conception arises that a leader should be paid at the rate that would be received from an ordinary employer by a

---

* The financial generosity which the leaders of big corporations show to themselves is too well known to require comment.

MICHELS: LIMITS OF DEMOCRACY

worker-member of the organization. This stage soon passes. As the organization grows and becomes established and powerful, the pay which the leaders receive from the organization goes rapidly up until it is far beyond the income level of the ordinary members. A trade-union official in this country at the present time frequently gets as much as a $25,000 salary, plus that or more in "expenses," as well as the "use" of union property such as houses, cars, and even airplanes. This financial privilege marks the dominance of the leaders over the organization, and at the same time, through the greater resources, cultural as well as material, which the high income places at the leaders' disposal, reinforces their dominance. In the beginning, at conventions and meetings, the members protest this development, which they rightly regard as autocratic and directed against themselves. But not successfully or for long. The leaders are beyond their control, and the delegates, some of them grumbling, vote the increases.

The process, as well as several other of the tendencies discussed in the last section, are particularly well illustrated in the proceedings of the 1942 convention of the United Automobile Workers. This great union is young, and therefore shows organizational tendencies in their growth, not as hidden and crystallized in established groups. In its first years, before a leadership stabilized (indeed, it has not yet fully stabilized), the U. A. W. went through a period of rapid administrative flux. It prided itself publicly on the fact that its officials sought no personal privilege from their work, and were paid at the rate of skilled auto workers. I quote now from the New York *Times* report of the session of the 1942 convention devoted to the salary question:

"The salary row started when the constitution committee moved that the salary of the international president be advanced to $10,000 a year; that that of the secretary-treasurer be increased from $5,000 to $9,500 and that of executive board members from $3,500 to $6,000 and that the pay of the new vice presidents be set at $8,000. [Modest enough sums, as union salaries go, but the power of a ruling class is not built in a day. The U. A. W. administration knows that more conventions will come tomorrow.]

"Mingled applause and boos drowned out the chairman's appeal for order as speakers on both sides of the question went into action. [When the U. A. W. is older, the ungrateful boos will disappear.] James Lindahl, chairman of the constitution committee, stated that U. A. W. had more than 600,000 members, that presidents of many local unions made almost as much as President Thomas [a revealing argument] and that an organization such as the U. A. W., which boasted of being 'the biggest union in the world,' could afford to pay its leaders salaries commensurate with those paid other union leaders.

"The sharpest opposition was expressed by William Mazey, delegate from Hudson Local 154 of Detroit, who was against any increase at all.

"'I feel our officers should be paid the same salary as the rank-and-file back in the shop,' he shouted. 'Pay them like bosses, and they begin to think like bosses!' [Delegate Mazey is one step behind: the leaders, thinking like bosses already, logically demand to be paid like bosses.]

"To this, another delegate retorted: 'We're treating them like the bosses try to treat us when we ask for a raise!' . . .

"President Thomas told the convention that if its delegates desired to do so, the committee could take the amendment back under consideration 'and cut our salaries.' He said the debate was embarrassing to him, and surrendered the gavel to James B. Carey, international secretary of the C. I. O. [A mild variant of the resignation device, combined with effective democratic piety.]

"Curt Murdock, president of Packard Local, 190, of Detroit, told the opponents of the measure that they ought to be ashamed of themselves and that the leaders of industry, to whom the union men would apply for their own raises, 'would be pleased to hear

MICHELS: LIMITS OF DEMOCRACY 155

our arguments against wage increases today.' [An appeal to the sentiment of gratitude, combined with a veiled threat that the delegates had better knuckle down for their own good.]"

However, this is only one, and on the whole a minor, effect of the power that the leaders wield through their control of the organization's finances. In passing, they may line their own pockets. But it does not really matter if, through conscience or fixed rules or scanty treasury, they do not. If the leaders are not well paid, they are more subject to temptation from without and less likely to be loyal to their own organization. Or, as often in democratic and labor politics, persons with independent means take over the leadership. In any case, the leaders decide the more important questions of the day-by-day use of what funds there are: what and who shall be strengthened, what and who weakened, who put on the pay-roll and who taken off, who favored and who financially frowned on. In these matters, nations are not different from unions: shall this local or that get the subsidy from the international? this town or that get the heaviest public-works appropriation?

Second, collaborating with financial control, "the press constitutes a potent instrument for the conquest, the preservation, and the consolidation of power on the part of the leaders." (P. 130.) Publicity and propaganda are carried on by all large organizations. Sometimes they are direct and open, where the organization (a political party, for example) publishes in its own name a paper and pamphlets and magazines, runs its own radio programs and speaking campaigns. Sometimes they are more indirect and informal, with advertising and publicity handouts, and subsidized journals, writers and speakers who remain nominally independent. "In all cases, the press [as well as publicity and propaganda generally] remains in the hands of the leaders and is never controlled by the rank and file." (P. 135.) The case for the leadership and its policies, therefore, can be and is always the preponderant burden of the organization's propaganda. "The press is the most suitable means of diffusing the fame of the individual leaders among the masses, for popularizing their names" (p. 130), and at the same time for undermining opponents either by denunciation or by keeping their names out of sight. By the nature of the case, the mass of the membership cannot control or conduct the press and propaganda; and no one therefore should be surprised that modern governments employ tens of thousands of publicists and raise the masters of propaganda to their highest posts.

A third powerful instrument of control possessed by the leaders results from the fact that they administer, in part or altogether, the disciplinary mechanism of the organization. In the state, this is open enough, since the leaders give orders to the police, the jailers, and the armed forces. Physical force is not unknown as a disciplinary weapon in organizations other than the state, but other punishments, such as fines and loss of rights or membership, can be equally effective from the point of view of protecting the leadership. In the case of trade unions, the loss of membership can be extremely serious, because it often means for the worker the loss of the right to make a living at his trade. Expulsion can obviously get rid of an opposition, though it is an unwelcome device since it means at least a temporary weakening of the organization as a whole. But the leaders have at their disposal a more subtle disciplinary procedure: namely, their effective control over much of the process of selecting delegates for conventions. The proper handling of this process can be, as all trained leaders know, a most intricate and fascinating talent.

* * *

We must be careful to distinguish the problem of government "by the people" from that of government "for the people." With

MICHELS: LIMITS OF DEMOCRACY

the latter, Michels' examination is not concerned. The argument has shown that, in established organizations of any size, including the state considered as a social organization, government is not by the people—that is, the mass of members does not control the leaders, but the leaders the mass. It may quite possibly be that this is, if not always, at least sometimes best "for the people"; that is, the interests of the members as a whole and of the majority of them individually, may be best served by leadership control.

This conclusion is maintained by those who defend democracy but at the same time are willing to recognize that normally the leaders are in charge. They then attempt to reconcile this paradox with democratic doctrine. "Those [professed democrats] who defend the arbitrary acts committed by the democracy, point out that the masses have at their disposal means whereby they can react against the violation of their rights. These means consist in the right of controlling and dismissing their leaders." (P. 156.) This brake on the leaders cannot be wholly disregarded, and it would be a mistake to suppose that it does not serve to differentiate democratic organizations from those completely subject to an autocratic structure. "Unquestionably this defense possesses a certain theoretical value, and the authoritarian inclinations of the leaders are in some degree attenuated by these possibilities. . . . In practice, however, the exercise of this theoretical right is interfered with by the working of the whole series of conservative tendencies to which allusion has previously been made, so that the supremacy of the autonomous and sovereign masses is rendered purely illusory." (P. 156.)

All those organizational facts that we have been reviewing unite to show that where a definite conflict arises between the leaders and the mass, the odds are overwhelmingly in favor of the leaders. Nevertheless, leaders are sometimes ousted. Does this violate the general principle of the supremacy of leadership? What exactly happens when leaders lose?

"When there is a struggle between the leaders and the masses, the former are always victorious if only they remain united." (P. 157.) The unled masses, less closely organized than the leaders, and perpetually weakened by the whole weight of the organizational pressures, never win against a united leadership. The existing leadership may be overthrown under two circumstances only, and not always under these.

In the first place, if a division occurs among the leaders, one section or both is forced to seek help from the masses of the membership, and is able to organize their strength. The opposition leadership is sometimes successful in eliminating the old leadership. Second, new leaders may, and do, arise as it were "spontaneously" out of the masses. If the existing leadership is unable or unwilling to crush or assimilate these "outside" leaders, then it may be overthrown. In both of these cases, however, though the process may appear to take the form of a successful struggle of the masses against their leaders, and thus to prove the supremacy of the masses, in reality it consists only of the substitution of a new leadership for the old. Leadership remains in control; "self-government" is as distant as ever.

This problem is given more extended and generalized treatment by Pareto, and I shall return to it in both Part VI and Part VII. I wish here, however, to remark, that Michels underestimates the indirect, if not direct, democratic significance of the "opposition." If it is true that in the end there can be no more than the substitution of one set of leaders for another, nevertheless through the opposition leadership the pressure of the masses is brought indirectly to bear upon the leadership as a whole. An opposition, so long as it remains an opposition, whatever its theories, is compelled to rest to some extent on a democratic basis and to defend democratic practices. The existence of an opposition is the firmest and the only firm check on the autocratic tendencies of the leaders.

There are, finally, certain tendencies of leadership which, though almost always present to a certain degree, do not get carried in every social organization to their full extreme. These tendencies, however, and especially their extreme development, are so profoundly important for democracy that they deserve a very special notice.

In established leaders there normally occurs what Michels calls a "psychological metamorphosis." "In the majority of instances, and above all at the opening of his career, the leader is sincerely convinced of the excellence of the principles he advocates. . . . He has been pushed forward by a clearer vision, by a profounder sentiment, and by a more ardent desire for the general good; he has been inspired by the elasticity and seriousness of his character and by his warm sympathy for his fellows. It is obvious that this will be true above all where the leader does not find already established a solid organization capable of offering remunerative employment, but where his first step must be to found his own party. But this must not be taken to mean that wherever a well-organized party already exists the leader seeks at the outset to gratify his personal interests." (Pp. 205-6.)

But these qualities do not long resist the habit of power. "He who has once attained to power will not readily be induced to return to the comparatively obscure position which he formerly occupied. . . . The consciousness of power always produces vanity, and undue belief in personal greatness. . . . In the leader, consciousness of his personal worth, and of the need which the mass feels for guidance, combine to induce in his mind a recognition of his own superiority (real or supposed), and awake, in addition, that spirit of command which exists in the germ in every man born of woman. We see from this that every human power seeks to enlarge its prerogatives. He who has acquired power will almost always endeavor to consolidate it and to extend it, to multiply the ramparts which defend his position, and to withdraw himself from the control of the masses." (Pp. 206-7.)

At a typical stage in this psychological metamorphosis, the leader identifies himself with the group—party or nation or whatever the group may be. "The bureaucrat identifies himself completely with the organization, confounding his own interests with its interests. All objective criticism of the party [or nation, if he is the leader of a nation] is taken by him as a personal affront. This is the cause of the obvious incapacity of all party leaders to take a serene and just view of hostile criticism. . . . If, on the other hand, the leader is attacked personally, his first care is to make it appear that the attack is directed against the party [or nation] as a whole." (P. 228.) Criticism of the group is personal libel against the leader; criticism of the leader is subversion and treason against the group. "The despotism of the leaders," moreover, "does not arise solely from a vulgar lust of power or from uncontrolled egoism, but is often the outcome of a profound and sincere conviction of their own value and of the services which they have rendered to the common cause." (P. 229.)

These psychological changes are themselves part of a larger process frequent in the development of democracy: the process of the growth of what Michels, and others, call "Bonapartism," a name derived from the regimes of the two Bonapartes, particularly from that of Napoleon III.

The despotic Bonapartist rule was not theoretically based, like most monarchies, upon any claims of God-given right or of inheritance. The theoretical and also the historical basis was democratic; democratic form was carefully and consistently preserved. Both Napoleons ruled as democratic representatives of the governed, the people. Their democratically legitimate right to act as delegates of the people's will was confirmed in a series of broad plebiscites. The first Napoleon was overwhelmingly elected as Consul, Consul for life, and then (1804) as Emperor; the second,

MICHELS: LIMITS OF DEMOCRACY

twice as President, and finally (1852) as Emperor. "Napoleon III did not merely recognize in popular sovereignty the source of his power, he further made that sovereignty the theoretical basis of all his practical activities. He made himself popular in France by declaring that he regarded himself as merely the executive organ of the collective will manifested in the elections, and that he was entirely at the disposition of that will, prepared in all things to accept its decisions. With great shrewdness, he continually repeated that he was no more than an instrument, a creature of the masses." (P. 216.)

The Bonapartist leader claims, with more than a show of justification, to be the most perfect embodiment of the will of the group, the people. Everything, therefore, is permitted to him, since he is merely the symbol of the group as a whole. The intermediary political organs—parliaments, for example—still continue; but they are now subordinate to the Bonapartist leader, for only he completely expresses the popular will; they are his agents, and only through him are they agents of the people. "Once elected, the chosen of the people can no longer be opposed in any way. He personifies the majority, and all resistance to his will is anti-democratic. The leader of such a democracy is irremovable, for the nation, having once spoken, cannot contradict itself. He is, moreover, infallible. . . . It is reasonable and necessary that the adversaries of the government should be exterminated in the name of popular sovereignty, for the chosen of the people acts within his rights as representative of the collective will, established in his position by a spontaneous decision. It is the electors themselves, we are assured, who demand from the chosen of the people that he should use severe repressive measures, should employ force, should concentrate all authority in his own hands." (Pp. 218-9.)

All this is much more than mere pretense. Once granted the principle of representation, Bonapartism can be regarded as the logical culmination of democracy. More than this: to judge from the experience not only of our own times but from that of the Greek city-states, the Roman Republic, and the medieval city-states, Bonapartism is likewise the normal—though not perhaps the invariable—historical culmination of democracy. Bonapartism, in one or another stage of development, is the most striking and typical political structure of our day. The great nations which, in the period since the Renaissance, adopted democratic political formulas and representative parliamentary practices, have without exception in this century exhibited a powerful tendency toward Bonapartism, a tendency which in Germany, Russia, and Italy has gone to full maturity, but which is no less plainly marked in, for example, England and the United States.

It is a grave historical error to identify Bonapartism with other forms of despotism. Bonapartism is not mere military dictatorship; it is not the traditional hereditary or God-derived despotism of absolute monarchies; it is not the oligarchical rule of a closed hereditary caste. Mature Bonapartism is a popular, a democratic despotism, founded on democratic doctrine, and, at least in its initiation, committed to democratic forms. If Bonapartism, in fact rather than in theory, denies democracy, it does so by bringing democracy to completion.

4. The Iron Law of Oligarchy

THE AUTOCRATIC TENDENCIES of organization have not, of course, escaped the notice of those proponents of democracy who have been both hard-headed and sincere. Recognizing them, a number of measures have been proposed in an effort to thwart these tendencies and to guard democracy. Michels discusses the results obtained from four of the chief of these: the referendum, "renunciation," syndicalism, and anarchism.

The device of the referendum has been tried both in governmental bodies (Switzerland, certain States of the United States) and in many lesser organizations. In theory, it serves to refer policy-making decisions to the entire membership of the group, and thus to operate in accordance with strict democratic principle. In practice, we find that it does not work. Usually only a small percentage of the membership participates in the referendum. It is easy for the leaders to put the referendum-question in such a form as to assure the outcome that they wish. "The referendum is open to criticism to the same extent and for the same reasons as is every other form of direct popular government. The two principal objections are the incompetence of the masses and the lack of time. Bernstein has said with good reason that even if none but the most important political and administrative questions are to be submitted to the popular vote, the happy citizen of the future will find every Sunday upon his desk such a number of interrogatories that he will soon lose all enthusiasm for the referendum. It is, however, especially in respect of questions demanding a prompt decision that the referendum proves impracticable." (P. 336.) We have already noted that these questions which demand prompt decision are just those that are most crucial in determining the fate of organizations.

The so-called "Ludlow Amendment," strongly advocated not long ago in this country, which provided for a referendum vote of the people before this country could go to war, was certainly a consistent application of democratic principle. The pretended arguments against it on the basis of democracy were either ignorant or hypocritical. Nevertheless, it was plainly ridiculous from the point of view of practice—a war was not going to wait for the conclusion of the unwieldy and elaborate mechanics of a general referendum. Indeed, the real as distinguished from the formal meaning of the agitation for the Ludlow Amendment had nothing to do with democracy, but was a struggle against the impending war and against the existing Administration.

The most conspicuous use of the referendum, it may further be observed, is in the Bonapartist plebiscite (Hitler and Stalin have followed the two Napoleons) where the vote attaches the fiction of the "popular will" to what has already been decided in historical fact.

By "renunciation," Michels refers to a device that has been frequently advocated for working-class organizations, and sometimes enforced by them. Reasoning that the anti-democratic habits of leaders follow from their possession of material privileges beyond those available to the rank-and-file, it is held that these tendencies will disappear if the privileges are made inaccessible, if the leaders are required to have the same income, conditions of life, social and cultural environment, as the members. It is certainly a fact that there is a most intimate connection between power and privilege. Nevertheless, the device of renunciation fails in practice. In the first place, except sometimes in small or persecuted organizations, the leaders never do renounce all privileges, and they can find very plausible excuses in both the nature and quality of their work for not doing so. Even where they do, renunciation does not produce simple democrats but fanatics, often more tyrannical than those leaders who are sometimes mellowed a little by privilege.

Third, the "syndicalist" policy aims to defend democracy. As we have seen in Part IV, syndicalism, noting the anti-democratic tendencies of the state and of political parties, tells the workers to have nothing to do with politics, but to confine themselves altogether to "their own" organizations, the trade unions (syndicates) and the labor co-operatives. The naïveté of this proposal is apparent enough. Trade unions and co-operatives are not exempt from the autocratic tendencies of organizations, are rather prime sources of these tendencies. Getting rid of political parties would not at all get rid of autocracy, but merely leave the union autocracy a field free of rivals.

Anarchism, finally, which was the first movement to study in detail the autocratic tendencies of organization, draws the clearest and most formally consistent conclusion. Since all organization leads to autocracy, then, in order to achieve democracy, there must be no organization at all, neither state nor party nor union. This viewpoint, which the history of anarchism shows is capable of producing very noble human individuals, is wholly divorced from the reality of human society, which necessarily includes organizations. Anarchism therefore can never be more than a faith —and a completely unrealistic faith, able to integrate an individual's own isolated life, but never a serious political movement. Anarchists are compelled, when they try to put their ideas into social practice, to accept organization. They ordinarily do so in the economic field and even, though they disguise it, among themselves. "But though the anarchist leaders are as a rule morally superior to the leaders of the organized parties working in the political field, we find in them some of the qualities and pretensions characteristic of all leadership. This is proved by a psychological analysis of the characteristics of the individual anarchist leader. The theoretical struggle . . . has not stifled in them the natural love of power. All that we can say is that the means of dominion employed by the anarchist leader belong to an epoch which political parties have already outlived. These are the means utilized by the apostle and the orator: the flaming power of thought, greatness of self-sacrifice, profundity of conviction. Their dominion is exercised, not over the organization, but over minds; it is the outcome, not of technical indispensability, but of intellectual ascendancy and moral superiority." (P. 358.)

It is not surprising that the test of experience shows that these and all other devices fail. Social life cannot dispense with organization. The mechanical, technical, psychological, and cultural conditions of organization require leadership, and guarantee that the leaders rather than the mass shall exercise control. The autocratic tendencies are neither arbitrary nor accidental nor temporary, but inherent in the nature of organization.

This, the general conclusion from Michels' entire study, he sums up as *the iron law of oligarchy,* a law which, upon the basis of the evidence at our disposal, would seem to hold for all social movements and all forms of society. The law shows that the democratic ideal of self-government is impossible. Whatever social changes occur, whatever happens to economic relations, whether property is in private hands or socialized, organization will remain, and through organization an oligarchical rule will be perpetuated. "The social revolution would not effect any real modification of the internal structure of the mass. The socialists might conquer, but not socialism, which would perish in the moment of its adherents' triumph." (P. 391.)

"These phenomena would seem to prove beyond dispute that society cannot exist without a 'dominant' or 'political' class, and that the ruling class, whilst its elements are subject to a frequent partial renewal, nevertheless constitutes the only factor of sufficiently durable efficacy in the history of human development.

MICHELS: LIMITS OF DEMOCRACY

According to this view, the government, or, if the phrase be preferred, the state, cannot be anything other than the organization of a minority. It is the aim of this minority to impose upon the rest of society a 'legal order,' which is the outcome of the exigencies of dominion and of the exploitation of the mass of helots effected by the ruling minority, and can never be truly representative of the majority. The majority is thus permanently incapable of self-government. . . . The majority of human beings, in a condition of eternal tutelage, are predestined by tragic necessity to submit to the dominion of a small minority, and must be content to constitute the pedestal of an oligarchy." (P. 390.)

However, from the iron law of oligarchy, Michels does not at all conclude that we should abandon the *struggle* for democracy, or, more strictly, for a reduction to the minimum possible of those autocratic tendencies which will nevertheless always remain. "Leadership is a necessary phenomenon in every form of social life. Consequently it is not the task of science to inquire whether this phenomenon is good or evil, or predominantly one or the other. But there is great scientific value in the demonstration that every system of leadership is incompatible with the most essential postulates of democracy. We are now aware that the law of the historic necessity of oligarchy is primarily based upon a series of facts of experience." (P. 400.) "The mass will never rule except *in abstracto*. Consequently the question . . . is not whether ideal democracy is realizable, but rather to what point and in what degree democracy is desirable, possible, and realizable at a given moment." (P. 402.) Oligarchy will always remain; but it may be possible to put some limit and restraint on the absoluteness of oligarchy. This cannot be effectively done by a utopian and sentimental idealism concerning the possibilities of democracy. "Nothing but a serene and frank examination of the oligarchical dangers of a democracy will enable us to minimize these dangers, even though they can never be entirely avoided." (P. 408.) "Those alone, perhaps, are in a position to pass a fair judgment upon democracy who, without lapsing into dilettantist sentimentalism, recognize that all scientific and human ideals have relative values. If we wish to estimate the value of democracy, we must do so in comparison with its converse, pure aristocracy. The defects inherent in democracy are obvious. It is none the less true that as a form of social life we must choose democracy as the least of evils." (P. 407.) "Democracy is a treasure which no one will ever discover by deliberate search. But in continuing our search, in laboring indefatigably to discover the undiscoverable, we shall perform a work which will have fertile results in the democratic sense." (P. 405.)

"The democratic currents of history resemble successive waves. They break ever on the same shoal. They are ever renewed. This enduring spectacle is simultaneously encouraging and depressing. When democracies have gained a certain stage of development, they undergo a gradual transformation, adopting the aristocratic spirit, and in many cases also the aristocratic forms, against which at the outset they struggled so fiercely. Now new accusers arise to denounce the traitors; after an era of glorious combats and of inglorious power, they end by fusing with the old dominant class; whereupon once more they are in their turn attacked by fresh opponents who appeal to the name of democracy. It is probable that this cruel game will continue without end." (P. 408.)

Part VI

PARETO: THE NATURE OF SOCIAL ACTION

1. *Logical and Non-logical Conduct*

VILFREDO PARETO, in his gigantic book, *Mind and Society*,* disavows any purpose other than to describe and correlate social facts. He is not offering any program for social improvement nor expressing any ideal of what society and government ought to be. He is trying merely to describe what society is like, and to discover some of the general laws in terms of which society operates. What could or should be done with this knowledge, once obtained, is a question he does not try to answer.

This restriction of the problem is more extreme than in the case of the other Machiavellians. They too, of course, try to describe and correlate social facts, and they never permit their goals or ideals or programs to distort their objective descriptions; they never, like Dante, mistake their wishes for reality. Nevertheless, they state also what kind of social order they feel to be desirable, and what the conditions are for the achievement of such a social order. In his earlier writings, particularly those on economic subjects, Pareto also expressed certain practical goals. He defended, for some while, the point of view of orthodox "liberal" economics —not what is nowadays called "liberalism," that strange mélange of sentimental confusion, but the classical liberalism of free trade

---

* This is the title which has been given to the English edition of Pareto's *Trattato di Sociologia Generale* (literally, "Treatise on General Sociology"), which was finished by Pareto in 1915 and first published in 1916. With the permission of the publishers, all my quotations are from, and my references to: *The Mind and Society* by Vilfredo Pareto, translated by Arthur Livingston and Andrew Bongiorno, copyright, 1935, by Harcourt, Brace and Company, Inc. The editor, Professor Livingston, notes that this work contains more than a million words. As is customary, I refer not to page numbers but to the numbers of the sections into which *Mind and Society* is divided. Pareto lived from 1848 to 1923.

and free markets. This point of view he gradually abandoned. It was not replaced by any other.

Critics have often argued that Pareto's disavowal of any practical goal is no more than pretense, and they have usually attributed to him this or that program. It may well be that, even though no goals are explicitly stated in *Mind and Society,* certain values and attitudes are suggested by the over-all tone of his remarks. However, about these nothing can be definitely settled. They are in any case irrelevant to my purpose, which is to show what Pareto added to the main trends of Machiavellian thought. Everybody can argue all night about how to save society; but only a rare few have told us any truths about society.

* * *

To understand Pareto's general analysis of society, we must first be entirely clear about the distinction he makes between "logical conduct" and "non-logical conduct." (*Mind and Society,* 151 *ff.*)

A man's conduct (that is, human action) is "logical" under the following circumstances: when his action is motivated by a deliberately held goal or purpose; when that goal is possible; when the steps or means he takes to reach the goal are in fact appropriate for reaching it.

Logical conduct is common in the arts, crafts, and sciences, and frequent in economic activity (Pareto calls the economic field, "interests"). For example: a carpenter wants to make a table (the production of the table is his deliberately held purpose); this goal is, normally, quite possible; he assembles lumber and tools, applies one to the other, and as a result gets the table—the means he takes are in fact appropriate to reach his goal. Thus his conduct, with respect to this activity, is logical. Or a scientist wants to test the efficacy of a new drug in curing some disease; he de-

PARETO: THE SOCIAL ACTION 173

vises proper experiments in accordance with the usual canons of scientific method, and determines whether the drug does accomplish a cure. Or a worker wants higher wages and, when the chance offers, quits one job for an available new one that does in fact pay more. Or an investor, wanting to maintain his funds in the most profitable manner, withdraws capital from a field of enterprise that is drying up in favor of a new and expanding industry. All of such activities are, in Pareto's sense, logical.

If, however, any one or more of the conditions for logical conduct are not present, then the actions are *non-logical*.

Actions may, for instance, have no deliberate motivation at all. This would be true of all or almost all of the behavior of animals; and Pareto, in spite of the prejudice of rationalists, believes it to be true of a surprising percentage of human actions. Taboos and other superstitious acts, which are by no means confined to primitive peoples, are obvious examples, as are many rituals, sports, and courtesies. Human beings simply do things, without any purpose at all; it is natural for them to be active, whether or not there is any consciously understood point in the activity.

Very common, also, are cases where the purpose or goal is impossible. The goal may be transcendent—that is, located outside of the real spatio-temporal world of life and history—and in all such cases it is, from Pareto's scientific standpoint, strictly impossible. So, if the goal is Heaven or Nirvana or the duplication of the cube or any other transcendent dream or illusion. On the other hand, the goal, if not impossible in strict logic, may nevertheless be impossible for all practical purposes, granted the real nature of the world. So, if the goal is a Tower of Babel to reach to the highest heaven, or a utopia of eternal peace and universal good will, or some fantastic personal goal as when a dreamer with no aptitude decides to become the greatest violinist in the world, or a child, just learning numbers, to count to a billion. In all these cases, conduct motivated by such goals or purposes is non-logical.

Pareto is strict with his definition. It might be that, though the deliberately held purpose is impossible, yet the activities carried out would yield a result that the person in question would judge desirable, if he stopped to think about it. Striving for utopia, a worker might get a 10% raise in standard of living. This result, doubtless, the worker might judge desirable so far as it went. Even in this case, however, the worker's conduct is non-logical, because it is not and could not be the logical consequence of the conscious purpose; the desirable result follows as a chance by-product, and the goal held in mind is logically irrelevant to it.

We have here the situation which I analyzed in discussing Dante. Where there is a disparity between the "formal" goal and the "real" goal of an action, then the action is non-logical. In logical action, the formal goal and the real goal are identical.

Finally, action is non-logical when the means taken to reach the goal are in fact inappropriate to that purpose. If the carpenter tried to pound his nails with a sponge, then his means would be inappropriate, no matter how suitable he might himself think them. So, too, if a surgeon used a pickaxe for an appendectomy; or if an oppressed people thought they could overcome a despotic social regime by an assassination or two; or if a democratic electorate believed that by voting a change of parties in power they might be guaranteed an era of endless prosperity.

Everyone knows that a certain amount of human conduct is non-logical. Pareto's stress is on the enormous scope of the non-logical—his book lists many thousands of examples, and each of these could suggest a thousand more of the same kind. Other writers on the nature of society have recognized the existence of non-logical conduct; some have even admitted that, quantitatively, it exceeds the logical; but almost all have in the end held that somehow the margin of logical conduct is what is "most distinctively human," and what is decisive for the development of government and society. Pareto not only shows that non-logical conduct is predominant; his crucial point is that the conduct which has a bearing on social and political structure, on what he calls the "social equilibrium," is above all the arena of the non-logical. What happens to society, whether it progresses or decays, is free or despotic, happy or miserable, poor or prosperous, is only to the slightest degree influenced by the deliberate, rational purposes held by human beings.

Taboos, magic, superstition, personified abstractions, myths, gods, empty verbalisms, in every culture and at every period of history express man's persisting non-logical impulses. The forms change, but the fundamentals remain. Gods and goddesses like Athena or Janus or Ammon are replaced by new divinities such as Progress and Humanity and even Science; hymns to Jupiter give way to invocations to the People; the magic of votes and electoral manipulations supersedes the magic of dolls and wands; faith in the Historical Process does duty for faith in the God of our Fathers.

It is impossible to review here the mass of evidence. Let us, rather, concentrate attention on certain types of human activity which are significantly related to political and social change, and discover whether these are logical or non-logical.

In the first place, we may note that so far as social development is determined by such factors as climate, geography, or in general by biological and physical characteristics, it is non-logically motivated. Temperature, rainfall, mountains and valleys are not logical products; they are simply given as the environment wherein human society develops. Few theorists nowadays would accept any of the extreme doctrines that try to explain all history by a single principle of climate or race or something of the sort; but few would deny that these have at least some influence on social change. It might, however, be argued that, when interpreting social change, we accept the physical and biological factors as historically irrelevant "constants"; and that, within the conditions which they admittedly set, logical conduct functions to decide what happens in history.

The social goals, ideals, or purposes that men presumably try to achieve in political and social life are capable of being put into words. Especially in modern times those goals that are of the widest significance and that are professed by great numbers of men are often written into great public documents: Constitutions, Programs, Codes, Declarations, Charters, and so on. These public goals, so expressed, are decisive for our present investigation. If the conduct that influences social change is logical, then these Constitutions, Declarations, and Charters, together with the human activities associated with them, will meet, at least to a considerable degree and a good part of the time, the tests that we have listed for logical conduct. Let us see what the facts are.

First, we may at once observe that most of the goals incorporated in these public documents are too ambiguous to determine one line of conduct as against another. They are so vague, indeed, that whatever is actually done can be subsequently interpreted as consistent with the alleged goal. The Declarations call, often, for "freedom." But "freedom," by itself, is a term with no content whatsoever. There is no freedom "in general"—only freedom *from* certain things or *for* certain things, which always involves restrictions in other specific respects. If I am to be free from being murdered by private individuals, then you are not free to murder me; if the state is free to compel sales of commodities at set prices, then the manufacturer is not free to sell them as he chooses; if an owner is free to do what he wants with his possessions, then others are not free from the effects of what he does.

Or take "liberty, equality, and fraternity," the great goals, it was believed, of the French Declaration of the Rights of Man, and of the French Revolution. Anything, or nothing, can be meant by these terms. No two men are or can be equal in all things; all are equal in some. Michels reminds us that, after the

Revolution, the three words appeared over the entrance of every French prison.

The Atlantic Charter, as drawn up by Churchill and Roosevelt, proclaims as one of the central aims of the United Nations, "Freedom from Want." Such a goal is strictly impossible. Man is, as we observed in another connection, a wanting animal; there is no possible end to his wants except death, as the philosophers of the East have always insisted.

The program of a political party declares in favor of "law and order." But what law and order, and whose law and order? All sovereignty, the Constitutions say, is vested in the people. But the most liberal parliament and the most despotic Bonapartist equally claim to respect the principle of popular sovereignty. The Nazis are to build "the new order"; but concentration camps and workers' houses can with equal ease be interpreted as part of a new order. The United States stands, it is said, for "freedom of the seas." But, in 1940, let us say, freedom of the seas did not mean freedom for United States ships to sail to German ports, nor freedom for German ships to sail anywhere. Japan is aiming, she says, at a Greater East-Asia Co-Prosperity Sphere; but this Sphere has no definable limits nor, apparently, much of what would normally be called prosperity.

The point is not that these slogans, ideals, programs, and declarations do not influence action. Under certain circumstances they undoubtedly do, and tremendously. But they are not and cannot be part of logical or rational action. I am not taking logical steps in pursuit of a goal if the presumed goal is nothing definite. I can say, no matter what happens, that I have attained the goal; and you can say I have not. In spite of what I may think, the expressed goal itself and the deductions I draw from it have no logical relation to what I do. My actions, whatever the appearances, are non-logical, and spring not from the goal but from other sources. Thus, in all cases—and these include the majority that is relevant to social change—where the goals are vague or ambiguous or meaningless, human conduct is non-logical.

However, there are other cases where the goal is sufficiently definite for us to determine objectively whether or not the actions taken are in accordance with it. Even in some of the instances cited above, the specific historical context may give a fairly definite meaning to terms which by themselves are wholly vague. How do matters stand when the goals are at least clear enough to be understood?

We discover, to begin with, that men who profess a certain goal are just about as likely to take actions contrary to it as in accordance with it. Nor can we generally attribute these contrary actions to duplicity; those who act contrary to the goal can continue at the same time believing sincerely in it, and not noting any contradiction. One of the Ten Commandments forbids killing; but all Jewish and Christian groups have frequently killed, without in the least altering their faith in the Commandment. In modern times there have been many pacifists; but the overwhelming majority of them support all wars in which their countries engage. Soviet Russia did not at all drop its belief in the Marxist ideal of a classless society while class differentiation steadily developed after the revolution. Communities with the strictest beliefs about monogamy and prohibition and the sinfulness of gambling are always able, in action, to display a good deal of sexual promiscuity, drinking, and gambling. The same Attorney-General can on the same day make an address in favor of free speech, and arrest individuals exercising free speech; the same legislator can praise free enterprise while preparing a law for new state controls over enterprise. A political party can get elected on a platform that promises a balanced budget; and can then use power to run up the biggest deficits in history.

Similarly, we may observe that various groups can profess the same goals and yet take differing and often directly conflicting lines of action. Reformist, syndicalist, Trotskyist, and Stalinist parties of the labor movement all cite the same texts of Marx while cutting each others' throats; all Christian nations have the New Testament and the Fathers on their clashing sides. In one state, the Seventh Commandment forbids capital punishment; in its neighbor, the same Commandment justifies capital punishment. England and the United States both believe in freedom of the seas; but for England this can mean capturing United States ships as contraband, and for the United States, sending them through the blockade. A belief in the immortality of the soul is compatible with a total disregard of material goods (this short life counting nothing against eternity) or total concentration on them (thus attesting, as Calvin taught, that the active soul is elected to blessedness in after life).

On the other hand, we find that groups can profess different and contrary goals, and yet carry out the same type of actions. Pareto cites many fascinating examples. There can be the most varying alleged moral codes governing sexual behavior, and yet just about the same kind of sexual behavior in practice. Intimate personal possessions are placed with dead bodies in the grave no matter what the belief or lack of any belief concerning an afterlife for the soul. The Soviet Union can be on the same side of a war with England and the United States, and Japan with Germany, even though in both cases the implications of official beliefs forbid the alliances. Germany proclaims doctrines of racial superiority, and the United States condemns them; nevertheless, the United States acts toward negroes very much as the Nazis toward Jews, and the United States retains in law and practice the Exclusion Acts directed against the yellow races. Stalin can speak in the name of the classless society of communism, Hitler in that of the hierarchical society of the *Herrenvolk*, but the differences between the Gestapo and the G. P. U. in action are not readily discerned.*

All these are not examples selected arbitrarily for the sake of proving a thesis. They are chosen at random and they could be indefinitely added to. Moreover, most of them are not the peculiar quirks of individuals, but involve the important group actions that have a significant bearing upon what happens in government and society. If the analysis of these and similar actions shows that they are not logical, that the professed goals are either too vague or, if definite, are as a general rule not in accordance with the actions that are taken in practice, then Pareto is right, and the reformers and rationalists and moralists are wrong. Rational, deliberate, conscious belief does not, then, in general at any rate, determine what is going to happen to society; social man is not, as he has been defined for so many centuries, a primarily "rational animal." When the reformers tell us that society can be improved by education, by increasing men's knowledge, by projecting the correct program and then taking action to realize that program, they are wrong because men in society do not act that way. Their actions, their socially decisive actions, spring not from logical but from non-logical roots.

This is not a question about which "one opinion is as good as another." Pareto presents evidence, a mass of evidence, drawn not from one nation and one time, but from many nations and classes and cultures and times. If he is wrong, he can be proved wrong only by evidence equally cogent.

But, assuming that non-logical conduct is, on the whole, predominant in those actions that affect the course of history, we may legitimately wonder why this has not been widely recognized. Pareto readily grants that "if non-logical actions are really as

---

*I assume it to be obvious—since Pareto died in 1923—that most of the examples I cite are my own and not Pareto's. I follow here the same practice as throughout this book: I am trying to concretize the exposition of Machiavellian principles by new, independent, and often contemporary illustrations.

PARETO: THE SOCIAL ACTION 181

important as our induction so far would lead us to suppose, it would be strange indeed that the many men of talent who have applied themselves to the study of human societies should not have noticed them in any way." (252.) The fact is that many writers on society, and many plain men and politicians as well or even better, have observed the importance of non-logical conduct. Nevertheless, they have almost never been willing to generalize the legitimate inference from their observations. Something seems to block them from accepting the conclusions of their own inquiries.

Pareto thinks that this is partly accounted for by the fact that few writers on society are content to describe and correlate facts, but are always going on to tell what ought to be, and how to reform society. He remarks of Aristotle, who recognized but refused to be consistent in recognizing, the importance of non-logical conduct: "Had Aristotle held to the course he in part so admirably followed, we would have had a scientific sociology in his early day. Why did he not do so? There may have been many reasons; but chief among them, probably, was that eagerness for premature practical applications which is ever obstructing the progress of science, along with a mania for preaching to people as to what they ought to do—an exceedingly bootless occupation —instead of finding out what they actually do." (277.) A desire to reform society seems to call for logical action—the deliberate adoption of suitable means to bring about the reforms. Therefore, those who wish above all for reform are likely in the end to minimize the influence of non-logical action.

An even greater obstacle to understanding derives from the fact that we have a powerful non-logical impulse to make our own and other human actions seem logical. We are unable to accept non-logical actions for what they are, so we conjure up a rational explanation for them. A taboo arises in some obscure way —against killing or incest, let us say. Later theorists give it a pseudo-logical explanation by saying that a god commanded and men accepted the command, whereas in reality the taboo long preceded any belief in a god. Still later, rationalist theorists decide that the taboo was derived from the "natural principle" that men wish to live co-operatively in society, or from an awareness of the "scientific truth" (which they somehow discover) that incest is biologically unsound. In fact, of course, no one dreamed of such principles or truths when the taboos arose, not to mention the fact that the pretended principles and truths are usually as absurd as the taboos themselves. Many Jews, following the lead given by the medieval rationalist, Maimonides, explain that the Hebraic taboo against eating pork was really the means used in the days of the Old Testament to guard the people against the lack of refrigeration for keeping pig-meat; with which explanation, which has not the remotest basis in historical evidence, the taboo becomes respectably logical.

Or (306 *ff.*) the principles of non-logical conduct are dismissed as unimportant, mere prejudices or absurdities or exceptions, or tricks used by chiefs or priests to deceive and rule their groups. Or various kinds of metaphysical and religious beings are invented, from whose nature and decrees the principles of non-logical conduct logically follow. Zeus or Poseidon or Morality or Truth or Progress or Natural Law demands that this or that be done, which was being done, from non-logical causes, long before Zeus or Progress was thought of. Or myths are taken as allegories or disguised historical facts, and are thus only picturesque versions of the logical.

This tendency, however, to logicalize the non-logical leads us to Pareto's more general analysis of "residues" and "derivations."

2. Residues and Derivations

WORDS ARE PERHAPS the most distinctive trait of human beings. If man is only in small degree a rational animal, he is pre-eminently a verbal animal. Words, spoken or written, are associated with most of his activities, and in particular with those activities that are of social and political significance. After finishing his discussion of non-logical conduct in general, Pareto restricts himself to those non-logical actions which include or are associated with words. Everyone will recognize that nearly all of non-verbal conduct, such as is found in animals or in the purely instinctive behavior of human beings, is also non-logical. The peculiar and deceptive problems arise in connection with conduct which is verbal but at the same time non-logical.

Pareto examines a vast number of examples of this sort of conduct, taken from many times and cultures. From this examination, Pareto concludes that two quite different phases may be discovered. There is, he says, a fairly small number of relatively constant factors (or "nuclei") which change little or not at all from age to age or from culture to culture. These constant factors he calls "residues." Along with these there are other factors which are variable, change rapidly, and are different from age to age and nation to nation. These variable factors he calls "derivations." *

Let us illustrate the distinction by examples. Pareto records a long list of non-logical practices in many tribes, groups, and na-

---

* Pareto sometimes uses the term "derivative" for the action as a whole. A derivative, therefore, is made up of the constant factor (residue or residues) plus the variable factors (derivations).

tions which have as their ostensible purpose the control of weather conditions. Sometimes the practice is to sacrifice a bull or a cock or a goat; sometimes to manipulate certain material objects; sometimes to repeat certain formulas. The most extreme concrete differences are observable. Often, along with the practice, there is a theory which supposedly explains why the practice is able to affect the weather—because a god is thereby propitiated, or something of the sort. These varying concrete practices together with the explanatory theories are all "derivations."

However, among all the variables, there is a common nucleus, the feeling that by means of some manipulation or another it is possible to control the weather. Once this common nucleus is understood, it is seen to be the same that is manifested in many other types of activities besides those related to weather-control: activities through which men bring together into a "combination" two or more elements of whatever kind, and for whatever supposed purpose or with no purpose at all. This nucleus, common to all this great area of actions, is the "residue," in this case what Pareto calls the Residue of Combinations.

Again: we find in all ages a great variety of verbalized activities connected with the sex impulse. Sometimes these take the form of pornographic literature and stories; sometimes of denunciations of sexual license, of asceticism or pruriency; sometimes of strict or licentious theories about proper sexual relations; sometimes of ideas about censorship; sometimes of religious or moral allegories. Throughout all these manifold derivations, nevertheless, runs the common sex nucleus, remarkably stable at all periods, changing style and mode, but always cropping up in some new expression when an old disappears or is suppressed. This common sex nucleus is therefore also a residue.

Or again: we find that everywhere and at all times men believe in the objective reality and persistence of entities like gods or spirits or "the state" or "progress" or "justice" or "freedom" or "humanity" or "the proletariat" or "the law." The names and special personalities of the entities change, sometimes rather quickly. So also do the theories that explain the entities—religions and philosophies and moralities. The names and special features and the theories are derivations. But always we find, however expressed, this common belief in the reality of such entities, so that here too we have a residue, the residue of "the persistence of abstractions."

The term, "residue," then, means simply the stable, common element which we may discover in social actions, the nucleus which is "left over" (hence, perhaps, Pareto's choice of the word "residue") when the variable elements are stripped away. It must be stressed that for Pareto "residue" is a sociological, not a psychological or biological term. Residues are discovered not by psychological or biological research, but by comparing and analyzing huge numbers of social actions. Presumably a residue corresponds to some fairly permanent human impulse or instinct or, as Pareto more often calls it, "sentiment." However, Pareto is not primarily interested in where residues come from, but in the fact that social actions may be analyzed in terms of them, whatever their origin. "Our detailed examination of one theory or another has in any case led to our perceiving that theories in the concrete may be divided into at least two elements, one of which is much more stable than the other. We say, accordingly, that in concrete theories, which we shall designate as *c* [derivatives], there are, besides factual data, two principal elements (or parts); a substantial element (part), which we shall designate as *a* (residue), and a contingent element (part), on the whole fairly variable, which we shall designate as *b* (derivation)." (798.) "The element *a* [residue] corresponds, we may guess, to certain instincts of man, or more exactly, men, because *a* has no objective existence and differs in different individuals; and it is probably because of its correspondence to instincts that it is virtually constant in social phenomena.

The element *b* [derivations] represents the work of the mind in accounting for *a*. That is why *b* is much more variable, as reflecting the play of the imagination." (850.) "The residues *a* must not be confused with the sentiments or instincts to which they correspond. The residues are manifestations of sentiments and instincts . . ." (875.)

Pareto is not always strict about these distinctions, and sometimes uses terms like "sentiment" or "instinct" where he should say "residue." No great harm need result, since from a rough common-sense point of view they are interchangeable. However, it is important to keep them theoretically distinct and to insist that a "residue" is a social and not a psychological term, in order to guard against the supposition that Pareto's social theories could be disproved by a psychological argument, by for example showing, if it could be shown, that an "instinct" theory of psychology is false. Pareto's theories, properly understood, do not depend upon any special psychological doctrine. Even if psychology says that men do not have any permanent instincts, it may still be true that there are certain permanent, or at least relatively constant, types of social activity.

Analysis can, Pareto believes, show that there are a good many residues operative in social action. For convenience, he divides them into six main classes, though other divisions might be substituted without altering the main theory. This list, with a brief explanation of each class, is as follows (888 and *ff.*):

Class I: Instinct for Combinations. This is the tendency which leads human beings to combine or manipulate various elements taken arbitrarily from experience. Many magical practices are a result of its operation: the manipulations to control weather or disease, to bring good luck, the supposed efficacy assigned to certain numbers (3 or 7 or 13, for example) suitably employed, totems, and so on. Supposed connections are established between

PARETO: THE SOCIAL ACTION

certain events, formulas, prayers, or words, and good or bad luck, happiness or terror or sorrow. At a complex level it is this residue that leads restless individuals to large-scale financial manipulations, merging and combining and re-combining of various economic enterprises, efforts to entangle and disentangle political units, to make and remake empires.

It is residues of Class I, also, that impel men to "system-making" —that is, to elaborate logical or rather pseudo-logical combinations of ideas and mental elements in general, to theologies and metaphysics and ideologies of all sorts. Thus it is this class of residue that chiefly accounts for "derivations," expressing man's need to make his own behavior seem rational.

Class II: Group-Persistences. When once any combination has been formed, forces come into play to keep that combination sustained and persisting. These are, one might say, "conservative" forces, present among animals as well as human beings, and sometimes referred to as "social inertia." They express themselves, for instance, in the powerful feeling that the family or the tribe or the city or the nation is a permanent and objective entity. So strong are they that the dead and the not-yet-living are included in the supposedly persisting unit, and we thus have all the many forms of ancestor-worship, belief in immortality, and social provisions made for a posterity that will not exist until all living persons are long dead. "Family pride," "class solidarity," patriotism, religious zeal are all quite direct modes of these residues.

They account also for the feeling that "property" becomes a permanent part of a man's being, so much so that certain objects are even placed with the dead body in the grave, or for the "love of the native soil." In another direction, they give persisting life to abstractions and personifications. Gods and heroes and Platonic Forms and "natural law" and "progress" and "the state" and "the moral will" and many other creatures of the dynamic human imagination are endowed with substance and enduring reality.

These Class II residues, as Pareto describes them, are usually accompanied by a willingness to use force in order to maintain the solidity and persistence of the entities in question—to "save the nation," or the "true faith," for example.

We shall later see that Pareto considers the Class I and Class II residues to be the most important in influencing changes in political and social structure.

Class III: Need of Expressing Sentiments by External Acts—Residues of Self-Expression and Activity. Most human beings constantly feel the need to "do something," whether or not the something done can accomplish any desired purpose. Ignorance of medical science in no way stops the family from bustling about when someone is ill. Most persons always feel that something must be done to improve political and economic conditions, even though they have not the slightest idea whether what they do— making speeches or campaigning for votes or advocating this or that reform—will in fact affect conditions favorably; and most people are very impatient with anyone who remains passive "while civilization is being destroyed." This class of residues is plainly connected with Class I—making "combinations" is one of the chief forms of activity.

Class IV: Residues Connected with Sociality. This class, and also Class V, as Pareto treats them, are related to residues of Class II, and it is somewhat arbitrary to separate them in theory. Indeed, with the exception of Class VI (sex residues), all residues tend to fall into two main classes—(1) "combinations," the tendencies to change, newness, manipulations, speculations, upsets, progress; and (2) "group-persistences," the tendencies to inertia, resistance to change, social solidarity, conservation, conformity.

However, under Class IV Pareto groups such factors as the need felt by the individual for conformity with the group, and his effort to force conformity on others; the distrust or hatred of innovation; the opposite but related social sentiments of pity and cruelty; the willingness to sacrifice life or comfort or property for the supposed good of others; the sentiments of social ranking and hierarchy present in most persons—feelings, that is, that some individuals are superior, some inferior in the social scale; and the almost universal need for group approval.

Most of these feelings, and the significant part they play in providing a foundation for social life, have been noted by writers on society from the time of the Greek philosophers. We should keep in mind that what is distinctive in Pareto's analysis of them is his general contention that they are all non-logical in origin. They may yield good or bad results—that will depend upon the circumstances—but they continue to function in any case, not from deliberate intention but independent of all processes of rational thought. We do not conform with the group and its customs because we have a theory that thereby our own life becomes more satisfactory; we begin with a tendency to conform, and only later do we invent or adopt a theory that this is "the best way of life." We do not sacrifice our life for our country because we believe in some complex philosophical theory, of which many are available, about the nature of social life and the state; a tendency to self-sacrifice is prior to the theories, and they are only an attempt, under the pressure of Class I Residues, to give the tendency a pleasing logical form.

Class V: Integrity of the Individual and His Appurtenances. In general, according to Pareto's account, these are the feelings that lead men to guard their personal integrity, to maintain themselves and the conditions of their existence, together with whatever they happen to identify with themselves and those conditions of existence. For example, there is the usual strong feeling against any serious alteration in the social structure. In a slave society, most people are indignant at a proposal for doing away with slaves; in a capitalist society, at attacks on "the rights of property"; and the indignation, which would seem natural enough in the case of slave-holders or capitalists, extends to the other members of the social group who do not have slaves or capital wealth. Many of those who fought most bravely on the Southern side during the Civil War never owned or could hope to own slaves; many of those fighting today in the United States Army, in order, so some of their leaders tell them, "to defend free enterprise," have never owned and will never own any share of that enterprise. Nevertheless, they identify the preservation of their own integrity with the preservation of the general social structure.

When something has gone wrong, has violated the integrity of the individual, he seeks to restore his integrity. A taboo has been broken, so a purification ceremony is performed (as in the case of baptism, the purification may be required because of the impiety of a very distant or even mythical ancestor). The individual must "re-assert" himself after a slip. A Purgatory must restore a balance that has been upset during real life. Or the integrity is restored by actions directed against the real or supposed violator—that is, vengeance must be carried out, the criminal punished, the heretic burned.

Pareto also holds this Class of Residues responsible for many of the feelings of social equality. Such feelings, he shows, are never what they seem to be, but are always in fact a drive toward extra privileges for the group that adheres to the doctrine of equality that may be in question. The post-Renaissance bourgeoisie, calling for "equality," wanted in fact the transfer of the major social privileges from the feudal aristocrats to themselves; analogously today in the case of the working-class demands for equality. From the point of view of this analysis, there is no contradiction in the evident fact that a nation fighting sincerely for equality can at the same time accept internal practices of racial and religious discrimination. The contradiction exists only in the words used, which are of slight influence, and not in the feeling which the words in their own curious way express.

Class VI: The Sex Residue. The merely biological sex urge is not, properly speaking, a residue. The sex residue functions only where it receives an expression that is at least partly verbal, where theories and literature and moral rules and religious doctrines are used as the ever-varying but always present disguises and distortions of the sex impulse. In his treatment of the sex residue and its "sublimations," Pareto is not unlike Freud, though he was apparently not directly acquainted with Freud's writings.

These six, then, or others of the same sort, are the major and relatively unchanging nuclei of non-logical conduct, the conduct that makes up the greater proportion of human action and in particular of those actions that affect the course of government and history.

* * *

Along with the more or less constant residues, which operate at all times and in all cultures, are found the shifting, variable elements, the manifestations of the residues, the outward forms, what Pareto calls the derivations. Of special interest to Pareto are the verbal explanations, dogmas, doctrines, theories with which man, with that passionate pretense of his that he is rational, clothes the non-logical bones of the residues. These verbal derivations* are themselves specifically evoked by the operation of one of the Combination Residues, as I have already remarked.

"Concrete theories in social connections are made up of residues and derivations. The residues are manifestations of sentiments. The derivations comprise logical reasonings, unsound reasonings, and manifestations of sentiments used for purposes of derivation: they are manifestations of the human being's hunger for thinking. If that hunger were satisfied by logico-experimental [i.e., empiri-

---

* "Derivation," in this narrower verbal sense, is a generalized term which includes a number of ideas which we have previously discussed: "political formula" (Mosca), "myth" (Sorel), "ideology" (Michels); and, for that matter, Freud's "rationalization."

cal-scientific] reasonings only, there would be no derivations; instead of them we should get logico-experimental [scientific] theories. But the human hunger for thinking is satisfied in any number of ways; by pseudo-experimental reasonings, by words that stir the sentiments, by fatuous, inconclusive 'talk.' So derivations come into being." (1401.)

Derivations—which include all or nearly all doctrines and beliefs and theories that figure in social struggles, principles of democracy and law and authority, moral and theological systems, justifications of this or that form of society, bills of rights and programs and charters—are divided by Pareto (1419) into four main classes:

Class I: Assertion. These, the simplest and most direct and often the most effective of derivations, are mere dogmatic assertions. They frequently take the form of maxims and aphorisms— "Honesty is the best policy," "Expect from another what you have done to another," "It is better to receive a wrong than to inflict one," the Golden Rule, and so on. The tone and feeling with which these simple assertions are made and accepted, especially if they are constantly repeated, may give them great persuasive value. This point is stressed in Hitler's discussions of propaganda in *Mein Kampf:* "Any effective propaganda must be confined to a very few points, and must use these as slogans until the very last man cannot help knowing what is meant. . . . Propaganda must limit itself to saying very little, and this little it must keep forever repeating. . . ."

Class II: Authority. This large variety of derivations argues by making an appeal to some authority: an individual or group of individuals; divine beings or personifications; or the authority of tradition and custom. There is seldom the slightest scientific justification for accepting the relevance of the authority's opinion— which besides is not seldom wholly unreal—but this does not weaken the effectiveness of the derivation. God's Will, the Bible,

PARETO: THE SOCIAL ACTION

what our forefathers did, Marx's "real meaning," a Farewell Address or a Testament to Posterity, remain cogent arguments from a non-logical standpoint.

Class III: Accords with Sentiment or Principles. With the help of Class II Residues, men convert sentiments into abstractions, persistent realities and everlasting principles. The power of these entities is derived from the feelings they express, not from their supposed logical or scientific rigor. Because of their power they too can serve as premises in the pseudo-logic of derivations. The theorist can appeal to "universal judgment" or "the collective mind" or "the will of the people" or "the opinion of all the best minds," and be persuasive without any need to take the trouble to gather the actual facts about what actual people think. A political program which serves the "best interests of humanity" or embodies the "principles of natural law" or respects the "eternal rights of individuals" is made acceptable without a tedious scientific assessment of just what its effects upon real society and real men would probably be.

Class IV: Verbal Proofs. These are the familiar derivations that depend upon verbal confusions and fallacies, ambiguous terms, the intrusion of emotive expressions in the place of statements of fact, metaphors and allegories taken for proofs, all of which have been recently so much discussed by the many writers on "semantics."

* * *

It will be evident from the examples and analysis given in this and the preceding section that Pareto believes derivations to have little effect in determining important social changes. Residues are the abiding, the significant and influential factor. When the complex of residues is given and while it remains, the general course of conduct is decided; the derivations can come and go, change and be changed, but nothing much is altered. The derivations cannot, it is true, be disregarded; but their importance is primarily as expressions of residues, not in themselves.

"Theologians, metaphysicists, philosophers, theorists of politics, law, and ethics, do not ordinarily accept the order indicated. They are inclined to assign first place to derivations. What we call residues are in their eyes axioms or dogmas, and the purpose [that is, the supposed goal of conduct which is in fact non-logical] is just the conclusion of a logical reasoning. But since they are not as a rule in any agreement on the derivation, they argue about it till they are blue in the face and think that they can change social conditions by proving a derivation fallacious. That is all an illusion on their part. They fail to realize that their hagglings never reach the majority of men, who could not make head or tail to them anyhow, and who in fact disregard them save as articles of faith to which they assent in deference to certain residues." (1415.)

"A politician is inspired to champion the theory of 'solidarity' by an ambition to obtain money, power, distinctions. Analysis of that theory would reveal but scant trace of his motives, which are, after all, the motives of virtually all politicians, whether they preach white or black. First prominence would be held by principles *a* that are effective in influencing others. If the politician were to say, 'Believe in "solidarity" because if you do it means money for me,' he would get many laughs and few votes. . . ." (854.)

The influence on people's actions and on the course of events that derivations—theories, doctrines, reasoning—seem at times to have is always deceiving the surface observer. At most the derivations strengthen already existing residues—a truth well realized by skilled propagandists; for the rest, they operate only indirectly. The seeming influence of the derivation is in reality the influence of the residue which it expresses. It is for this reason that the "logical" refutation of theories used in politics never accomplishes anything so long as the residues remain intact. Scientists can prove with the greatest ease that the Nazi racial theories are altogether false, but that has no effect at all in getting Nazis to abandon those theories; and even if they should abandon them, they would merely substitute some new derivation to express the same residues.

Pareto, as well as the other Machiavellians, is often charged by sentimentalists with "neglecting human ideals" and "disregarding men's goals." No charge could be more inappropriate. It is the Machiavellians, perhaps more than any other school, who have paid closest attention to ideals. However, as I have already more than once stated, they do not take ideals and the theories accompanying them at face value. They insist on relating the ideals and theories to the whole complex of human behavior, and interpreting what men do, not merely by their words, but by their words related to the rest of their actions. Recognizing that moral, social, and political doctrines have little or no genuinely scientific content, they do not try to evaluate them through a superficial examination of the words that appear in them, nor do they expect to understand and predict the course of social events by accepting the verbal nonsense that a Constitution or Platform or political speech may contain. Often they discover that the actual effects of a doctrine are completely at variance with the results that it claims to be able to accomplish—a discovery not without its practical importance, if we are interested in the welfare of society. Let us take as another example of their method a brief analysis by Pareto of the widespread modern derivation, "humanitarianism":

"The weakness of the humanitarian religion does not lie in the logico-experimental deficiencies of its derivations. From that standpoint they are no better and no worse than the derivations of other religions. But some of these contain residues beneficial to individuals and society, whereas the humanitarian religion is sadly lacking in such residues. But how can a religion that has the good of humanity solely at heart, and which is called 'humanitarian' for that very reason, be so destitute in residues correlated with society's welfare? . . . The principles from which the humanitarian doctrine is logically derived in no way correspond with the facts. They merely express in objective form a subjective sentiment of asceticism. The intent of sincere humanitarians is to do good to society, just as the intent of the child who kills a bird by too much fondling is to do good to the bird. We are not, for that matter, forgetting that humanitarianism has had some socially desirable effects. For one thing, it has contributed to the mitigation of criminal penalties; and if among these some were beneficial, so that society has suffered from their mitigation, there were others that were useless, so that by their mitigation society has gained. . . . And so for the democratic religion in general. The many varieties of Socialism, Syndicalism, Radicalism, Tolstoyism, pacifism, humanitarianism, Solidarism, and so on, form a sum that may be said to belong to the democratic religion, much as there was a sum of numberless sects in the early days of the Christian religion. We are now witnessing the rise and dominance of the democratic religion, just as the men of the first centuries of our era witnessed the rise of the Christian religion and the beginnings of its dominion. The two phenomena present many profoundly significant analogies. To get at their substance we have to brush derivations aside and reach down to residues. The social value of both those two religions lies not in the least in their respective theologies, but in the sentiments that they express. As regards determining the social value of Marxism, to know whether Marx's theory of 'surplus value' is false or true is about as important as knowing whether and how baptism eradicates sin in trying to determine the social value of Christianity—and that is of no importance at all. . . ." (1859.)

3. Social Utility

SINCE THE BEGINNING of systematic thought—that is, for about 2500 years in western culture—there has been constant discussion of the problem of "the good community," "the ideal society," "the best form of government." Tens of thousands of persons have given time and intelligence to arguments over these questions, and have devised nearly as many answers. After all this while, men have not reached any generally accepted conclusions, and there is no indication that we have advanced in these matters a single step beyond the reasonings of the ancient Greeks and Romans. This fact, and the contrast it presents to the advances made in solving the problems of the physical sciences, are enough to show that the attempted answers to these questions are not scientifically credible theories, but non-logical expressions, that is to say, derivations. Derivations, not being subject to the controls of logic, clarity and evidence, never reach any objective stability, but come and go with every shift of sentiment and cultural fashion.

Disputes over the best form of society and government can be interpreted in terms of the notion of "social utility." When we are asking whether some law or economic measure or belief or war or revolution will be best for society, we are wondering if it will contribute to the community's welfare or utility. In connection with the idea of "social utility," Pareto makes certain distinctions which help to clarify what is meant by this whole type of problem.

To begin with, it may readily be observed that a community (a nation, for example) is heterogeneous. It is not composed of identical elements, but sub-divided into various groups and classes:

rulers and ruled in one rough way, but with many more intricate and elaborate divisions—economic classes, religious sects, and so on. Ordinarily, the philosophers, reformers, and social writers speak of "the community" or "the society"; but these are vague and distant abstractions. It is to be expected, and it is ordinarily the case, that any given proposal should be useful to some subgroups of the community, and detrimental to others: a benefit to the rulers, a detriment to the ruled; good for the workers, but hurtful to employers. . . . The spokesmen for the various groups never, of course, put things in this distinct way. They make use of derivations, and always put a program, the consequences of which would be favorable to their own group, forward in the name of the community as a whole. From this habit not a little confusion results.

A war wherein defeat would result in death or enslavement for the whole population is directly related to the welfare of the entire community; but in modern times this is not usually what happens as a result of defeat in war. At least some sections of the defeated communities prosper even in and through the defeat. More plainly, in the case of such measures as tariffs and subsidies, is it pointless to speak of the community as a whole. There are benefits for some sections; hurts for others. It is by no means true, to take a prominent current example, that inflation harms everyone. A certain amount of inflation, under certain circumstances, can, by stimulating the economy, help nearly everyone. More usually, inflations harm some groups—those living on relatively fixed incomes; and aid others—those whose incomes vary easily, or who are expert speculators and manipulators. Does force contribute to social utility? The general question is meaningless. We must first determine what force is under discussion, to be used by whom and against whom and for what purposes. Force used against the state and the ruling class, for instance, is very different in its effects from force used by the state and the ruling class.

But even a proper analysis in terms of sub-groups and classes will not sufficiently clarify the meaning of utility (welfare, happiness). We must, in Pareto's language, distinguish further between the utility *"of* a community" and the utility *"for* a community."

By the utility *of* a community Pareto refers to what might be called the community's survival value, its strength and power of resistance as against other communities. By the utility *for* a community Pareto means its internal welfare, the happiness and satisfactions of its members.

The first of these may be objectively studied. We can observe whether the community endures in its struggles with external rivals, or is overthrown, and disappears as a separate community. The second utility, however, is purely subjective or relative, since what is internally useful for the community will depend upon what the members of the community want, what they regard as constituting happiness and satisfaction.

Granted that we accept some particular conception of internal utility (material prosperity would be suitable in the case of most modern nations), we must note that these two utilities, the internal and the external utility, seldom coincide. Those factors which give a community survival value, strength and endurance as against other communities, are usually not the factors that can contribute most to the happiness of its members.

There are many fairly obvious examples of this divergence. Lengthy and adequate war preparations absorb time, require a discipline most men find unpleasant, and reduce the volume of material goods available for current satisfactions. Nevertheless, they greatly increase the utility *of* the community. Again, large numbers of children usually increase the utility *of* the community, its survival value against other communities, at least up to the limit of the physical means for subsistence. However, in many cases, they decrease the pleasures and satisfactions of the constituent members of the community. In general, measures which provide more adequately for the strength of the community in the future, especially in a future some years or generations distant, diminish the satisfactions of the existing generation.

Which, then, is better: a shorter historical life for the community, to end in its destruction, with more internal satisfactions as it goes along, or a longer life with fewer satisfactions? This seems to be frequently, perhaps always, the choice. The answer, needless to say, is never given by deliberate, logical decision. And it may be that there is no way in which this question could be objectively answered.

Let us turn to another fundamental question raised by the problem of social utility. There are, in every community, prevailing norms or standards of conduct, embodied in customs, codes, laws, moral philosophies, and religions. By various devices, ranging from the automatic pressure of social approval and disapproval through education to physical force, each individual member of the community is called upon to observe these standards. As usual, men are not content merely to try to bring about conformity. There must be a theory to explain why the individual "ought" to conform—that is, there must be a derivation. This type of derivation is the substance of most systems of ethics or moral philosophy.

The question suggested by the facts is: Does an individual in truth realize a maximum happiness for himself by conforming to the prevailing standards of his community? If the community norm says to be honest, patriotic, faithful in marriage, is it true that an individual member of the community will be happier by not stealing, by sacrificing his life in war, by foregoing adultery? The overwhelming majority of moral philosophies unite in holding that these things indeed are true, that the individual best secures his own private happiness by conforming to his community's standards. By a careful analysis (1897 ff.), Pareto shows that the reasonings of the moral philosophies are almost without exception derivations, depending upon those non-scientific devices briefly outlined in the preceding section. There is never, or almost never, an objective examination of the facts themselves, but a reliance upon vagueness, ambiguity, empty abstraction, and sentiment. And if it should nevertheless appear that some miscreant *seems* happy though he lives a life of wickedness, self-indulgence, and disregard for duty, then the philosophers tell us that this is only appearance and that he is not "really happy."

There are a few philosophies, in contrast, that take a pessimistic view. They deny that the individual secures his own happiness by following the standards of the group. These philosophies, too, are derivations. "Such [pessimistic] solutions count for little in the social equilibrium. They are never popular. They have vogue primarily among men of letters and philosophers, and are valuable only as manifestations of the psychic state of this or that individual. In moments of discouragement many people repeat, as we saw, with Brutus, 'Virtue, thou art but a name.' Oftentimes pessimism acts as a spur to material enjoyments, and many people of literary inclinations will repeat the maxim: 'Let us eat, drink, and be merry, for tomorrow we die.' In Russia, after the war with Japan, there was a movement for revolution, with eager hopes of an exciting future. The revolution was put down, the hopes were dispelled. A period of discouragement followed, with a marked impulse towards purely physical enjoyments." (1999, 2000.)

What is the truth about this problem, apart from derivations? The truth seems to be that no general conclusion can be drawn. Sometimes the individual best secures his own happiness by conforming to the group standards; sometimes by disregarding or violating the standards. It all depends upon the individual in question, and upon the circumstances.

Nevertheless, though this is the truth, it would, generally speaking, be disadvantageous to society for this truth to be known. Almost always it is socially useful, it contributes to social welfare, to have people *believe* that their own individual happiness is bound up with acceptance of the community standards: or, as moral philosophers put it, that there is a direct correspondence between the welfare of the individual and the welfare of society.

Here, however, we have reached a principle with much wider application than to this particular problem. Is the truth, or rather a knowledge of the truth, always advantageous to society? is falsehood, or nonsense, always harmful? To both of these questions, the facts compel us to answer, No. The great rationalistic dream of modern times, believing that social actions are or can be primarily logical, has taught the illusion that the True and the Good are identical, that if men knew the truth about themselves and their social and political life, then society would become ever better; and that falsehood and absurdity always hurt social welfare. But things do not stand in that simple way. Sometimes the truth aids society. But often a widespread knowledge of the truth may weaken or destroy sentiments, habits, attitudes upon which the integrity of social life, above all in times of crisis, may depend. False beliefs do sometimes produce evil social results; but they often, also, benefit the community. Again no general conclusion is possible. We must examine each concrete case, each specific truth and falsehood in its specific circumstances.

We are not, therefore, entitled to judge that it is invariably a "bad thing" that men believe derivations, ideologies, myths, formulas, these verbal constructions which from a scientific standpoint always contain a large measure of the false and the absurd. The myths are, in the first place, a necessary ingredient of social life. A society in which they would be eliminated in favor of exclusively scientific beliefs would have nothing in common with the human societies that have existed and do exist in the real world, and is a merely imaginary fantasy. Here once more our investigation must be concrete. Certain derivations or myths under certain circumstances are socially useful, others detrimental; when the circumstances change, so may the effects of the myths. The doctrine of the divine right of kings is scientifically ridiculous. From this it does not follow that it would always be better if men understood that it was ridiculous, nor that a belief in it always hurts society. The democratic ideology is equally ridiculous from the point of view of scientific truth. Belief in it may, nevertheless, in one historical context greatly aid, in another gravely injure, the welfare of society. Society is not so simple as a problem in mathematics, which is fully solved once ignorance is overcome. Not only is it impossible that all men should know the scientific truth about society and act in accordance with this knowledge; it is far from clear that this would improve society even if it were possible.

Those who believe that all social difficulties could be overcome if the truth about society were known "recognize only one tie [obstacle]—ignorance. Ignorance being eliminated, they have no doubt that society will follow the course they think is the best. The tie of ignorance may legitimately be said to have been suppressed, at least in great part; for it is certain that there are educated people in our time just as there have been educated people in the past; and in society as a whole knowledge has increased in the course of the ages. So far, therefore, no obstacle blocks our path; but one rises insuperable in that part of the argument which holds that the tie of ignorance is the only tie that has to be removed before the conclusion is possible. If the most intelligent people we know—the 'best-educated,' to use a current term—were also the people who make most extensive use of logico-experimental [scientific] principles in social matters to the exclusion of all other principles, it would be legitimate to conclude that, in course of time, such people would reject everything of a non-experimental character; and that other people, more or less their equals in knowledge, would also be more or less like them in their exclusive acceptance of logico-experimental principles. But the facts do not stand that way. If theologians have diminished in number among our educated people and lost much of their power, metaphysicians, properly so called, are still prospering and enjoying fame and influence, to say nothing of those metaphysicians who call themselves 'positivists' or under some other name are merrily overstepping the boundaries of the logico-experimental. Many scientists who are supremely great in the natural sciences, where they use logico-experimental principles exclusively or almost so, forget them entirely when they venture into the social sciences.* As regards the masses in the large, what one observes is an unending alternation of theologies and systems of metaphysics rather than any reduction in the total number of them." (1881.)

* How easily we observe this in the United States, with the examples before us of great natural scientists like Millikan and Conant and Boas and Urey and Compton, whose not infrequent remarks on social affairs are, scientifically, much below the level reached by the average factory worker.

4. The Circulation of the Elites

BY "SOCIAL EQUILIBRIUM," Pareto means the general state and structure of society, considered dynamically, at any given moment. That is, the term refers to the state of society insofar as it involves the interplay of those forces that both determine what it is at any given moment, and at the same time, through their operation, work to change its state and structure. What are these forces that determine the social equilibrium, that make society what it is and bring about changes in society? Pareto believes the chief of them to be the following:

1. The physical environment—climate, geographical factors, and the like—is plainly of great importance, but, since it alters very slowly during historic periods, may be treated as a constant and disregarded when trying to discover the laws of social change and development.

2. Residues are very influential. Residues, Pareto finds, change slowly, remaining surprisingly stable especially within each organized social group. In the end, however, these slow changes alter the whole fabric of social life. Quicker and more obvious in their effect are changes not so much in the residues that are present as in the distribution of residues in the various strata of society. The study of these changes in the distribution of residues can be incorporated in the discussion of (5) below.

3. Economic factors—what Pareto calls "interests"—have also a major role, as is recognized by almost all modern historians and sociologists. In *Mind and Society,* however, Pareto does not treat the economic factors at great length.

4. Derivations, too, have a certain influence on the social equi-

librium, though Pareto, as we have seen, believes this to be minor and for the most part indirect compared to the other major factors. These non-logical beliefs, myths, formulas, are chiefly notable as expressions of residues or interests, and for their indirect ability to reinforce residues or to alter the pattern of the circulation of the élites.

5. Finally, there functions what Pareto calls "the circulation of the élites." The analysis of this conception will occupy the greater part of this section.

Pareto, like all Machiavellians, has thus a pluralistic theory of history. Changes in society do not result from the exclusive impact of any single cause, but rather from the interdependent and reciprocal influences of a variety of causes, principally, though not only, these five.

* * *

"Whether certain theorists like it or not, the fact is that human society is not a homogeneous thing, that individuals are physically, morally, and intellectually different.... Of that fact, therefore, we have to take account. And we must also take account of another fact: that the social classes are not entirely distinct, even in countries where a caste system prevails; and that in modern civilized countries circulation among the various classes is exceedingly rapid.... We shall consider the problem [in order to simplify it] only in its bearing on the social equilibrium and try to reduce as far as possible the numbers of the groups and the modes of circulation, putting under one head phenomena that prove to be roughly and after a fashion similar." (2025.)

"Let us assume that in every branch of human activity each individual is given an index which stands as a sign of his capacity, very much the way grades are given in the various subjects in examinations in school. The highest type of lawyer, for instance, will be given 10. The man who does not get a client will be given

1—reserving zero for the man who is an out-and-out idiot. To the man who has made his millions—honestly or dishonestly as the case may be—we will give 10. To the man who has earned his thousands we will give 6; to such as just manage to keep out of the poor-house, 1, keeping zero for those who get in. To the woman 'in politics,' such as the Aspasia of Pericles, the Maintenon of Louis XIV, the Pompadour of Louis XV, who has managed to infatuate a man of power and play a part in the man's career, we shall give some higher number, such as 8 or 9; to the strumpet who merely satisfies the senses of such a man and exerts no influence on public affairs, we shall give zero. To a clever rascal who knows how to fool people and still keep clear of the penitentiary, we shall give 8, 9, or 10, according to the number of geese he has plucked and the amount of money he has been able to get out of them. To the sneak-thief who snatches a piece of silver from a restaurant table and runs away into the arms of a policeman, we shall give 1. To a poet like Carducci we shall give 8 or 9 according to our tastes; to a scribbler who puts people to rout with his sonnets we shall give zero. For chess-players we can get very precise indices, noting what matches, and how many, they have won. And so on for all the branches of human activity." (2027.)

In some such way we shall be able to distinguish, at least roughly, the *élite* or better the *élites* in society from the mass. We shall quickly observe, moreover, that human beings are not distributed evenly over the scale. At the top there are very few, considerably more in the middle; but the overwhelming majority are grouped near the bottom. The élite is always a small minority.

Within the élite we may further distinguish a "governing élite" from a "non-governing élite." The élite within many branches of human activity—chess-playing, for example, from the list quoted—does not exert any appreciable influence on political affairs and social structure.

The character of a society, Pareto holds, is above all the character of its élite; its accomplishments are the accomplishments of its élite; its history is properly understood as the history of its élite; successful predictions about its future are based upon evidence drawn from the study of the composition and structure of its élite. Pareto's conclusions here are the same as those reached by Mosca in his analysis of the narrower but similar concept of the "ruling class."

The élite in any society is never static. Its structure, its composition, and the way in which it is related to the rest of the society are always changing. Most obviously the élite changes through the death of its individual members, and their replacement by other individuals. In itself, however, this is of no significance. If each dead individual were replaced by another of the same type, the élite as a historical grouping would remain unaltered. What influences social development is not the mere shift of individuals, but change in the types of individual, and in the relations of various types to each other and to the rest of society.

If, in the selection of members of the élite, there existed a condition of perfectly free competition, so that each individual could, without any obstacle, rise just as high in the social scale as his talents and ambition permitted, the élite could be presumed to include, at every moment and in the right order, just those persons best fitted for membership in it. Under such circumstances —which Pareto seems to imagine after the analogy of the theoretical free market of classical economics, or the biological arena of the struggle for survival—society would remain dynamic and strong, automatically correcting its own weaknesses.

However, a condition of this sort is never found in reality. There are always obstacles, or "ties" as Pareto calls them, that interfere with the free circulation of individuals up and down the social scale. Special principles of selection, different in different societies, affect the composition of the élite so that it no longer includes all those persons best fitted for social rule. Weaknesses set in; and, not compensated by a gradual day-by-day circulation, if they go far enough they are corrected sharply by social revolution: that is, by the sudden intrusion into the élite of large numbers of individuals hitherto prevented by the obstacles from finding their natural social level.

The most evident and universal of the obstacles to free circulation is the aristocratic principle. The children of members of the élite are helped to a position in the élite regardless of their own capacities and at the sacrifice of individuals of greater capacity appearing among the non-élite. If this principle is carried far enough, if the élite becomes "closed" or almost so, degeneration is bound to set in. The percentage of weak and inferior persons within the élite necessarily increases, while at the same time superior persons accumulate among the non-élite. A point is reached where the élite will be overthrown and destroyed.

This, for example, is what happened to Sparta. The doors of entrance to the Spartan élite (the Citizens) were firmly closed to the other classes of the population (the Perioeci and the Helots). The élite to some extent guarded its internal health by the negative device of killing its weak and feeble children, but this was not enough. In spite of an unmatched tradition of self-sacrifice and discipline, the élite declined gravely in numbers and even more in quality until it was utterly defeated, in the 4th century, at the battle of Leuctra, by the people of a city (Thebes) which Sparta had for generations thought of as little more than a second-rate ally. From this defeat, which might in a nation less rigidly organized have become the stimulus to rejuvenation, Sparta never recovered.

From these considerations it follows that a relatively free circulation of the élites—both up and down the social scale—is a requisite for a healthy and a strong society. Conversely, it follows that when in a society the élite becomes closed or nearly closed, that society is threatened either with internal revolution or with destruction from outside. It must be added that Pareto is discussing here not the law or theory dealing with entrance to the élite, but the facts. In theory—as in almost all modern nations, for example—entrance to the élite may be open to all comers. This is of no importance if, in fact, by one device or another—as, again, is true of many modern nations especially since the end of the 19th century—newcomers are kept out. In the United States, everyone has the theoretic right to become a millionaire and the owner of a great industry. In fact, however, at about the time of the first World War, newcomers, with less than a handful of exceptions, stopped becoming millionaires or big owners. Conversely, there have been societies where, though in theory the élite was closed (by rigid hereditary regulations), it was in fact opened, at least sometimes, by such means as adoption or clientage or re-definition of citizenship. This was true at certain periods in Athens and in Rome.

But, since a perfectly free circulation according to ability is never found, a healthy and strong society is not assured merely by keeping the élite more or less open. The additional problem remains of the kind of individuals admitted to or excluded from the élite. We have noted that, according to Pareto, the basic residues within a given society change little and slowly. However, the character of the society is determined not only by the basic residues present in the entire population, but also by the *distribution* of residues among the various social classes; and this distribution may change quite rapidly. To put the matter simply: a given society will include a certain and relatively stable percentage of, for example, clever individuals; but an enormous difference to the society and its development will result from the extent to which these clever individuals are concentrated in its élite, or spread evenly throughout the entire population, or even concentrated in the non-élite.

PARETO: THE SOCIAL ACTION

The residues which, in their circulation, are of chief influence on the social equilibrium are those belonging to Class I and Class II. Indeed, in discussing the circulation of the élites, Pareto expands his definition of these two Classes so that the whole problem can be summed up roughly in terms of them.

Individuals marked primarily by Class I (Combinations) residues are the "Foxes" of Machiavelli. They live by their wits; they put their reliance on fraud, deceit, and shrewdness. They do not have strong attachment to family, church, nation, and traditions (though they may exploit these attachments in others). They live in the present, taking little thought of the future, and are always ready for change, novelty, and adventure. In economic affairs, they incline toward speculation, promotion, innovation. They are not adept, as a rule, in the use of force. They are inventive and chance-taking.

Individuals marked by Class II (Group-Persistences) residues are Machiavelli's "Lions." They are able and ready to use force, relying on it rather than brains to solve their problems. They are conservative, patriotic, loyal to tradition, and solidly tied to supraindividual groups like family or Church or nation. They are concerned for posterity and the future. In economic affairs they are cautious, saving and orthodox. They distrust the new, and praise "character" and "duty" rather than wits.

Pareto cites ancient Athens as a typical example of a state with a heavy proportion of Class I residues in its élite, and an unusually large proportion even in the non-élite (where Class II residues almost always greatly predominate). From this distribution sprang many of the glories of Athens, as well as the extraordinarily rapid shifts in its fortunes. In every field, economic, political, and cultural, Athens welcomed the new, and was ready for any adventure. After the defeat of Persia at Salamis, Athens could not return to the old ways. Taking immediate advantage of the fleet which had been built up for the war, she went on to establish her commercial empire in the eastern Mediterranean. When the tribute from the alliance was no longer needed for war, it was used to build the wonderful temples and statues. Philosophers and poets were honored for attacking the old, traditional ways of life. But her glories were comparatively short-lived. She was always weakened from within by the numerous Class I individuals who were constantly forming factions, plotting with internal or external enemies, and organizing rebellions. And Athens could not endure the long-drawn-out trials of the Peloponnesian Wars. On the one hand, the Class I tendencies led her to attempt too much: she refused peace when it could have been made with honor and profit, and launched the Sicilian Expedition which in its outcome proved her ruin. On the other, wit and shrewdness were not a firm enough foundation to sustain the shock of plague, death, siege, weariness, and defeat.

Sparta, in extreme contrast, was a nation where Class II residues were wholly predominant both in the general population and in the élite. Innovation in Sparta was a crime; everything was regulated by ancient custom and religion and time-sanctified tradition. The individual counted for nothing, the group for all. Adventure was always to be distrusted. From these roots Sparta derived a tremendous power of endurance when faced with adversity. But she always stopped short of anything spectacular. She produced no philosophy, no liquid wealth, and little art. She never tried to establish a great empire. Her own armies went home after the Persians were defeated. In spite of defeats and crushing hardships, she finally conquered in the Peloponnesian Wars; but in the 4th century, when the conditions of life and warfare greatly changed, she too was lost. Because of her lack of Class I residues, Sparta could not adapt herself to new ways; so, defending the old, she perished.

The social combination that is strongest against external enemies, and at the same time able to bring about a fairly high internal level of culture and material prosperity, is that wherein (1) Class II residues are widespread and active among the masses (the non-élite); (2) the individuals with a high level of Class I residues are concentrated in the élite; (3) a fair percentage of Class II residues nevertheless still remains within the élite; (4) the élite is comparatively open, so that at least a comparatively free circulation can take place.

The meaning of this optimum combination can be translated as follows into more usual terms: (1) The masses have faith in an integrating myth or ideology, a strong sense of group solidarity, a willingness to endure physical hardship and sacrifice. (2) The best and most active brains of the community are concentrated in the élite, and ready to take advantage of whatever opportunities the historical situation presents. (3) At the same time the élite is not cynical, and does not depend exclusively upon its wits, but is able to be firm, to use force, if the internal or external condition calls for it. (4) The élite is prevented from gross degeneration through the ability of new elements to rise into its ranks.

A combination of this sort does not, however, as a rule last long. The typical, though not universal, pattern of development of organized societies goes along some such lines as these: The community (nation) becomes established and consolidated after a period of wars of conquest or of internal revolutions. At this point the governing élite is strongly weighted with Class II residues—revolutions and great wars put a premium on faith, powers of endurance, and force. After the consolidation, activities due to Class I residues increase in importance and are able to flourish. The relative percentage of Class I residues in the élite increases; the Foxes replace the Lions. The proportion of Class II residues remains high, as always, in the masses. A time of great material prosperity may follow, under the impulse and manipulations of the Class I residues. But the élite has lost its faith, its self-identification with the group; it thinks all things can be solved by shrewdness, deceit, combinations; it is no longer willing and able to use force. It reaches a point where it cannot withstand the attack from an external enemy, stronger in Class II residues; or from within, when the masses, one way or another, get a leadership able to organize their potential strength. The combinationist élite is destroyed, very often carrying its whole society to ruin along with it.

Let us put this process in the simplest possible terms by reducing it to the problem of force (noting that a willingness and ability to use force is primarily an expression of Class II Residues). "To ask whether or not force ought to be used in a society, whether the use of force is or is not beneficial, is to ask a question that has no meaning; for force is used by those who wish to preserve certain uniformities [e.g., the existing class structure of society, the status quo] and by those who wish to overstep them; and the violence of the ones stands in contrast and in conflict with the violence of the others. In truth, if a partisan of a governing class disavows the use of force, he means that he disavows the use of force by insurgents trying to escape from the norms of the given uniformity. On the other hand, if he says he approves of the use of force, what he really means is that he approves of the use of force by the public authority to constrain insurgents to conformity. Conversely, if a partisan of the subject class says he detests the use of force in society, what he really detests is the use of force by constituted authorities in forcing dissidents to conform; and if, instead, he lauds the use of force, he is thinking of the use of force by those who would break away from certain social uniformities." (2174.) *

* The analysis here stated with reference to internal relations would hold also for international relations. Pacifism as advocated by the dominant powers means a disavowal of force directed against the international status quo, and an acceptance of force in upholding that status quo. Pacifism means just the reverse when advocated by the less favored nations. In the latter case, it is a method of ideological attack on the international status quo, supplementing, not contradicting, the violence of the "have-nots."

That is one side of the matter. But, in addition, the argument may be carried further, and directed against the use of force in any sense whatever. Such arguments express a concentration of Class I residues, at the expense of Class II, in the élite whose spokesmen formulate the arguments. "The dispute is really as to the relative merits of shrewdness and force, and to decide it in the sense that never never, not even in the exceptional case, is it useful to meet wits with violence, it would be necessary first to show that the use of cunning is always, without exception, more advisable than the use of force. Suppose a certain country has a governing class A, that assimilates the best elements, as regards intelligence, in the whole population. In that case the subject class, B, is largely stripped of such elements and can have little or no hope of ever overcoming the Class A so long as it is a battle of wits. If intelligence were to be combined with force, the dominion of the A's would be perpetual. . . . But such a happy combination occurs only for a few individuals. In the majority of cases people who rely on their wits are or become less fitted to use violence, and *vice versa*. So concentration in the class A of the individuals most adept at chicanery leads to a concentration in class B of the individuals most adept at violence; and if that process is long continued, the equilibrium tends to become unstable, because the A's are long in cunning but short in the courage to use force and in the force itself; whereas the B's have the force and the courage to use it, but are short in the skill required for exploiting those advantages. But if they chance to find leaders who have the skill—and history shows that such leadership is usually supplied by dissatisfied A's—they have all they need for driving the A's from power. Of just that development history affords countless examples from remotest times all the way down to the present." (2190.)

The result of such a revolution—for the passage just quoted is simply the generalized description of the form of social revolutions—is to get rid of the weaker elements of the old élite, open up the élite to the rapid influx of new elements, and to alter the balance of residues in the élite in favor of those from Class II. In spite of the cost of revolution in bloodshed and suffering, it may, under certain circumstances, be both necessary and socially beneficial. Even in the latter case, however, it is always an illusion to suppose that the masses themselves take power through a revolution. The masses can never successfully revolt until they acquire a leadership, which is always made up in part of able and ambitious individuals from their own ranks who cannot gain entrance into the governing élite, and in part of disgruntled members of the existing élite (members of the nobility, for example, in the opening stages of the French Revolution, or dissatisfied intellectuals and middle-class persons in the Russian Revolution). So long, therefore, as the governing élite is both willing and in a position to destroy or to assimilate all such individuals, it has a virtual guarantee against internal revolution. If the revolution does take place, we merely find a new élite—or more properly a renewed élite, for the old is almost never wholly wiped out—in the saddle. Nevertheless, the change may quite possibly be for the benefit of the community as a whole and specifically of the masses who, remaining the ruled and not rulers, may yet be better off than before.

Pareto's theory of the circulation of the élites is thus a theory of social change, of revolution, and of social development and degeneration. It is a re-statement, in new and more intricate terms, of the point of view common to the modern Machiavellians and found, more crude, in Machiavelli himself.

Pareto claims, as we have seen, that, though we can come to objective conclusions about the strength of a society relative to other societies, we cannot make any objective judgment about what type of social structure is "best" from the point of view of internal welfare. However, a certain tendency in his own feelings becomes evident from his anaylsis. To begin with, he plainly puts external strength first, since it is a pre-condition of everything else: that is, if a nation cannot survive, it is rather pointless to argue in the abstract whether or not it is a "good society." In order to survive, a society must have a fairly free class-circulation; the élite must not bar its doors too rigidly. This freedom will at the same time on the whole operate to increase the internal well-being of the society.

Second, in discussing the distribution of residues, Pareto implicity joins the other Machiavellians in an evident preference for social checks and balances. The strongest and healthiest societies balance a predominance of Class I residues in the élite with a predominance of Class II residues in the non-élite. But Class II residues must not be altogether excluded from the élite. If Class II residues prevail in all classes, the nation develops no active culture, degenerates in a slough of brutality and stubborn prejudice, in the end is unable to overcome new forces in its environment, and meets disaster. Disaster, too, awaits the nation given over wholly to Class I residues, with no regard for the morrow, for discipline or tradition, with a blind confidence in clever tricks as the sufficient means for salvation.

The laws of the circulation of the élites serve not only to clarify our understanding of societies of the past; they illuminate also our analysis of present societies, and even, sometimes, permit us to predict the future course of social events. Writing in the years just prior to the first World War, Pareto analyzed at length the United States and the principal nations of Europe. He found that the mode of circulation of the élites during the preceding century had brought most of these nations into a condition where the ruling classes were heavily over-weighted with Class I residues, and were subject to debilitating forms of humanitarian beliefs.

The results of such a condition he summarizes in general terms as follows: "1. A mere handful of citizens, so long as they are willing to use violence, can force their will upon public officials who are not inclined to meet violence with equal violence. If the reluctance of the officials to resort to force is primarily motivated by humanitarian sentiments, that result ensues very readily; but if they refrain from violence because they deem it wiser to use some other means, the effect is often the following: 2. To prevent or resist violence, the governing class resorts to 'diplomacy,' fraud, corruption—governmental authority passes, in a word, from the lions to the foxes. The governing class bows its head under the threat of violence, but it surrenders only in appearances, trying to turn the flank of the obstacle it cannot demolish in frontal attack. In the long run that sort of procedure comes to exercise a far-reaching influence on the selection of the governing class, which is now recruited only from the foxes, while the lions are black-balled. The individual who best knows the arts of sapping the strength of the foes of 'graft' and of winning back by fraud and deceit what seemed to have been surrendered under pressure of force, is now leader of leaders. The man who has bursts of rebellion, and does not know how to crook his spine at the proper times and places, is the worst of leaders, and his presence is tolerated among them only if other distinguished endowments offset that defect. 3. So it comes about that the residues of the combination-instinct (Class I) are intensified in the governing class, and the residues of group-persistence (Class II) debilitated; for the combination-residues supply, precisely, the artistry and resourcefulness required for evolving ingenious expedients as substitutes for open resistance, while the residues of group-persistence stimulate open resistance, since a strong sentiment of group-persistence cures the spine of all tendencies to curvature. 4. Policies of the governing class are not planned too far ahead in time. Predominance of the combination instincts and enfeeblement of the sentiments of group-persistence result in making the governing class more satisfied with the present and less thoughtful of the future.

The individual comes to prevail, and by far, over family, community, nation. Material interests and interests of the present or a near future come to prevail over the ideal interests of community or nation and interests of the distant future. The impulse is to enjoy the present without too much thought for the morrow. 5. Some of these phenomena become observable in international relations as well. Wars become essentially economic. Efforts are made to avoid conflicts with the powerful and the sword is rattled only before the weak. Wars are regarded more than anything else as speculations. A country is often unwittingly edged towards war by nursings of economic conflicts which, it is expected, will never get out of control and turn into armed conflicts. Not seldom, however, a war will be forced upon a country by peoples who are not so far advanced in the evolution that leads to the predominance of Class I residues." (2179.)

Confronted with these circumstances, Pareto believed that analogies from comparable processes in the past made plain what was to be expected. In one way or another, probably catastrophically, the social unbalance within the élites would be corrected. Internal revolutions and the impact of external wars would re-introduce into the élites large numbers of individuals strong in the residues of group-persistence (Class II) and able and willing to use force in the maintenance of social organization. This development might mean the almost total destruction of certain of the existing élites, and, along with them, of the nations which they ruled. In other cases, a sufficient alteration in the character of the élite might take place in time to preserve the community, though greatly changed.

This survey should seem familiar today. Pareto was writing, in advance, an outline history of the generation just passed, and the present. Munich, in 1938 was, in its way, a definitive expression of his theory of the circulation of the élites. At Munich, there was demonstrated the impotence of an exclusive reliance on Class I residues: combinations, no matter how shrewdly conceived, could no longer meet the challenge of the matured world social problems. And at the same time Munich revealed that only those two nations—Russia and Germany—where a redistribution of the élites had already taken place, had been able to prepare seriously for the war which was so evidently sure to come.

Part VII

POLITICS AND TRUTH

1. *The Nature of the Present*

I SHALL NOW summarize the main principles of Machiavellism, those principles which are common to all Machiavellians and which, taken together, define Machiavellism as a distinctive tradition of political thought. These general principles constitute a way of looking at social life, an instrument for social and political analysis. They are capable of being applied concretely in the study of any historical period, including our own, that may interest us. They are to be found, implicit as a rule, in the writings of Machiavelli himself. The modern Machiavellians, with a vastly increased number of historical facts at their disposal, have explicitly formulated them.

In each case, in the list that follows, I shall state in parentheses the contrary point of view which is opposed to the Machiavellian principle. In order to understand what a thing is, we must understand also what it is not.

1. An objective science of politics, and of society, comparable in its methods to the other empirical sciences, is possible. Such a science will describe and correlate observable social facts, and, on the basis of the facts of the past, will state more or less probable hypotheses about the future. Such a science will be neutral with respect to any practical political goal: that is, like any other science, its statements will be tested by facts accessible to any observer, rich or poor, ruler or ruled, and will in no way be dependent upon the acceptance of some particular ethical aim or ideal.

(Contrary views hold that a science of politics is not possible, because of the peculiarity of "human nature" or for some similar reason; or that political analysis is always dependent upon some practical program for the improvement—or destruction—of society; or that any political science must be a "class science"—true for the "bourgeoisie," but not for the "protetariat," as, for example, the Marxists claim.)

2. The primary subject-matter of political science is the struggle for social power in its diverse open and concealed forms.

(Contrary views hold that political thought deals with the general welfare, the common good, and other such entities that are from time to time invented by the theorists.)

3. The laws of political life cannot be discovered by an analysis which takes men's words and beliefs, spoken or written, at their face value. Words, programs, declarations, constitutions, laws, theories, philosophies, must be related to the whole complex of social facts in order to understand their real political and historical meaning.

(The contrary view pays chief attention to words, believing that what men say they are doing or propose to do or have done is the best evidence for what they actually do.)

4. Logical or rational action plays a relatively minor part in political and social change. For the most part it is a delusion to believe that in social life men take deliberate steps to achieve consciously held goals. Non-logical action, spurred by environmental changes, instinct, impulse, interest, is the usual social rule.

(The contrary views assign an important or the primary place to rational action. History is conceived as the record of the rational attempts of men to achieve their goals.)

5. For an understanding of the social process, the most significant social division to be recognized is that between the ruling class and the ruled, between the élite and the non-élite.

(Contrary views either deny that such a division exists, or consider that it is unimportant, or believe that it is scheduled to disappear.)

6. Historical and political science is above all the study of the

élite, its composition, its structure, and the mode of its relation to the non-élite.

(Contrary views hold that history is primarily the study of the masses, or of individual great men, or purely of institutional arrangements.)

7. The primary object of every élite, or ruling class, is to maintain its own power and privilege.

(The contrary view holds that the primary object of the rulers is to serve the community. This view is almost invariably held by all spokesmen for an élite, at least with respect to the élite for which they are speaking. Among such spokesmen are to be numbered almost all of those who write on political and social matters.)

8. The rule of the élite is based upon force and fraud. The force may, to be sure, be much of the time hidden or only threatened; and the fraud may not entail any conscious deception.

(The contrary views hold that social rule is established fundamentally upon God-given or natural right, reason, or justice.)

9. The social structure as a whole is integrated and sustained by a political formula, which is usually correlated with a generally accepted religion, ideology, or myth.

(Contrary views hold either that the formulas and myths are "truths" or that they are unimportant as social factors.)

10. The rule of an élite will coincide now more, now less with the interests of the non-élite. Thus, in spite of the fact that the primary object of every élite is to maintain its own power and privilege, there are nevertheless real and significant differences in social structures from the point of view of the masses. These differences, however, cannot be properly evaluated in terms of formal meanings, verbalisms, and ideologies, but by: (a) the strength of the community in relation to other communities; (b) the level of civilization reached by the community—its ability, that is to say, to release a wide variety of creative interests and to

attain a high measure of material and cultural advance; and (c) liberty—that is, the security of individuals against the arbitrary and irresponsible exercise of power.

(Contrary views either deny that there are any significant differences among social structures, or, more frequently, estimate the differences in formal or verbal terms—by, for example, comparing the philosophies of two periods or their ideals.)

11. Two opposing tendencies always operate in the case of every élite: (a) an aristocratic tendency whereby the élite seeks to preserve the ruling position of its members and their descendants, and to prevent others from entering its ranks; (b) a democratic tendency whereby new elements force their way into the élite from below.

(Though few views would deny the existence of these tendencies, some would maintain that one of them could be suppressed, so that an élite could become either completely closed or completely open.)

12. In the long run, the second of these tendencies always prevails. From this it follows that no social structure is permanent and no static utopia is possible. The social or class struggle always continues, and its record is history.

(Contrary views conceive a possible stabilization of the social structure. The class struggle, they say, can, should, and will be eliminated in a Heaven on Earth or a "classless society," not understanding that the elimination of the class struggle would, like the elimination of blood-circulation in the individual organism, while no doubt getting rid of many ailments, at the same time mean death.)

13. There occur periodically very rapid shifts in the composition and structure of élites: that is, social revolutions.

(Contrary views either deny the reality of revolutions or hold that they are unfortunate accidents that could readily be avoided.)

It may be remarked that these Machiavellian principles are

much closer to the more or less instinctive views of "practical men" who are themselves active in the social struggle than to the views of theorists, reformers and philosophers. This is natural, because the principles are simply the generalized statement of what practical men do and have been doing; whereas the theorists, most often comparatively isolated from direct participation in the social struggle, are able to imagine society and its laws to be as they would wish to have them.

In terms of these Machiavellian principles, I shall now analyze three problems: (1) What is the nature of the present historical period? (2) What is the meaning of democracy? (3) Can politics be scientific?

* * *

During the past two or three years it has become fashionable to say that we are in the midst of a revolution. There is something rather ludicrous in the spectacle of well-paid ministers telling their congregations all about the great revolution in which they live, or a 75-year-old bank president explaining world revolution to an after-dinner audience—the congregation and the audience, as likely as not, feeling excited and thrilled at the prospect.

When we examine what is said, it becomes doubtful how seriously we should take the revolutionary phrases. The strict communists tell us that Russia is the revolution, and all the rest of the world capitalist and counter-revolutionary. Others, like Hermann Rauschning, say that Nazi Germany is the revolution, and that what the world needs is a "conservative counter-revolution" to be led by England and the United States. Still others, like Herbert Agar or Vice-President Wallace, say that two revolutions are going on: a bad revolution led by the Nazis, and a good revolution of the "people" or the "common man" led or to be led by the United Nations. As for the kind of revolution, it is indiscriminately labeled as communist or socialist or internationalist or national-socialist or people's or fascist or monopolist. We may reasonably conclude that a majority, at least, of the revolutionary commentators have not made up their minds what they are talking about.

This is a case, however, where words express more than the speakers are usually aware. For there really is a revolution, and we are in truth living in the midst of it. In *The Managerial Revolution*,* I tried to summarize the general character of the revolution. I did so, in the analysis I therein made, primarily in institutional, especially in economic, terms. I propose here to redefine the nature of the revolution through the use of the Machiavellian principles. This is not at all arbitrary, since the present revolution was in fact anticipated and its general course predicted by the modern Machiavellians, more than a generation ago. Their predictions are, indeed, a powerful confirmation of their principles. Moreover, there is no necessary conflict among several possible modes of analyzing historical events. Economic, political, sociological, cultural approaches to history do not have to contradict each other, since these various social factors are at least to some extent interdependently correlated. It is for this reason that we can often reach approximately the same conclusions about history from any of a number of quite different approaches.

From a Machiavellian point of view, a social revolution means a comparatively rapid shift in the composition and structure of the élite and in the mode of its relation to the non-élite. It is possible to state the conditions under which such a rapid shift takes place. The principal of these conditions are the following:

1. When the institutional structure, and the élite which has the ruling position within this structure, are unable to handle possibilities opened up by technological advances and by the growth, for whatever reason, of new social forces.

2. When a considerable percentage of the ruling class devotes

---

* Published by The John Day Company, New York. 1941.

little attention to the business of ruling, and turns its interests to such fields as culture, art, philosophy, and the pursuit of sensuous pleasure.

3. When an élite is unable or unwilling to assimilate rising new elements from the masses or from its own lower ranks.

4. When large sections of the élite lose confidence in themselves and the legitimacy of their own rule; and when in both élite and non-élite there is a loss of faith in the political formulas and myths that have held the social structure together.

5. When the ruling class, or much of it, is unable or unwilling to use force in a firm and determined way, and instead tries to rely almost exclusively on manipulation, compromise, deceit, and fraud.

These are the general pre-conditions of social revolution in any culture. They characterized the age just ending, as the modern Machiavellians understood.

During the past several centuries, the major and most privileged section of the ruling class of the chief nations consisted of the capitalists, or bourgeoisie, together with the closely related parliamentary type of politician. Soldiers, military men, who had been so prominent in many ruling classes of the past, sometimes the exclusive rulers, were in a decidedly minor position. The legal formula which expressed the privileged position of the capitalists was summed up in the conception of individual property rights in the instruments of social production, which were accepted as giving the owner control over those instruments and a preferred share in their products.

The five revolutionary pre-conditions may readily be seen to hold for this private-capitalist ruling class in the generation or more which has just concluded:

1. Technological advance, exceeding during the past 150 years what took place during all prior history, and the growth of elaborately sub-divided mass industry, made anachronistic both

private-capitalist enterprise and the political system of post-Renaissance nationalism. The private owners, dependent for existence upon a market economy, have shown themselves unable to handle integrated mass enterprise, the functional requirements of which are incompatible with a market economy. Similarly, the private owners are unable to organize either a world polity or the great regional states which are the political minimum that is needed in order to permit contemporary social and economic life to continue operating. In addition, the private capitalists have proved unable to organize and control the mass labor movement, brought into being, as the greatest new social force, by the structural changes in modern economy. Leadership over this force has already gone into other hands.

2. During the last generation in this country and some decades earlier in Europe, many members of the capitalist ruling class, particularly from its highest strata, have largely given up active political and economic life in favor of the pursuit of pleasure or of culture.

3. Toward the end of the last century in Europe, and since the first World War in this country, admission to the capitalist ruling class became much more difficult for new aspirants. The top rank of the ruling class became almost completely closed. This development was especially significant because during the greater part of the 19th century class circulation was more rapid and extensive than in any previous social era except for revolutionary crises. The difference is plainly seen in the changed attitude of the youth: young ambitions were no longer directed toward the goal of becoming a great capitalist, but more and more toward such outlets as a high place in the labor movement or in government.

4. Equally noteworthy have been the loss of confidence by the capitalist élite in its own right to rule and in the formulas which upheld its rule, as well as the decay of mass faith in the sustaining capitalist-parliamentary myths. The self-confident myth of Prog-

ress, so bright in the late 18th and throughout most of the 19th centuries, began to fade, in Europe, before the end of the 19th century. Today it is scarcely even referred to except to be "exposed" and refuted by pessimistic interpretations of world history. Prominent children of the ruling class have taken up Communism, Socialism, and anti-capitalist versions of fascism. The results of the first World War produced a great wave of disillusionment which engulfed especially the capitalists themselves. Both élite and masses have become susceptible in the highest degree to formulas that abandon those key terms which, when they were written into the Constitutions and Declarations of the late 18th century, seemed like eternal and irrefutable truths.

5. The unwillingness or inability to use force effectively was shown in the unprecedented growth of humanitarian sentiments and their attempted expression in all fields of social life. Reform instead of punishment was to solve the problem of domestic crime. Arbitration was to replace strikes and riots in settling internal class disputes. Imperialism was to be done away with. War was to be abolished by a League of Nations and recorded signatures on a Kellogg Pact. Such ideas, carried to such extremes, were in their own way merely reflecting the inability of the old élite to face any longer the facts of social life.

Thus, as always under analogous circumstances, a social revolution takes place. In order to remove these conditions, to solve at least sufficiently the problems out of which they grow, there occurs a drastic renewal and re-organization of the ruling class. Moreover, the general character of the new élite, though not its specific personnel, becomes clear simply through the analysis of the pre-conditions of the revolution.

The new, or re-newed, élite (as we have seen, the old élite is never wholly wiped out) must include men who are able to control contemporary mass industry, the massed labor force, and a supra-national form of political organization. This means, in place of private owners skilled in the manipulation of financial profits or losses on the market, and of the old sort of parliamentary politician, those whom I call "managers"—the production executives and organizers of the industrial process, officials trained in the manipulation of the great labor organizations, and the administrators, bureau chiefs and commissars developed in the executive branch of the unlimited modern state machines. And, that the managers may function, the economic and political structure must be modified, as it is now being modified, so as to rest no longer on private ownership and small-scale nationalist sovereignty, but primarily upon state control of the economy, and continental or vast regional world political organization.

The renewed élite will not only incorporate a large percentage of fresh elements, with a greater self-confidence and faith in the myths of a new order, but will permit—at least for a while, until it too, under the pressure of the aristocratic tendency, begins to harden—a readier entry into its own ranks. We may be sure that the soldiers, the men of force, the Lions, will be much more prominent among the new rulers than in the ruling class of the past century. This shift of weight toward the soldiers is already clear enough on a world scale. Most naturally, the war promotes it. We must, however, recognize that it is not, this time, a mere accident of war, but a far more fundamental realignment of a social unbalance which has been accumulating over many generations.

Few changes to be brought by the revolution will be more striking than this for the United States, and few are being more stubbornly disregarded. Up to the present, soldiers have had a lesser place in the social life of this country than, probably, in the case of any other great nation in history. Compared to religion, agriculture, commerce, industry, labor, finance, the army has been a social force of most trivial influence. The men with *virtù*, the ruler-types, have seldom felt any attractive pull from the military field: it offered too small a scope to those who were serious about the struggle for power.

Those days have ended. This time the soldiers are here to stay. Never again, in our time or our childrens', will the army dry up into a small puddle on the fringe of the social pond. The armed forces will henceforth be not merely quantitatively large. They will also become a major arena for the contests of the ambitious and powerful, will supply a considerable section of the ruling class of the future, and will exert a great, perhaps sometimes the decisive, influence on the social equilibrium. In what direction, internally, will the weight of the army fall? Our columnists and editors, who can discover the fate of the country depending upon some minor escapade of a labor leader or a farm lobbyist, do not seem even to have asked themselves this mighty question. But some of the soldiers, already, are beginning to ask it.*

There is only one revolution now going on. It is at different stages and proceeds through different paths in the different nations. It is, however, the first genuinely world revolution. Once, in the classical world, a social revolution could be confined to a single small city-state. Most of Europe and the Mediterranean basin took part in the revolution that led from the Roman Empire to medieval feudalism. The capitalist revolution spread still further, and its indirect effects were felt almost everywhere. Our

---

* In *The Managerial Revolution* I failed to give enough attention to this phase of the revolution. I continue to believe, as I stated in that book, that under the complex socio-economic conditions of modern civilization a stable ruling class made up almost entirely of soldiers, as were many ruling classes under more primitive conditions, cannot develop. The ruling class in our age must include those able to direct the intricate social forces of our day, and this the soldiers cannot do, except perhaps during some brief period of crisis. Nevertheless, the heightened influence which the soldiers are gaining, and will for some while maintain, constitutes one of the most significant features of the managerial revolution.

revolution, today, directly involves every part of the world. How plain this should be from the events of the war—for this war is, also for the first time, in the most strictly literal sense, a world war.

We should understand that, beginning in 1914 and prepared for some while before then, a double war has been going on, and continues. The double nature of the war corresponds to the fact that the world élite is organized in terms of two different structures: it is broken up into localized segments as the ruling class of this or that nation; and, within and across national boundaries, it is stratified into various social sub-classes and groups (capitalists, workers, farmers, managers, soldiers, and so on). Thus at one and the same time the national sections struggle for world domination, and the social sub-classes strive either to resist the general revolution or to assure their own leading positions within the new élite of the new order.

The two phases of the war are inter-related, with now one, now the other, becoming the more prominent. From 1914-7, the struggle seemed to be only between the national sections; but in 1917 the Russian Revolution brought the internal social contest into the open. Today, also, the national aspect is, for a while, the more obvious. During the intervening years, however, events in Italy and Germany and then in Spain were reminders of the second phase. In the summer of 1942 that phase again shot to the surface, with the beginning of the Indian revolution. In each of the warring nations, moreover, the internal struggle proceeds at varying intensities in a variety of forms, along with the international contest. Washington, like Moscow and Berlin, is a focus of both wars, not of one only. Not all of the participants in the revolution have yet openly appeared. There are many shocks still awaiting those who believe that this is nothing more than a very big war of one coalition of allies against another, which will end with one side, intact and victorious, writing a new Versailles.

The present war, let it be repeated once again, is a stage in a world social revolution. The real struggle is not to recapture the past, but to conquer the future. It may well be that those who most clearly understand this will emerge the victors.

2. The Meaning of Democracy

"DEMOCRACY" IS USUALLY DEFINED in some such terms as "self-government" or "government by the people." Historical experience forces us to conclude that democracy, in this sense, is impossible. The Machiavellians have shown that the practical impossibility of democracy depends upon a variety of factors: upon psychological tendencies which are apparently constant in social life, and, most decisively of all, upon the necessary technical conditions of social organization. Since our expectations of the future can be based only upon the evidence from the past, and since there is no reason to suppose that the tendencies and conditions which prevented democracy in the past will cease to hold for the future, we must, from a scientific standpoint, believe that democratic self-government is ruled out for the future as it has been absent from the past.

The theory of democracy as self-government must, therefore, be understood as a myth, formula, or derivation. It does not correspond to any actual or possible social reality. Debates over the merits of the theory are almost wholly valueless in throwing light on social facts.

It does not, however, follow that the theory of democracy (I continue to refer to democracy in the sense of "self-government" or "government by the people") is without any influence on the social structure. The theory does not correctly describe any social facts. No societies are governed by the people, by a majority; all societies, including societies called democratic, are ruled by a minority. But the ruling minority always seeks to justify and legitimize its rule in part through a formula, without which the social structure would disintegrate. The positive significance of democratic theory is as a political formula of this kind. Moreover, certain political practices are associated with the democratic formula: of particular importance, the practice of suffrage extended to a considerable proportion of the adult members of the society, whereby some questions, including the naming of certain state officials, pass through the electoral process.

The democratic formula and the practice of suffrage do not mean the self-government of the people by themselves. They do, however, constitute a special mechanism of rule by the minority élite, differing from other mechanisms. As a special mechanism of rule, they have effects upon the social structure which differ from the effects of other mechanisms of rule. In general, they exercise a particular kind of influence on the selection of members of the ruling class. When, for example, there exists in society an established ruling class that uses a non-democratic formula (an aristocratic formula, let us say) to justify its position, the influence of the democratic formula and of the suffrage machinery tends to weaken the position of that established ruling class. In addition, the existence in society of the suffrage machinery naturally tends to favor those individuals who are adept at using the machinery; just as, in a society where rule is founded directly on force, the ablest fighting men are favored against the rest.

We can see how this influence worked during the 18th century. At that time, there still existed in many nations an aristocratic section of the ruling class which used non-democratic formulas, and neither liked nor was able to manipulate the suffrage machinery. Under those conditions, the democratic formula and the introduction of wider suffrage machinery weakened the position of the older, non-democratic aristocracy, and greatly aided the newer, capitalist élite. The spread of the democratic formula and the electoral practices were an important, even essential, factor, in the rise of the capitalists to the dominant place in the modern ruling class.

However, we cannot conclude that the influence of the democratic formula and the suffrage mechanism is always the same. When circumstances change, the influence may well have quite different results, just as planting seeds may have quite different results in autumn from those that follow in spring. Circumstances today are not those of the 18th century: for one thing, there no longer exists an established ruling class making use of a non-democratic formula.

If we ask what are the primary effects in our own time of the democratic formula of self-government and the suffrage machinery, we must reply, as we noted in Part V, that they are to strengthen the international trend toward Bonapartism. It can hardly be denied that this trend exists, that it is the most indisputable political tendency of our generation. In every advanced nation we observe the evolution of the form of government toward that wherein a small group of leaders, or a single leader, claims to represent and speak for the whole people. As the embodiment of the will of the whole people, the leader claims an unlimited authority, and considers all intermediary political bodies, such as parliaments or local governments, to be wholly dependent on the central sovereignty which can alone stand legitimately for the people. The regime is democratically legalized by the use of the suffrage mechanism in the form of plebiscites. These are the characteristics of Bonapartism. We find them completely developed in Germany and Russia; and more and more closely approximated in England and the United States.

Bonapartism is a type of government very dissimilar to what men in the 19th century ordinarily thought of as democracy. Nevertheless, as we have already seen, Bonapartism does not violate the formula of democracy nor the place assigned to suffrage. Rather can Bonapartist theory plausibly claim to be the logical as well as the historical culmination of the democratic formula, just as the plebiscite can claim to be the most perfect form of democratic suffrage. The Bonapartist leader can regard himself, and be regarded, as the quintessential democrat; his despotism is simply the omnipotent people ruling and disciplining itself. This is just what the Bonapartist leaders themselves, and their spokesmen, argue. When democracy is defined in terms of self-government, there can be no convincing democratic answer.

When we translate formal meanings into real meanings, by the method used in Part I to unravel Dante's politics, "the people's century," "the century of the common man," become, like "the people's state" and "the classless society," variant expressions the real meaning of which is "the century of political Bonapartism" or "the Bonapartist state."

Striking support for this conclusion is provided by the speeches and writings of Vice-President Wallace, who is the major prophet, in this country, of the Bonapartist *mystique*. Wallace, it may be recalled, never held elective office prior to 1941. It is unanimously agreed that he is in his present position solely because of the personal demand of the President, which was counter to the prior wishes of almost all the delegates to the 1940 Convention of the Democratic party. Wallace's nomination by the Convention, and his share in Roosevelt's electoral victory, was, thus, not a voluntary expression of the will of either the delegates or the people at large, but a plebiscitary confirmation of a decision made in fact by a leader.

Wallace's most remarkable expression, so far, of his point of view was the speech which he delivered at Madison Square Garden, New York City, on November 8, 1942. His mere presence at the meeting was sufficiently indicative. It was organized by a committee, created by the American representatives of the Communist International, which called itself the "Congress of American-Soviet Friendship." Its occasion was the celebration of the 25th anniversary of "the Russian revolution." The press overlooked the detail that the revolution in question was not the revolution against Czarism, which took place in March, 1917, but the November Bolshevik revolution against the parliamentary-democratic government of Kerensky, the revolution which in its development has led to the most extreme totalitarian-Bonapartist government in history. Wallace opened his speech as follows: "We have been helping the Russians celebrate this afternoon a glorious birthday."

Only the first three paragraphs of the speech contain any references to the present war. The rest is a comparative social commentary on Russia and the United States, and a statement of social program. After quoting some century-old words of Tocqueville on Russia, Wallace discovers that "Russia and the United States are far closer than Tocqueville could possibly have imagined." "Both," he declares, "are striving for the education, the productivity and the enduring happiness of the common man."

Wallace's goal, in common with Russia's, is "the new democracy, the democracy of the common man." This new democracy "includes not only the Bill of Rights, but also economic democracy, ethnic democracy, educational democracy, and democracy in the treatment of the sexes," all of which "must be woven together into a harmonious whole." Of these five types which make up the harmonious whole of the democracy of the common man, Wallace finds Russia today to be far superior in four, all but "Bill of Rights democracy." Let us not imagine that this is a Russian defect. "Some in the United States"—and the context makes clear that Wallace numbers himself among them—"believe that we have over-emphasized what might be called political or Bill-of-Rights democracy. Carried to its extreme form, it leads to rugged individualism, exploitation, impractical emphasis on States' rights, and even to anarchy." *

Two months before this speech of Wallace's, an interesting expression of another facet of Bonapartist doctrine occurred in the sudden message by which the President ordered Congress to pass new anti-inflation legislation. The President said: "I ask the Congress to take this action by the first of October. Inaction on your part by that date will leave me with an inescapable responsibility to the people of the country to see to it that the war effort is no longer imperiled by threat of economic chaos. In the event that the Congress should fail to act, and act adequately, I shall accept the responsibility, and I will act. At the same time that farm prices are stabilized, wages can and will be stabilized also. This I will do. . . . When the war is won, the powers under which I act automatically revert to the people—to whom they belong." In this short passage, there is much rich material for future research in United States constitutional history. It is particularly enlightening to understand that the Executive, as the directly responsible agent of the people, is now able to supersede Congress, and that the powers under which the Executive is now acting are derived not from Congressional legislation but, again, directly from the people—who, to judge from the implication of the last sentence, have for the time being turned them over to the Executive, who can exercise them as unlimited attorney (if the people had not given up their powers to the Executive, there would be no meaning in the promise that, after the war, the powers would "revert to the people").

* My quotations are from the text printed in the New York *Times,* Nov. 9, 1942. As in the case of all derivations, Wallace's words have no correlation whatever with the facts. Disregarding the fantastic statements he made about Russian conditions (which I have not quoted), the above notions about the social consequences of "Bill of Rights democracy" are utter nonsense from the point of view of historical science. They are nonetheless significant as expressions of attitudes and residues.

When we keep in mind the connection between Bonapartism and the formula of democracy as government by the people, we should not be surprised by what might otherwise seem to be a paradoxical political phenomenon: the rapidly growing number of individuals in this country who may properly be called "democratic totalitarians." Pathological newspapers like New York's *PM,* frustrated poets like Archibald MacLeish, choleric bureaucrats like Harold Ickes, gutter-columnists, like Walter Winchell, trying to crawl out of the gutter, guilt-ridden bankers' sons, like Corliss Lamont, authors, like Walter Millis, trying to lead the public to forget that once they thought there was something to be said against war, ambitious detective-story writers, like Rex Stout, ministers enjoying the platforms that they get from fellow-traveling with the Communist party—these people are, as we can readily discover from their speeches and articles and books, the most extreme democrats in the country and quite possibly in the world. In the name of their democracy, they preach the attitudes of Bonapartism, and they advocate the suppression of the specific institutions and the specific rights and freedoms that still protect the individual from the advance of the unbridled state.

Huey Long knew much more about politics than these persons will ever know. When he said that if fascism destroys democracy in this country, it will do so in the name of democracy, he was correctly predicting the role that the democratic totalitarians are today playing. His opinion, expanded into the language we have been using, may be put as follows: the Bonapartist development of the democratic formula of self-government will be used in the attempt to destroy those concrete individual and social rights which were once also associated with the idea of democracy.

It should not be imagined that this phenomenon is confined to the United States. Some people have the naïve opinion that in other countries despotism was established in the name of despotism, that dictators who were in the process of destroying freedom made clear to the people that they were doing just that. Naturally, it never happens that way. The modern despotisms have all marched to the tune of "the workers" or "the people." The Stalinist Constitution of 1936 is, we are assured, the most democratic in the world. Nazism expresses, according to its own account, the aspirations and highest freedom of the entire German people, and, indeed, when Europe begins to get conquered by Germany, of all European peoples; and would doubtless do the same for the peoples of the whole world, if Nazi arms should be fully successful. Honest men have never been able to get an exclusive patent on the words of democracy.

* * *

Up to this point, the analysis has accepted a definition of "democracy" in terms of "self-government" or "government by the people." The analysis holds only for democracy interpreted in this way. The truth is, however, that there are other meanings commonly associated with the word "democracy," which have nothing to do with "self-government." *

If we examine, not the verbal definitions that most people, including dictionary-makers, give for "democracy," but the way in which they use the word in practical application to affairs of our time, we will discover that it does not have anything to do with self-government—which is not surprising, because there is no such thing. In practice, in the real world rather than the mythical world of ideologies, a "democracy" means a political system in which there exists "liberty": that is, what Mosca calls "juridical

---

* One such meaning, as we have seen, refers to a social structure in which there is fairly rapid class circulation, in which it is relatively easy for members of the non-élite or their children to rise into the élite. I am not concerned here with this meaning, which has already been discussed at some length. The Machiavellians unanimously believe that rapid class circulation contributes to the strength and happiness of a society.

defense," a measure of security for the individual which protects him from the arbitrary and irresponsible exercise of personally held power. Liberty or juridical defense, moreover, is summed up and focused in the *right of opposition,* the right of opponents of the currently governing élite to express publicly their opposition views and to organize to implement those views.

Democracy so defined, in terms of liberty, of the right of opposition, is not in the least a formula or myth. We will never be able to decide whether the democratic wills of their respective peoples are more truly represented by the governments of the United States and England than by the governments of Japan, Germany, Russia, and Italy. We cannot decide because the whole problem is fictitious and the disputes in connection with it purely verbal.* But it is a fact, an objective and observable fact, that liberty exists in some societies and not in others; or, more exactly speaking, that it exists more in some societies, less in others. It is a fact that today there exists more liberty, much more, in England or the United States, than in Germany, Russia, Italy or Japan; and it is also a fact that in the United States today there is less liberty than 15 or even 2 or 3 years ago.

The modern Machiavellians, like Machiavelli himself, do not waste time arguing the merits or demerits of the myth of democracy defined as self-government. But they are very profoundly concerned with the reality of democracy defined as liberty. They know that the degree of liberty present within a society is a fact of the greatest consequence for the character of the whole social structure and for the individuals living within that structure.

What does liberty, juridical defense, the right of opposition, mean for a society? Let us examine the conclusions reached by

---

* This is the reason, by the way, why democratic statesmen are always getting themselves into a jam when they promise, as seems to be required by the democratic formula, that all peoples shall have governments of their own choosing. Someone can always raise the awkard point that the German people may prefer Hitler, or the Japanese, the Mikado.

the Machiavellian analysis of this question. I shall disregard the effect of the presence or absence of liberty on individual self-development (great and significant as this seems to me to be) because this would lead to problems of subjective moral evaluation which I wish to avoid; I shall confine myself to observable distinctions of a sort that may be called sociological.

Within any field of human interest, liberty is a necessary condition of scientific advance. This follows because science can proceed only where there is complete freedom to advance hypotheses contrary to prevailing opinion. Pareto, indeed, considers liberty to be an indispensable requirement of scientific method: "It follows that before a theory can be considered true, it is virtually indispensable that there be perfect freedom to impugn it. Any limitation, even indirect and however remote, imposed on anyone choosing to contradict it is enough to cast suspicion upon it. Hence freedom to express one's thought, even counter to the opinion of the majority or of all, even when it offends the sentiments of the few or of the many, even when it is generally reputed absurd or criminal, always proves favorable to the discovery of objective truth." * It must be added that it is possible for liberty to remain within restricted scientific fields (the physical sciences, for example) even when it has disappeared in political and social affairs generally. Nevertheless, under such conditions, its continuance in the restricted fields would seem to be precarious, as is indicated by the political intervention of modern totalitarian governments (especially Russia and Germany) to suppress or lessen liberty in fields like biology, and even physics.

Experience seems to show that, almost always, liberty is a condition for an advanced "level of civilization," in the sense that Mosca uses this expression. That is, liberty is needed to permit

* From *Mind and Society* (568), by Vilfredo Pareto, translated by Arthur Livingston and Andrew Bongiorno, copyright, 1935, by Harcourt, Brace and Company, Inc.

the fullest release of the potential social forces and creative impulses present in society, and their maximum development. With liberty absent, great development may occur along certain restricted lines—in religion, perhaps, or the technique of war, or a conventionalized art style—but the compulsory conformity to official opinion limits variety and stultifies creative freshness not only in the arts and sciences, but in economic and political affairs as well.

Liberty or freedom* means above all, as I have said, the existence of a public opposition to the governing élite. The crucial difference that freedom makes to a society is found in the fact that the existence of a public opposition (or oppositions) is the only effective check on the power of the governing élite.

The Machiavellians are the only ones who have told us the full truth about power. Other writers have at most told the truth only about groups other than the ones for which they themselves speak. The Machiavellians present the complete record: the primary object, in practice, of all rulers is to serve their own interest, to maintain their own power and privilege. There are no exceptions. No theory, no promises, no morality, no amount of good will, no religion will restrain power. Neither priests nor soldiers, neither labor leaders nor businessmen, neither bureaucrats nor feudal lords will differ from each other in the basic use which they will seek to make of power. Individual saints, exempt in individual intention from the law of power, will nevertheless be always bound to it through the disciples, associates, and followers to whom they cannot, in organized social life, avoid being tied.

Only power restrains power. That restraining power is expressed in the existence and activity of oppositions. Oddly and fortunately, it is observable that the restraining influence of an opposition much exceeds its apparent strength. As anyone with

---

* I am using the term "freedom" as equivalent in meaning to "liberty."

experience in any organization knows, even a small opposition, provided it really exists and is active, can block to a remarkable degree the excesses of the leadership. But when all opposition is destroyed, there is no longer any limit to what power may do. A despotism, any kind of despotism, can be benevolent only by accident.

It may, however, be argued, as it is by anarchists and by the sectarian wing of Marxism, that the influence of the opposition in restraining the power of the rulers is after all of small importance to the non-élite, to the masses. When an opposition exists, this means only that there is a division in the ruling class; if an "out-élite" replaces the governing élite, this is only a change in the personnel of the rulers. The masses remain still the ruled. Why should they be concerned? and of what interest is the whole process for the great majority?

It is true that the opposition is only a section of the élite as a whole. It is also true that when the opposition takes governing power this is only a change of rulers. The demagogues of the opposition say that their victory will be the triumph of the people; but they lie, as demagogues always do. Nevertheless, the seeming conclusion does not follow; it is not true that the activities of the oppositions are a matter of indifference for the masses. Through a curious and indirect route by way of freedom, we return to self-government, which we were unable to discover by any direct path.

The existence of an opposition means a cleavage in the ruling class. Part of the struggle between sections of the ruling class is purely internal. Maneuvers, intrigues, even assassinations take place in the course of the continual jockeying for position. When, however, the opposition is public, this means that the conflicts cannot be solved merely by internal changes in the existing élite. The opposition is forced to undertake external moves, beyond the limits of the ruling class. Since rule depends upon the ability to control the existing social forces, the opposition seeks to draw forces to its side, and to win over new leaders who are coming up from the ranks of society. In this attempt it must promise certain benefits to various groups; if successful, it must keep at least a few of the promises. At the same time, the struggle stimulates new demands by many groups, even by the non-élite. Finally, the opposition must seek to destroy the prestige of the governing élite by exposing the inequities of its rule, which it knows much better than do the masses.

Confronted with this multiple attack, the governing élite, in order to try to keep control, is in turn compelled to grant certain concessions and to correct at least some of the more glaring abuses. The net indirect result of the struggle, which from one point of view is only a fight among two sets of leaders, can thus be benefits for large sections of the masses. The masses, blocked by the iron law of oligarchy from directly and deliberately ruling themselves, are able to limit and control, indirectly, the power of their rulers. The myth of self-government is translated into a measure of reality by the fact of freedom.

These, then, are the primary effects of political liberty, of freedom, upon the social structure. However, the question of liberty does not end, as the Machiavellians again relentlessly show, at the bare political level. They explain not merely what liberty is, what it means for society, but also what the conditions are for its preservation. The right of public opposition to the rulers, the heart of freedom, will not be kept alive merely by wishing—and it is besides very doubtful that a majority of men are much concerned about it one way or the other. It requires the existence in society of a number of relatively autonomous "social forces," as Mosca calls them. It demands that no single social force—the army or liquid wealth or the Church or industrial management or agriculture or labor or the state machine, whatever it might be—shall be strong enough to swallow up the rest and thereby be in a position to dominate all phases of social life. When this happens, there cannot be a significant opposition to the rulers, because the opposition cannot have any social weight and therefore cannot restrain the power of the rulers. It is only when there are several different major social forces, not wholly subordinated to any one social force, that there can be any assurance of liberty, since only then is there the mutual check and balance that is able to chain power. There is no one force, no group, and no class that is the preserver of liberty. Liberty is preserved by those who are against the existing chief power. Oppositions which do not express genuine social forces are as trivial, in relation to entrenched power, as the old court jesters.

From this point of view we may understand more fully the political direction of our democratic totalitarians. The state, they say, when it is led by their leader—and it will always be, because they take as their leader the one who happens to be in the saddle—is the people. Democracy is the supremacy of the people. Therefore, democracy is the supremacy of the state. Whenever the state absorbs another phase of social life, that is a victory for democracy. And therefore, more particularly: a serious critic of the state or its policies is a fifth columnist and a traitor. "Pressure groups," as they call them—that is, those groups whose activities simply represent the interplay of autonomous social forces, which is the only foundation for liberty—are saboteurs of democracy. The Church is fascist if it wants to have its own schools, independent of the state-controlled educational system. John L. Lewis is a Nazi if he refuses to allow his section of the labor movement to be integrated into the state labor machinery. Industrial management is playing the game of the enemy if it points out that even state bureaus are wrong when they declare that more steel can be made by following abstract political aims than by accepting the consequences of modern technology. Teachers are spies if they wish to control, on the claim of expert knowledge and proficiency, the presentation of their subjects. Farmers are slackers if they argue that they cannot raise more dairy products with no hands to milk their cows. Skeptics are notorious reactionaries if they doubt, however mildly, that state control will of itself draw all the viciousness from private monopolies, or free the press and radio from all distortion of the news.

The policies of the democratic totalitarians are consistent with each other, and consistent with what they mean by "democracy." And they are consistent also in being uniformly directed against the foundations of freedom. Not unity but difference, not the modern state but whatever is able to maintain itself against the state, not leaders but the unyielding opponents of leaders, not conformity with official opinion but persisting criticism, are the defenses of freedom.

A considerable degree of liberty is not usual in human society. If we review the history of humanity, so far as we know it, it is apparent that despotic regimes are far more frequent than free regimes, and it would therefore seem that despotism is more nearly than freedom in accord with human nature. Moreover, special circumstances of our time count heavily against freedom. Pareto shows how the maximum external strength of a community in its struggle against other communities for survival need not at all coincide with a maximum of internal welfare for the members of the community. We are now at a period when the external struggle for survival is at the most acute possible juncture. Many sincere men feel that liberty, even though it may contribute most to internal welfare, cannot stand up against despotism in the external struggle. Liberty, they argue, means too much dissipation of energy, too much delay, too much division. These feelings make it easier for them to accept the loss of liberty as an inevitable destiny.

Then, in the economic structure, the economic arrangements which during the past several centuries aided political liberty, are being rapidly swept away. Private-capitalist ownership of the economy meant a dispersion of economic power and a partial separation between economic and other social forces in a manner that prevented the concentration of an overwhelming single social force. Today the advance of the managerial revolution is everywhere concentrating economic power in the state apparatus, where it tends to unite with control over the other great social forces—the army, education, labor, law, the political bureaucracy, art, and science even. This development, too, tends to destroy the basis for those social oppositions that keep freedom alive.

It would be absurd to deny how much these two factors darken the prospects of freedom for our time. Nevertheless, I am not yet convinced that they are sufficient to make freedom impossible. The argument that a free structure of society is not so strong externally as a despotic structure, and therefore must be given up in an era of wars and revolutions, seems to me unproved, and not a little suspicious. Whether valid or not, the argument is certainly a convenient cover under which a despotic regime may be imposed upon a free society.

Liberty, with its right of public opposition, does often delay decisions, and undoubtedly expends social energies on internal conflicts. Both of these consequences make for external weakness. But it may well be that this is more than compensated for by two other consequences of liberty, as against despotism. Under a free regime there is more chance for the development and utilization of creative forces and individuals that cannot get expression under a despotism. And, second, public criticism by an opposition exposes, and tends to force correction of, mistakes on the part of the governing élite which might prove fatal if too long and stubbornly maintained.

The importance to survival of this critical function of an opposition, which can be effective only where freedom is retained, may be illustrated by direct examples, both positive and negative.

On many occasions during the Civil War, the activities of the extremist "Black Republicans" in Congress were a temporary handicap; but it is very doubtful that the North would have won the war if it had not been for their bitter and relentless criticism of the Administration and the compromisers. During the War of 1914, a wider leeway for public opposition would almost surely have forced the British leadership to adopt the tank at least a year sooner than it did, with a probable consequent saving of many lives, and a quicker victory. In the present War, Germany might well have avoided some grave strategic errors, particularly in connection with the Russian campaigns, if a measure of freedom in Germany had permitted the existence of an active, public opposition. In this country, the extreme airpower advocates have not made their total view acceptable; but their vigorous public propaganda has undoubtedly been a major influence in correcting somewhat the hopelessly out-dated views that prevailed at the top of the armed forces and the Administration. Without the public criticism of the production program, especially in steel, oil, and rubber, and the critical work of the Congressional investigating committees, the internal war program would by now be close to collapse.

As for the economic threat, it would seem to be true that, since economic power comprises in all so large a percentage of total social power, the full concentration of all economic power in a centralized state apparatus would necessarily destroy the foundations of liberty. This conclusion, demonstrated theoretically by the modern Machiavellians, has been proved empirically by the history of the Soviet Union. No other social force can, under such circumstances, retain sufficient independence to support liberty. All social forces are either eliminated or absorbed by the centralized state. Private-capitalist property rights in the instruments of production meant—even under trust or monopoly conditions in many branches of industry—a sufficient fragmentation of economic power to provide a basis for freedom. Nevertheless, it does not follow that the elimination of private-capitalist property rights must do away with every possible basis for political freedom. Freedom or liberty, in the specific meaning that is being given to these terms in this chapter, has existed, at least in some degree, along with economic structures which were not capitalist: under slave or feudal structures, for example. Freedom does require that all economic power should not be centralized, but there are other means than capitalist property rights to prevent such centralization.

During the past generation, capitalist property rights have in any case been becoming more and more nominal. If they were largely done away with, if most property rights in the instruments of production were vested formally in the state, economic power could still be divided. The state itself, for instance, could be decentralized. Or the economic forces could be divided along functional or syndicalist lines: management, workers, consumers, or differing branches of industry, could operate as separate organized groups with relative independence. Instead of the old capitalist economic market, constituted by the operations of individual owners, there would be a new kind of market constituted by the operations of the functional and syndicalist groups as units, and by the various relevant institutions of the state. A development of this kind, far from being a fantasy, is already prepared for in many respects by the structural economic changes of recent decades.

The Marxists and the democratic totalitarians claim that freedom can now be secured only by concentrating all social forces and especially economic forces in the state which, when they or their friends are running it, they identify with the people. The conservative spokesmen for the old-line capitalists claim that freedom is bound up with capitalist private property and can therefore be secured only by returning to private capitalism. The two groups are, though for different reasons, both wrong; or, rather, their arguments and programs are both simply myths that express, not movements for political liberty, but a contest for control over the despotic and Bonapartist political order which they both anticipate. The concentration of all social forces in the state would in fact destroy all possibility of freedom. On the other hand, it is false that capitalist private property is the only foundation for political freedom; and it is in any case impossible to return to private capitalism.

We cannot, I think, state with any assurance what chances freedom has for surviving during the next historical period. But we do know something of the conditions under which it is possible for freedom to survive. We know that its fate will not be decided by the war nor by economic changes alone nor even by the general character of the great social revolution through which we are traveling. Political freedom is the resultant of unresolved conflicts among various sections of the élite. The existence of these conflicts is in turn correlated with the interplay of diverse social forces that preserve at least a considerable degree of independence. The future of liberty will, therefore, depend upon the extent to which, whether by necessary accident or conscious design, society is kept from freezing.

3. Can Politics Be Scientific?

DURING THE 18th and 19th centuries, and still in many quarters at the present time, theorists have raised the question whether politics can be scientific. It has generally been assumed that an affirmative answer would be a ground for optimism: that is, if politics could be and were scientific, it has been assumed that this would contribute to the welfare of mankind. John Dewey, the leading American philosopher, and his followers continue to debate this problem, to give an affirmative answer, and to maintain an attitude of social optimism.

It was natural that the question should be raised. From the 16th century on, the application of scientific method to one after another field of human interest, other than social affairs, has uniformly resulted in human triumphs with respect to those fields. In every field, science has solved relevant problems; indeed, science is in one sense merely the systematic method for solving relevant problems. If this is the case with mathematics, astronomy, physics, chemistry, geology, why should it not also be with society? Why could we not solve the most important problems of all, those of social and political life, by applying science?

These hopes in science reflected a wider optimism, both about what science could do and about the possibilities of social progress, which, from the point of view of the social achievements of the 18th and 19th centuries, seemed unlimited. In our time an anti-scientific attitude has been forming, at least toward the question of applying science to society. This, in turn, seems to reflect a pessimism both about what science can do and about all utopian social ideals. The idea of progress is running the usual course from self-evident article of faith to empty illusion.

Let us try to answer this question by reference to the facts, without attempting to justify an attitude of either optimism or pessimism. Granted the facts, optimism and pessimism are, after all, a matter of temperament. It is at once apparent that the broad question, "Can politics be scientific?" is ambiguous. It must be resolved into several more precise questions before answers become possible. The three of these with which I shall deal are the following: (1) Can there be a science of politics (and of society, since politics is a phase of social life)? (2) Can the masses act scientifically in political affairs? (3) Can the élite, or some section of the élite, act scientifically in political affairs?

The first of these narrower questions can be answered easily and with assurance: Yes, there can be a science of politics and of society. There is no insuperable obstacle to such a science. It is certainly the case that in the field of political and social affairs there are observable events. These events may be recorded and systematically described. On the basis of the observations, we may formulate generalizations and hypotheses. These can then be tested through predictions about future events, or about the results of further research. In order to make a science possible in any field, nothing further is required.

Of course it may be readily granted that there are serious practical difficulties in the way of social and political science. It is often argued that the subject-matter—human group actions—is extremely complicated; and this is so, though the subject-matter of a number of the other sciences is also rather complicated. A more direct and peculiar difficulty consists in the unwillingness of men to adopt a scientific attitude toward the study of political and social events, or to apply the canons of scientific procedure. "Sentiment," as Pareto would call it, interferes. A physicist would find it ludicrous if every treatise in his field habitually included a plan for curing the ills of mankind, and selected facts—and fictions—with the chief aim of proving the desirability of that plan. Yet, in 99% of the articles and books which pretend to tell us the way society works, such a method is accepted, without comment, as normal. More particularly and deliberately, the public application of scientific method to politics is interfered with by those who are powerful. They do not want genuine political knowledge to be available, and they block freedom of inquiry whenever it threatens, as it so often threatens, to undermine their power. From the time of the Greek sophists until today, everyone who, by objective inquiry, discloses some of the truth about power has been denounced by official opinion as subversive.

Because of these obstacles, which do not seem to be temporary, we should not expect too much in the way of results from political and social science. Nevertheless, such a science is not a mere theoretical possibility. We have already at our disposal a science of society, incomplete and undeveloped no doubt, but actual. The truths so far discovered by this science are of two kinds.

Fairly exact results have been obtained about problems of limited range. When care is taken not to project the conclusions too far beyond the temporal and spatial boundaries within which the data have been gathered, statistical conclusions dealing with mortality, diseases, certain economic facts, suicide, crime, literacy, trade movements, all illustrate these results. They are the primary and most fruitful achievement of academic social research.

At the other end, rough laws have been discovered about large-scale and long-term social and political movements. These are the achievement of, for example and outstandingly, the Machiavellians; many instances are given in this book. However, most of them may also be found (often somewhat differently worded, but similar in content) in the works of other social scientists from the time of Karl Marx* onward.

We have available, indeed, much more knowledge about society than is ordinarily recognized—and far more than is ever used. There is a widespread misunderstanding about the nature of scientific knowledge, partly fostered by academic scientists who prefer their profession to remain an esoteric cult. The statements, for example, that bodies when unsupported fall toward the surface of the earth and that water runs down hill, are a long way from the mathematically formulated law of gravity. Interpreted literally, they are in fact false, as the behavior of feathers and airplanes and siphons and pumps shows. Nevertheless, they are genuinely scientific, and, at a somewhat crude level of experience, they may properly be considered true. They are what Pareto calls "first approximations," and correctly enough generalize a vast number of observable facts. Moreover, they are very useful pieces of knowledge as guides to deliberate action. We may, on their basis, be advised to take pains to avoid a stone if we see it toppling over a building or a cliff above us; or to build a house or a village below rather than above a spring if we want the water to flow in. It would seem rather pedantic for an expert in physics to tell us, first, that our crude generalization about falling bodies is absolutely false because there are facts (as there are) which disagree with it; and, second, that therefore we have no right, on the basis of such falsity, to step aside from the path of the stone. This, however, is just the way that some of the academic experts reason and advise about social matters.

We have at our disposal a considerable body of knowledge of this "first approximation" sort. One example would be the rough

* Pareto had little use for Marx' economic theories, which he considered for the most part absurd metaphysics. However, in *Les systèmes socialistes,* he writes: "The sociological part of Marx' work is, from a scientific standpoint, far superior to the economic part." (Vol. II, p. 386.) In particular he notes that the conception of the class struggle is "profoundly true" (Vol. II, p. 393).

POLITICS AND TRUTH

laws of social revolution which we have examined in their application to the present period; or the summary list of Machiavellian principles stated at the beginning of this Part, as well as innumerable applications which can be made of these principles. There is enough knowledge at hand to have enabled us to realize that the Kellogg Pact was powerless to prevent war, and that the "Stimson doctrine" of non-recognition of territorial changes made by force never has and never will stop changes from being made by force. Professional New York gamblers, it is interesting to note, have never since the Civil War been wrong about the outcome of a Presidential election.* We know enough to be able to say now that there will almost certainly be a terrific economic crisis shortly after the end of the present war—though this expectation will be carefully obscured by the parties at interest. We can predict, with reasonable assurance, that the public debt of this and of almost all other countries will either be repudiated outright, or reduced indirectly through a lowering of interest rates, inflation, or some other similar device. Reasoning on the analogy of comparable historical periods, we may conclude that the trend away from private capitalism is irreversible.

Our scientific statements about social matters must often, it is true, be put in conditional form: if other things remain the same, if such-and-such does not take place, then so-and-so will probably happen. (There is, however, an implied condition in most if not all the statements within all the sciences.) Thus we now may know, with considerable probability, that: if the state absorbs under centralized control all major social forces, then political

---

* I base this statement on my personal knowledge from the Harding (1920) election on; and, for the elections prior to 1920, on the memory and research of Jack Doyle, who was, until his death in December, 1942, the outstanding authority in this field. He had been unable to trace the record back beyond the Civil War. During most of the 1916 campaign, the professional odds favored Hughes; but they were changed to favor Wilson forty-eight hours before the election took place.

liberty will disappear; if, after this war, Europe is again divided into a considerable number of independent sovereign states, then a new war will begin in Europe within a comparatively short time; if the present plan of military strategy (i.e., submarine attrition warfare, and "island-hopping") continues unchanged in the East, then Japan will not be definitely crushed for many, many years, and perhaps never; if the present Administration plans to remain in office after 1944, then it will have to curtail political liberty further; and so on. Such knowledge and much more is available: available but not, of course, used.

Let us turn to the second question into which we have analyzed the general problem of science and politics: can the masses act scientifically in political affairs? To act scientifically would mean to act "logically" in Pareto's sense; that is, to select, consciously and deliberately, real goals (goals which are not transcendental or fanciful or impossible), and then to take practical steps which are, in fact, appropriate for reaching those goals. The goals might be peace or a higher level of material prosperity or economic equality—though conceivably they might be quite different: war or conquest or moral license; we should not make the mistake of supposing that everyone really wants the things that moralists say they ought to want. In any case, the goals would be explicit, deliberately chosen; and the actions would really achieve or at least approach the goals.

This question, as Professor Dewey has often shown, is very similar to the question whether full and genuine self-government of the masses by themselves is possible. For a group to act scientifically presupposes that its decisions are reached on a democratic basis, because otherwise the decisions are not deliberate from the point of view of the group itself. In concluding that self-government of the masses is impossible, it therefore also follows that it is impossible for the masses to act scientifically in political affairs.

The Machiavellian analysis, confirmed and re-confirmed by the evidence of history, shows that the masses simply do not think scientifically about political and social aims; and that, even if they did, the technical and administrative means for implementing their scientific thought would necessarily be lacking. Beliefs, ideals, do sometimes influence the political actions of the masses; these are not, however, scientific beliefs and ideals, but myths or derivations.

There is, moreover, no reason to expect a change in this respect in the foreseeable future. During the 19th century it was thought by many that universal education would enable the masses to be scientific about politics and thereby reach a perfect democracy. This expectation has proved unfounded. In most great nations, illiteracy has been almost done away with. Nevertheless, the masses act no more scientifically today than a century or a millennium ago. In political affairs, the scientific potentialities of wider literacy have been more than counter-balanced by the new opportunities which mass education gives to non-scientific propaganda. At the same time, the ever-increasing size and complexity of modern social structures raise constantly new technical obstacles to the direct application of scientific procedures by the masses to their own political problems.

Many modern politicians habitually tell the people that "their fate is in their own hands," they rule themselves, they make the final and fundamental decisions, they are the court of last appeal. Remarks of this kind are all derivations expressing some variant of the democratic formulas. Their real purpose is to enable the politicians, while ruling in their own interests, to protect their regime by the moral sanction of the myth of the popular will.

An honest statement to the masses, which by the nature of the case a politician cannot give, would have to say: you cannot rule yourselves; distrust all leaders, and above all those who tell you that they are merely expressing or representing your will; erect and cherish every possible safeguard against the unchecked exercise of power. Even though such a statement is never made, there are many among the masses who understand its meaning without being told. The great anti-fascist novelist, Ignazio Silone, writes: * "The *cafone* [which may be approximately translated as 'small farmer' or 'sharecropper'] is by no means primitive; in one sense he is overcivilized. The experience of generations makes him believe that the State is merely a better organized Camorra [i.e., racket]. . . . Marx often speaks of the peasants as having torpid minds, but what did he know about them? I imagine that he watched them in the marketplace at Trier and observed that they were sullen and tongue-tied. He would not stop to think that they had assumed this role deliberately." An American Silone might mention, in the same connection, groups of farmers or industrial workers who passively listen, one day, to patriotic rhetoric about "equal sacrifice"; and, the next, demand higher prices or wages. It is by adopting attitudes of this kind that the masses come closest to being scientific about politics.

It is ludicrous for the authors of books like this one—that is, serious books about society—to pretend to speak to "the people." The great bulk of the people in this country neither buys nor reads any books at all—thereby avoiding a great quantity of nonsense. The potential audience for this sort of book is, as statistics show, limited to a comparatively small section of the élite.† The absurdity does not at all prevent the authors from covering page after page with rhetorical advice to the masses about what they can and should do to run society for their own welfare and interest.

The words of the politicians do, however, reach the masses; and when the politicians say these things, it is not absurd but

* *The New Republic*, Nov. 2, 1942.
† The average sale is less than 2,000 copies, with a rare maximum of 40,000 or 50,000.

ominous. When it is accepted that the rulers rule as the mere agents for the will of the masses, then their rule becomes irresponsible. The rulers are no longer personally accountable for their actions: they may go to war, persecute, steal, violate freedoms, fail to prepare for social or military crises, and yet never be brought to task for whatever crime or failure—they have only, they say, carried out the people's will; if the masses are stupid or selfish or easy-going or short-sighted, who are their humble rulers to be blamed? * Small wonder that rulers do not encourage the growth of a science of politics!

There remains, then, the question whether some sections of the élite can act scientifically about political affairs. It is necessary to raise the question in this modified form, rather than about the élite as a whole, because the élite is not ordinarily a homogeneous group.

There is little doubt that an individual can conduct his political affairs scientifically or logically. For example, an individual, granted certain capacities and some luck, can decide to rise in the social scale, and can take appropriate steps that will have a fair chance of achieving that aim. In some cases, individuals can, by deliberate scientific means, rise into the very top rank of social and political power.

It is to be observed in these latter cases that ordinarily the single individual is not operating as an isolated unit. There are associated with him various other individuals, together forming a group more or less large. The most conspicuous individual may become premier or king or dictator; but power is really acquired by the group, not by any single individual. Nowadays these

* This is the underlying thesis of the State Department's "White Paper," *Peace and War*, which was issued in January, 1943. As the magazine, *Life*, correctly notes: "It justifies itself for doing what [the State Department claims that] the people wanted by proving that the Department knew all along that what the people wanted was wrong."

groups will include, as a rule, certain experts in propaganda, public relations, and organizational skills, as well as one or more "theoreticians."

This sort of group constitutes a section of the élite, and there seems in general to be no reason why sections of the élite cannot function scientifically, at least within limits.

The inability of the masses to function scientifically in politics rests primarily on the following factors: the huge size of the mass group, which makes it too unwieldy for the use of scientific techniques; the ignorance, on the part of the masses, of the methods of administration and rule; the necessity, for the masses, of spending most of their energies on the bare making of a living, which leaves little energy or time for gaining more knowledge about politics or carrying out practical political tasks; the lack, in most people, of a sufficient degree of those psychological qualities—ambition, ruthlessness, and so on—that are prerequisites for active political life.

The deficiences can all be overcome in the case of sections of the élite. These are comparatively small in size. Their members can and do acquire a good deal of knowledge about administration and rule. Since their members either inherit or discover a way of extracting a living from others without too much effort on their own part, they have available time and energy in which to cultivate political skills. They are careful not to overburden their ranks with squeamish idealists. There would thus seem to be no theoretic reason why sections of the élite should not be scientific about political affairs. If our reference is to the governing élite, we are asking whether rulers can rule scientifically; and the answer would seem to be that, up to a certain point, they can. We may add that, at certain periods in certain societies, they have done so, or come close to it.

What exactly would this mean, for the rulers or some other

POLITICS AND TRUTH   265

section of the élite to be scientific about political affairs? And, if they were, would it be to the benefit of society as a whole?

It would mean, as always when conduct is scientific, that the section in question would pursue consciously understood and deliberately chosen goals. The goals would have to be real and possible. From these conditions it follows that the choice of alternative goals would be confined within very narrow limits. All utopias would be excluded, all those mirages of permanent and universal peace and plenty and joy. Moreover, since the general pattern of social development is determined by technological change and by other factors quite beyond the likelihood of human control, a scientific élite would have to accept that general pattern. It was an illusion, in 1800, to think that society could revive the social structure appropriate to the pre-steam-engine era; so today is it an illusion to dream that the 19th century structure can be retained on the technological basis of the assembly line, the airplane, electricity, and radio. From this point of view, we may say that a scientific élite would have to be "opportunist"— not in the narrower sense in which opportunism means taking the easiest course today with no clear thought of tomorrow, but in the broader perspective of not trying to buck the main stream of development, not fighting for causes that are already lost when the battle begins.

In short, a scientific ruling group would not guide its political actions by myths. We must, however, repeat that our concern is only with political actions. Just as a man thoroughly scientific in the field of physics can accept the most naïve myths in the field of politics, so can another whose political actions are consistently scientific nevertheless believe all sorts of myths in other fields. We find a remarkable demonstration of this in the history of the Catholic Church. The upper hierarchy of the Church advocates and presumably believes very many non-scientific theories. However, since the time when St. Augustine made the wonderfully useful distinction between the "City of God" and the "City of Man," this has not prevented the hierarchy, on frequent occasions and sometimes for centuries together, from acting scientifically in the field of organization and politics.

We have seen that the primary real goal of every ruling group is the maintenance of its own power and privilege. Scientific conduct on the part of the group would not destroy this social fact, but, on the contrary, would require the group to recognize it frankly, and to take appropriate steps to insure power and privilege. Would it not seem, then, that scientific rulers would be the worst of all, that a scientific ruling class would mean in practice an eternal tyranny? Should the ruled not rather rejoice at every error, every illusion, every absurdity of the rulers?

Under some circumstances this would undoubtedly be the sensible attitude on the part of the ruled. Nevertheless, there is often a certain correlation between the interests of the ruler and the ruled in spite of the fact that the primary goal of the rulers is to serve their own interest. Examples are not at all hard to find. Everyone will doubtless admit that James C. Petrillo runs the Musicians' Union first of all to his own benefit; and, if the published reports of his salary and other perquisites of office are correct, he does very well by himself. However, it is also plain enough that his regime has greatly improved the economic lot of the musician members of the union. During the 5th century in Athens, or in the Roman Empire, the ruled and the rulers flourished together and together met disaster, and so it often happens. The fate of an entire society is frequently—whether one likes it or not, and unjust as it may seem usually to be—bound up with the fate of its ruling class. The collapse of the French ruling class a few years ago meant a harsh tragedy for the entire French people, blameless as the French masses might properly be considered from a moral standpoint. Surely it would have been better for the French people if they had been ruled by an élite which knew its business, knew, among other things, how to keep itself in social power, and which was firm enough to take the necessary steps to do so. If the generals are no good, the army will be defeated; but the soldiers also—in fact, primarily —will be the ones who are slaughtered. A society—a city or a nation or an empire—may become as a whole so thoroughly rotten that it is better that it should be destroyed as a social organism; but this too is seldom fortunate for the individual members of the society, ruled as well as rulers.

The lessons of history show that a ruling class can seldom continue long in power unless it is prepared to open its ranks to able and ambitious newcomers from below. A scientific ruling class will therefore keep its ranks open; and this will also be to the benefit of the ruled both in providing an outlet for dynamic individuals, and even more through permitting a greater expansion of creative social energies. Political liberty, too, in the longer run, usually aids both rulers and ruled. We have already seen that this is so from the point of view of the ruled; from the side of the rulers, liberty is a safeguard against bureaucratic degeneration, a check on errors, and a protection against revolution.

If a considerable section of the élite proceeded more or less scientifically, catastrophic revolutions would be much less likely. It may not be so immediately clear that the elimination of revolutions would promote the welfare of society as a whole. The net result of at least some revolutions would seem to be to the benefit of the masses, at least when measured against the old regimes. However, the point is that a scientific ruling class could avoid catastrophic revolution not by stopping revolutionary change in society but only by guiding the change, controlling it, and thus bringing it about in a more orderly manner. Catastrophic revolutions occur when the conditions that require a drastic change in the social structure are present but the changes themselves are blocked; then, sooner or later, they burst out in full eruption. There is seldom anything inevitable about this process. The broad changes will take place in any event. If they can be carried through without the immeasurable blood and terror and brutality and chaos which are the sure accompaniments of modern mass revolutions, there are few who would be losers. But revolutions will nonetheless certainly come if their causes are not removed; and only a responsible leadership, understanding the laws of society and acting on that understanding, ready to sacrifice as it would have to sacrifice many of its own immediate interests, and blessed, moreover, with not a little luck besides, would have a chance of removing those causes.

It should not be imagined that even the most thoroughly scientific procedures on the part of a ruling class could "solve" all the problems of society. We have already remarked that the broad patterns of social change are established by factors beyond deliberate human control. Scientific action could, therefore, make a difference only within the framework of these general patterns. Many important social problems—permanent peace or permanent economic prosperity, for example—are very probably insoluble. Moreover, a scientific ruling class could never hope to do more than make the best possible use of what was at its disposal: if it led a nation poor in resources and numbers, it and its society might still be crushed no matter how brilliantly scientific its leadership.

However much might be accomplished, for itself and for the society it led, by a scientific élite, there are obstacles in the way of scientific political action by an élite, which, if they are not quite insuperable as in the case of the masses, are nevertheless very formidable. It is in general, as we have repeatedly seen, exceedingly difficult for men to be scientific, or logical, about social and political problems. If the élite has an advantage over the masses in this respect through the possession of more knowledge, more time free from the burden of getting food and shelter, and no doubt certain talents also, the members of the élite, in partial compensation, are subject to the inescapable corruptions of power and privilege. Those who have privileges almost always develop false or distorted ideas about themselves. They are under a compulsion to deceive themselves as well as others through some kind of irrational theory which will seek to justify their monopoly of those privileges, rather than to explain the annoying truths about how the privileges are in fact acquired and held.

A dilemma confronts any section of the élite that tries to act scientifically. The political life of the masses and the cohesion of society demand the acceptance of myths. A scientific attitude toward society does not permit belief in the truth of the myths. But the leaders must profess, indeed foster, belief in the myths, or the fabric of society will crack and they be overthrown. In short, the leaders, if they themselves are scientific, must lie. It is hard to lie all the time in public but to keep privately an objective regard for the truth. Not only is it hard; it is often ineffective, for lies are often not convincing when told with a divided heart. The tendency is for the deceivers to become self-deceived, to believe their own myths. When this happens, they are no longer scientific. Sincerity is bought at the price of truth.

In the light of these obstacles and this tragic dilemma, it would seem that the possibility of scientific political action, even on the part of a section of the élite, which is itself only a small section of society, depends upon favorable and temporary circumstances. From my own acquaintance with history, I should say that these have been most nearly realized at certain periods in the history of Rome, of the Catholic Church, of the Venetian Republic, and of England. They have evidently not existed, up to now, in the present century. Our leaders—not only the governing élites but those other sections of the élites, such as that grown out of the labor movement, which have been moving toward increased power—are for the most part non-scientific and even anti-scientific in their handling of major social issues, while at the same time they have adopted scientific techniques in dealing with narrower problems of mass-manipulation. The programs which they profess, as well as those upon which they act, are devoid of reality in their failure to recognize the general pattern of our age. They are content not simply with myths, but with remnants of outworn myths. They admit no responsibility except to the fiction of the mass, which is only the projection of their own unloosed will to power. Proceeding in this manner, with the material resources devised by physical science at their disposal, they have brought civilization to the most shattering crisis of recorded history.

It is probable that civilized society will, somehow, survive. It will not survive, however, if the course of the ruling class continues in the direction of the present, and of the past forty years. In that direction there lies destruction of rulers and ruled alike. But, during the monstrous wars and revolutions of our time, there has already begun on a vast scale a purge of the ranks of the ruling class. That purge, and the recruitment of new leaders which accompanies it, may be expected to continue until they bring about a change in the present course. Though the change will never lead to the perfect society of our dreams, we may hope that it will permit human beings at least that minimum of moral dignity which alone can justify the strange accident of man's existence.